Therapy with Displaced Highly Mobile Individuals

A Guide for In-Person and Online Practitioners

Anastasia Piatakhina Giré

Routledge
Taylor & Francis Group

LONDON AND NEW YORK

Designed cover image: © Getty | Alexey Grachev

First published 2024
by Routledge
4 Park Square, Milton Park, Abingdon, Oxon OX14 4RN

and by Routledge
605 Third Avenue, New York, NY 10158

Routledge is an imprint of the Taylor & Francis Group, an informa business

British Library Cataloguing-in-Publication Data
A catalogue record for this book is available from the British Library

ISBN: 978-0-367-70102-4 (hbk)
ISBN: 978-0-367-70101-7 (pbk)
ISBN: 978-1-003-14458-8 (ebk)

DOI: 10.4324/9781003144588

Typeset in Times New Roman
by Taylor & Francis Books

Therapy with Displaced and Highly Mobile Individuals

This book provides therapists with an understanding of displacement-related issues to help them better serve potential clients such as emigrants, expats, migrants, digital nomads – all those who have left their original home country behind and moved to a different culture and place.

With the spread of communication technologies, psychotherapists are expanding their practice to the online setting and into the unfamiliar waters of transcultural counselling with highly mobile and displaced individuals. Building on her research, the author brings up new concepts in therapy practice with emigrants, calling for a displacement-focused, transcultural approach for a modern psychotherapy practice, blended or online, in a world shaped by ubiquitous displacement. Giré's own experience of relocations and multicultural families have helped her develop a personal approach to universal topics of the therapeutic endeavour, such as displacement, multilingualism, and shame.

Meeting displaced individuals' mental health needs is a priority for the mental health community. *Therapy with Displaced and Highly Mobile Individuals* will be of interest to all therapists working online with this client group, and for all those interested in psychotherapy (therapists or not), who want to learn about the psychological issues created by displacement.

Anastasia Piatakhina Giré is accredited with the UKCP and holds the European Certificate of Psychotherapy. She has practised online therapy for over a decade, with clients around the world. She now lives and works in Paris, France and is finalising her DPsych at Middlesex University, London. She is also a faculty member of the Online Therapy Institute, London.

Contents

Figure

Foreword

Are you a displaced person? Are you a child or a grandchild of people who migrated? Are any of your clients? *Online Therapy with Displaced and Highly Mobile Individuals* by Anastasia Piatakhina Giré is essential reading if you work therapeutically with displaced and highly mobile clients online. Anastasia Piatakhina Giré considers, in depth, the essential, topical, existential issue of displacement, at the personal, social, and political levels. Anastasia's focus is on working online with therapy clients who are displaced, but the book is relevant for anyone interested in the notion of displacement, be they a therapist, a client, or a member of the general public.

The online therapy space is characterised as "A room with an angle", and Anastasia proposes that reflecting on displacement from every angle can facilitate identity integration for families, couples, and individuals who have lived their lives across countries, cultures, languages, and religious practices. In fact, this is one of the explicit goals of this book. High mobility and displacement, whether moving physically or figuratively away from, towards or back to a place, make online therapy especially relevant beyond the era of lockdowns undertaken during the Covid-19 pandemic.

Drawing on research studies, theoretical frameworks of psychotherapy, applied linguistics and psychology, together with broader cultural references, Anastasia makes the case for the particular assets that online therapy can offer a displaced client, beyond practical convenience. The online presence of the therapist offers a consistency which is not linked to a specific location. It provides a virtual space for the exploration of decision-making processes about migration, where dreams, mythologies, and fantasies about what home may have been and what it can be are explored. It is a space to consider what leaving and returning may feel like. The online space provides neutrality to explore the meanings of attachments to and losses of geographical places. It provides enough space to hide and to be seen.

The online therapist offers a safe enough attachment figure, fellow-traveller, and a witness of the journeys already undertaken and the journeys that await.

Anastasia reminds us of how frequently exile produces shame, including linguistic shame, and of just how sneaky shame can be. She encourages therapists to address their own displacement and shame narratives so that they can develop "displacement rabbit ears" that can detect, rather than avoid or collude with shame in its hidden guises: "This alienation from the self and the desire to escape one's own skin, which is consistently rejected by others, is at the very core of the debilitating shame that individuals belonging to any marginalised and persecuted group will almost unavoidably suffer from."

She recommends having a displacement-savvy supervisor to help with this process. She examines the relationships we have with our languages, those remembered and those forgotten: "earlier linguistic history can impact our relationship with a language that we encounter later in displacement".

This book is packed full of ideas connected to theoretical concepts which cross therapeutic modalities. It is meticulously researched and contains selected quotations from academic and practitioner papers, and transcultural and multilingual authors from the literary tradition. Like the many translingual writers who are quoted in this book, Anastasia encourages us to view aspects of displacement and the affordance of a second language, not just as a means to provide distance and safety but as a means to occupy creative and playful positions in relation to our lives.

But at the very heart of this book are the rich fictionalised stories where the patients come to life, their inner worlds unlocked by Anastasia's considerable therapeutic skills.

The stories are beautifully told, often deeply moving and unfailingly authentic. Authentic, partly because the author draws on her extensive experience of working with displaced clients online. Authentic also because Anastasia is bold in her willingness to examine her own displacement story and to hold herself accountable for the impact that unexplored aspects of her story may have on her patients. Because she is bold, she is able to stay alongside her clients as a fellow traveller while the clients search for and recognise parts of their selves, acknowledging them, or simply mourning their loss, as they attempt to discover and to rediscover the path they want to travel.

To be bold, as a therapist, and to be authentic can be construed as an act of love. Anastasia chooses love to close this impressive, beautifully written book.

> So, love it will be. Love for the misplaced, misunderstood, and dislocated parts of us.

Read this book if you are working with or considering working online across cultures, across languages, and across geographies with displaced people. Read this book if you are displaced yourself. Aren't we all, at some time in our lives?

Beverley Costa, D.Psych., UKCP approved supervisor, MBACP, author of
Other Tongues: Psychological Therapies in a Multilingual World

Preface

The initial idea for this book was born well before the COVID-19 pandemic, and as I am finishing writing it, the world has changed and there are more changes to come that will be a direct result of this major global crisis.

All over the world, the pandemic crisis has impacted the way therapists practise. To adapt to the new social distancing reality, they had to widely rely on digital communication technologies. As a result, the profession's transition to the online space has been furiously accelerated. "Online therapy had moved, almost overnight, from a minority provision to a universal solution" (Dunn & Wilson, 2021). Therapists have had to acquire new skills extremely quickly, often on the go, and the need for resources and training for adapting to online therapy has surged. Many therapists will keep offering therapy online after the pandemic (McBeath et al., 2020; Aafjes-van Doorn et al., 2021). The uncertainty in the aftermath of the COVID-19 crisis will also present opportunities for integration of counselling and psychotherapy into new service models for the most vulnerable, which may include wider use of digital approaches (Vostanis & Bell, 2020) and the further emergence of mixed delivery methods.

As I kept meeting online with my displaced clients during the lockdown, I was able to appreciate the challenges that they were facing during this time. Some of them had to self-isolate in a foreign country; others had to make an emergency return to the home they had fled years ago. This suggests that any exterior crisis hits the displaced population particularly hard; their displaced condition makes their experience even more extreme.

Another impact of the pandemic has been a sudden increase in the number of digital nomads. Airbnb reported in *Travel & Living* that 11% of their customers booking long-term stays in 2021 declared living a nomadic lifestyle, and 5% planned to give up their main homes.[1] Once exonerated from the necessity to go to the office daily, these previously settled professionals moved to places better suited for their needs. This increased mobility has resulted in a growing number of digital nomads all around the globe. They have often had to make these decisions quickly, sometimes as a way of coping with the crisis. In this growing population of displaced individuals, who often rely on their laptops for work, many will be seeking psychological support, and they are likely to use the same technologies for this as those they use daily for work. Therapists working online must be prepared to address their particular displacement-related needs.

Now, in the aftermath of the lockdowns all over the world, the mental health profession is facing another crisis—a psychological one that is hitting society in the wake of such a collective trauma. The peak of the pandemic seems well behind us but mental health providers are now in the front line responding to this crisis. This book will equip them with some additional skills that have become essential nowadays.

Note

1 https://news.airbnb.com/wp-content/uploads/sites/4/2021/05/Airbnb-Report-on-Tra vel-Living.pdf

References

Aafjes-van Doorn, K., Békés, V., & Prout, T. A. (2021). Grappling with our therapeutic relationship and professional self-doubt during COVID-19: Will we use video therapy again? *Counselling Psychology Quarterly*, 34(3–4),473–484. doi:10.1080/09515070.2020.1773404.

Dunn, K., & Wilson, J. (2021). When online and face to face counseling work together: Assessing the impact of blended or hybrid approaches, where clients move between face-to-face and online meetings. *Null*, 20(4), 312–326. doi:10.1080/14779757.2021.1993970.

McBeath, A. G., du Plock, S., & Bager-Charleson, S. (2020). The challenges and experiences of psychotherapists working remotely during the coronavirus pandemic. *Counselling and Psychotherapy Research*, 20(3), 394–405. doi:10.1002/capr.12326.

Vostanis, P., & Bell, C. A. (2020). Counselling and psychotherapy post-COVID-19. *Counselling and Psychotherapy Research*, 20(3), 389–393. doi:10.1002/capr.12325.

Introduction

This book was inspired by my own personal experience of psychotherapy as a client, but also as a therapist working with individuals who are constantly on the move and struggling with different sorts of mental health issues whilst away from their home country.

I once faced a challenging international move with my family, causing me a lot of emotional turmoil. It was not my first expatriation, but this time it hit me hard—I was feeling uprooted against my will, angry at the circumstances and literally sick with anxiety. I was moved to a country where I did not speak the language well enough to reach out to a local therapist, therefore an online therapist who offered sessions via a videoconferencing platform seemed like my best shot.

My other challenge was that as a therapist in training I needed to start seeing clients in order to build up my clinical hours towards professional accreditation. Advertising my psychotherapy services online (as well) seemed like the only viable path to develop my practice in a place where—at least at the beginning—I did not belong. Thus, I found myself in the fortunate situation of experiencing online therapy from both sides of the screen. I did not know then how much this would re-shape my professional and personal life, or how meaningful this experience would become.

This book is the result of more than a decade of actively researching the subject, engaging in various dialogues with friends and colleagues who offer their counselling services online, and practising psychotherapy online with displaced individuals. It is deeply anchored in the clinical practice, as well as the research that it evolves from:

> Practice, however, is not simply a way to verify theory. Practice creates something new altogether that was not contained in the object previously explored or explained by theory. When we apply theory to the existing world, the world becomes something different as it embraces new facts created by the practical application of the theory itself. Thus practice, even when it is based on a particular theory, cannot simply

be reduced to that theory. It creates a possibility for new theories that in turn create possibilities for new practices.

(Epstein, 2012: 58)

The ideas developed in this book stem from my integrative and relational stance but are not modality- or approach-specific. The topics discussed here are existential in their nature, like displacement or shame. Reflecting on them can nourish the work of any therapist, working with displaced clients online or in-person, no matter what her main professional orientation is.

My purpose here is to provide therapists with theory and practice, which should help them work more efficiently with their displaced clients.

Since the day I switched on my camera to see the face of my first online client, I have been asking myself the following questions:

- Is there a natural relation between the psychological experience of displacement and online therapy?
- What are the main themes that naturally come up in therapy with displaced individuals?
- How can we better address the psychological experience of displacement in online therapy?

In those first years of practising online, I was actively blogging. Writing has helped me deepen my own thinking, practise reflectively, and has also kept me connected to some of my peers encountering the same challenges of online therapy and displacement. These earlier writings have nourished this book with illustrative vignettes.

As the American sociologist and researcher in narrative medicine, Arthur W. Frank humbly points out, no one can ever say anything new about his subject of choice, so we should abandon the hope of saying anything original, but "this does not mean abandoning the hope of saying something useful and interesting that leads people to imagine different possibilities for how their lives are formed and informed—much as a story leads people to imagine different possible lives" (Frank, 2010: 17–18).

I hope that this book can help practitioners imagine different possibilities of practice with displaced clients. Following closely the advice of the academic writing expert William Germano (Germano, 2014) and the inspiring steps of the applied linguistics scholar Aneta Pavlenko (Pavlenko in Casanave & Vandrick, 2003), I conceive this book as an unfinished quest, which only awaits colleagues from various horizons adding their own voices to the dialogue that it initiates.

References

Casanave, C., & Vandrick, S. (Eds.) (2003). *Writing for scholarly publication: Behind the scenes in language education.* London: Taylor & Francis.

Epstein, M. (2012). *The transformative humanities: A manifesto.* London: Bloomsbury.

Frank, W. A. (2010). *Letting stories breathe.* Chicago and London: University of Chicago Press.

Germano, W. (2014). *From dissertation to book* (2nd edn). Chicago: University of Chicago Press.

Acknowledgments

I would like to express my gratitude to all those who made this book possible.

First comes my wonderful academic advisor Stephen Goss, who was always interested in what I had to say, even when my thoughts or my English were confused and uncertain. Thank you, Stephen.

To my exceptional friend and colleague Joseph Burgo, who shared my passion for the topic of online therapy and shame. His always positive and curious presence and example of hard work helped me keep going. Thank you, Joseph.

An on-going encouragement of my dear friend Victor Yalom made me believe in my writing. Thank you, Victor for giving it a space to develop.

And, most importantly, to my French husband and critical friend, who although not a psychotherapist nor a native English speaker, read, edited, and kept asking annoying questions until my text got more precise.

Chapter 1

Displacement

This book's focus is on the displaced population: emigrants, expatriates, and migrants—all those who have left their original home country and moved to a different culture and place.

The variety of the displacement vocabulary reflects the multiplicity of this condition. The different types of geographic displacement have been sporadically discussed in literature on migration studies and in literary criticism (Brown, 2015; Klekowski von Koppenfels, 2014; Ryan & Mulholland, 2014; Suleiman, 1998). The definitions of displacement include generic terms such as nomads, refugees, exiles, migrants, or emigrants, and can be more specific, as with assigned or self-initiated expatriates, cosmopolitans, or digital nomads (Andresen et al., 2014). The typology and criteria for demarcation of these forms of human mobility are often unclear and hard to navigate for a therapist who wants to have a better sense of the variety of displacement conditions.

There are certainly endless psychological nuances in these landscapes of abandonment and loss. For a war refugee fleeing famine and death, or for an expat relocated for a professional assignment, these landscapes will not look the same, but their core existential themes will probably be similar: loss and alienation will lay dark shadows above their inner lands.

Today, thinking about the millions of people migrating to survive, Brodsky's words sound as true as ever:

> Whatever the proper name for these people, whatever their motives, origins, and destinations, whatever their impact on the societies which they abandon and to which they come may amount to—one thing is absolutely clear: they make it difficult to talk about the plight of the writer in exile with a straight face.
>
> (Brodsky, 1991: 1)

The expatriates who voluntarily migrated and feel privileged may keep silent, especially when they compare their lives with that of economic or political migrants, but they nevertheless experience shame linked to migration, which justifies including them in the wider displaced population. This type of shame

DOI: 10.4324/9781003144588-1

often prevents expatriates from seeking help or opening up in therapy about their struggles.

"Yet talk we must", Brodsky continues, having in mind literature, the only form of moral insurance that a society can get. Despite his shame, Brodsky takes it as his moral duty as a poet to talk about society's blind spots. For us therapists, our own moral duty is to help our clients explore their blind spots, one of the major ones probably being displacement. No one leaves home without a good reason. That reason, especially when invisible and unconscious, is always worth exploring.

Whatever the type of displacement, the existential condition of migration is what has to be worked on in therapy. Those who are fleeing famine on foot and those who take planes to escape the emotional abuse or neglect experienced in their original location will ultimately carry a similar emotional burden.

The definition of displacement that is relevant here focuses on interpersonal and relational impact and is borrowed from the environmental psychology: "Dis-PLACE-ment is, by definition, a rupture of the geographic and the social. Disruptions of this kind force people to remake their emotional connections, including those we know as 'place attachment'" (Fullilove in Manzo & Devine-Wright, 2014: 141). I opted for the umbrella term "displacement" because it is broader and more inclusive than other terms like "migrant" or "refugee", from which it is too easy to distance oneself, and not feel concerned. I am a displaced person myself, and it took me years to recognise this and finally accept displacement as an intrinsic part of my identity. This may be the case of many practitioners who are well-settled emigrants or even second-generation emigrants. Reflecting on this part of their life experience can lead them to a better personal integration and an enhanced capacity to help their displaced clients. Facilitating this kind of reflexivity is one of this book's main goals.

Vignettes in this book offer clinical examples, individual stories of voluntary displacement from the kind of people that constitute the main group in my online practice: emigrants, expatriates, digital nomads, international students, and people moving for professional assignments; all of them chose at some point in their lives to leave their original place.

Categories of placement and displacement have been widely explored in the contemporary literature. Postmodern discourse abounds in travel metaphors, but as Kaplan stresses: "Immigrants, refugees, exiles, nomads, and the homeless also move in and out of these discourses as metaphors, tropes, and symbols but rarely as historically recognized producers of critical discourses themselves" (Kaplan, 1996: 2).

As qualitative methods have been further developed in the social sciences, researchers have been giving voice to some representatives of these displaced groups. The extensive use of vignettes and case discussions in this book aims to let some of these voices into the narrative, as the voices of the displaced—especially those of the highly mobile individuals—can be easily lost by research projects which often require keeping in contact with the studied subjects. Traditional psychotherapy can offer these individuals a space for creating a personal narrative of displacement and its critical exploration; online therapy expands this space further for those who would not have been able to access mental health facilities due to their remote locations, mobility, lack of language skills, or limited local resources. The ways in which high mobility and displacement can naturally lead to choosing online therapy will be further discussed in Chapter 2.

The psychotherapeutic tradition itself is rooted in the culture of emigration (Makari, 2008; Laub, 2013). Personal stories of displacement have informed early psychoanalytic thought, although the paramount importance of this inner experience has not been directly addressed in psychoanalytic writings until recently (Nayar-Akhtar, 2015; Kuriloff, 2001; Szekacs-Weisz, 2016; Beltsiou, 2015). Psychoanalysts had to leave time and space after the personal and collective trauma of the Holocaust and exile before they could start an active exploration of the role displacement trauma had been playing in the genesis of psychoanalytical thought (Kuriloff, 2001).

Only in the 1980s, with León and Rebeca Grinberg's breakthrough book *Psychoanalytic Perspectives on Migration and Exile*, did psychoanalysis start directly addressing the unconscious processes activated in the individual psyche challenged with leaving the familiar world. The authors, psycho-analysts exiled from Argentina to Spain, put the emphasis on the existential quality of the displaced condition that they shared with many of their patients: "Using migration as a metaphor, human development itself can be seen as a succession of migrations whereby one gradually moves further and further away from his first objects" (Grinberg & Grinberg, 1984: 191). Any therapist working across different cultures, no matter what their approach, will find this existential lens an essential tool. I discuss in Chapter 3 how to integrate it in one's practice.

Back in the 1980s, the understanding by León and Rebeka Grinberg of migration as a trauma and a crisis raised some eyebrows, but it has now become a truism. High mobility comes with a high psychological cost (Rosen, 1992; Schwartz et al., 1996). Displacement is a traumatic experience with significant short- and long-term health consequences, not just for the dis-placed individuals but also for the communities they have left behind, and for the communities where they land (Greene et al., 2011).

Several studies have pointed out the wide spread of affective and psychotic disorders in the newly emigrated population (Buchwald et al., 1993; Mezey, 1960; Tyhurst, 1951). Various underlying reasons for these mental health issues have been given, such as pre-emigration factors (for example war), or the stress linked to the emigration process, the loss of social connections (Krupinski et al., 1965), or the absence of guaranteed social benefits (Brodsky, 1988). The link between displacement and mental health issues remains firm and strong.

Various authors have been building on the classic Grinberg and Grinberg volume stating that migration is a complex psychosocial process with significant and lasting effects on an individual's identity (Ainslie et al., 2013; Akhtar, 2004). Some focus on the loss and unresolved mourning (Conci, 2013; Clewell, 2004; Kogan, 2010), others on the importance of offering a transitional space to work through separation from their original objects during treatment of emigrants (Knafo, 1998).

"Irreparable losses, tragedies, broken dreams: the continuity of being is interrupted, over and over again and the identity of people becomes conditional and fragmented", Szekacs-Weisz sums up in her reflective paper, making a case for addressing the emigration experience in psychotherapy (Szekacs-Weisz, 2016). In psychodynamic psychotherapy, immigration is conceptualised as a complex precipitating factor, involving interrelated processes of mourning, imbalance between the change and continuity components of identity, and deregulation of self-esteem (Halperin, 2004). Halperin highlights the relevance of the immigration process in psychotherapy with displaced clients: "Cross-cultural moves precipitate experiences, behaviours and symptoms, which emerge from the dynamic shifts that parallel the geographic changes, and [...] the form and content of the patient's symptomatology depend on the individual's history and personality" (Halperin, 2004: 2). I will develop this idea further in Chapter 7, focusing on the emotion of shame as an intrinsic part of any dislocation.

No book had addressed the experience of emigration from a relational and interpersonal perspective until Beltsiou, in her collective volume, gathered several personal accounts from displaced psychoanalysts, addressing their shared experience of displacement with their clients during their therapy sessions (Beltsiou, 2015). My scope here is to build on this work and apply it to a relational approach to the psychotherapy practice rooted in any humanistic modality.

During the four decades since Grinberg and Grinberg's critical contribution, migration has grown dramatically all over the world; developments in communication technologies (internet, videoconferencing, smartphones) have significantly expanded migrants' capacity to keep in touch with those whom they have left behind. The same communication tools have also weakened the relationship between physical and social "place" (Meyrowitz, 1985). Displacement and simultaneous connectedness are now the inner and outer realities of an ever-growing mobile population (UN International Migration Report, 2017). Psychotherapy has not been left untouched by these changes and has had to adapt to ever more mobility. All over the world, therapists are now using various technologies to connect with their distant clients. With the recent pandemic, their number has grown dramatically; online therapy has gained more credibility as, during the series of global lockdowns, we all had to rely on remote communication tools more heavily than ever before.

The growing number of displaced individuals around the globe and the synchronous developments in communication technologies call for a renewed inquiry into what constitutes the psychological experience of displacement, as well as its implications for the online practice of psychotherapy.

References

Ainslie, R. C., Tummala-Narra, P., Harlem, A., Barbanel, L., & Ruth, R. (2013). Contemporary psychoanalytic views on the experience of immigration. *Psychoanalytic Psychology*, 30(4), 663.

Akhtar, S. (2004). *Immigration and identity*. Oxford: Rowman & Littlefield.

Andresen, M., Bergdolt, F., Margenfeld, J., & Dickmann, M. (2014). Addressing international mobility confusion—developing definitions and differentiations for self-initiated and assigned expatriates as well as migrants. *International Journal of Human Resource Management*, 25(16), 2295–2318. doi:10.1080/09585192.2013.877058.

Beltsiou, J. (Ed.) (2015). *Immigration in psychoanalysis. Locating ourselves*. London and New York: Routledge.

Brodsky, B. (1988). Mental health attitudes and practices of Soviet Jewish immigrants. *Health Social Work*, 13(2).

Brodsky, J. (1991). The condition we call exile. *Renaissance and Modern Studies*, 34, 1.

Brown, J. (2015). Home from home? Locational choices of international "creative class" workers. *European Planning Studies*, 23(12), 2336–2355. doi:10.1080/09654313.2014.988012.

Buchwald, D., Klacsanzky, G., & Manson, S. M. (1993). Psychiatric disorders among recently-arrived eastern europeans seen through a us refugee counseling service. *International Journal of Social Psychiatry*, 39(3), 221–227. doi:10.1177/002076409303900308.

Clewell, T. (2004). Mourning beyond melancholia: Freud's psychoanalysis of loss. *Journal of the American Psychoanalytic Association*, 52(1), 43–67. doi:10.1177/00030651040520010601.

Conci, M. (2013). Freud, Ossipow and the psychoanalysis of migration: *Briefwechsel 1921–1929* by Sigmund Freud and Nikolaj J. Ossipow, edited by Eugenia Fischer, René Fischer, Hans-Heinrich Otto and Hans-Joachim Rothe (Frankfurt-am-Main: Brandes & Apsel, 2009; 268 pp); reviewed by Marco Conci. *Psychoanalysis and History*, 15(2), 221–227. doi:10.3366/pah.2013.0134.

Greene, D., Tehranifar, P., Hernandez-Cordero, L. J., & Fullilove, M. T. (2011). I used to cry every day: A model of the family process of managing displacement. *Journal of Urban Health*, 88(3), 403–416. doi:10.1007/s11524-011-9583-4.

Grinberg, L., & Grinberg, R. (1984). *Psychoanalytic perspectives on migration and exile*. New Haven & London: Yale University Press.

Halperin, S. (2004). The relevance of immigration in the psychodynamic formulation of psychotherapy with immigrants. *International Journal of Applied Psychoanalytic Studies*, 1(2), 99–120. doi:10.1002/aps.62.

Kaplan, C. (1996). *Questions of travel: Postmodern discourses of displacement*. Durham, N.C; London: Duke University Press.

Klekowski von Koppenfels, A. (2014). *Migrants or expatriates?: Americans in Europe*. Palgrave Macmillan.

Knafo, D. (1998). Transitional space in the treatment of immigrants. *Israel Journal of Psychiatry and Related Sciences*, 35, 48–55.

Kogan, I. (2010). Migration and identity: Different perspectives. *The International Journal of Psycho-Analysis*, 91(5), 1206.

Krupinski, J., Schaechter, F., & Cade, J. F. J. (1965). Factors influencing the incidence of mental disorders among migrants. *Medical Journal of Australia*, 2(7), 269–277. doi:10.5694/j.1326-5377.1965.tb25240.x.

Kuriloff, E. (2001). A two-culture psychology: The role of national and ethnic origin in the therapeutic dyad. *Contemporary Psychoanalysis*, 37(4), 673–681. doi:10.1080/00107530.2001.10746435.

Laub, D. (2013). On leaving home and the flight from trauma. *Psychoanalytic Dialogues*, 23(5), 568–580. doi:10.1080/10481885.2013.832602.

Makari, G. (2008). *Revolution in mind*. New York: HarperCollins.

Manzo, L. C., & Devine-Wright, P. (2014). *Place attachment*. London and New York: Routledge.

Meyrowitz, J. (1985). *No sense of place: The impact of electronic media on social behavior*. New York: Oxford: Oxford University Press.

Mezey, A. G. (1960). Psychiatric aspects of human migrations. *International Journal of Social Psychiatry*, 5(4), 245–260. doi:10.1177/002076406000500401.

Nayar-Akhtar, M. (2015). *Identities in transition: The growth and development of a multicultural therapist*. London: Karnac Books.

Rosen, P. B. (1992). The trauma of moving: Psychological issues for women. *Journal of Feminist Family Therapy*, 4(3/4), 120.

Ryan, L., & Mulholland, J. (2014). Trading places: French highly skilled migrants negotiating mobility and emplacement in London. *Journal of Ethnic and Migration Studies*, 40(4), 584–600. doi:10.1080/1369183X.2013.787514.

Schwartz, A., Eilenberg, J., & Fullilove, M. T. (1996). Gloria's despair: Struggling against the odds [clinical conference]. *American Journal of Psychiatry*, 153(10), 1334–1338. doi:10.1176/ajp.153.10.1334.

Suleiman, S. R. (1998). *Exile and creativity: Signposts, travelers, outsiders, backward glances*. Durham NC: Duke University Press.

Szekacs-Weisz, J. (2016). Emigration from within. *American Journal of Psychoanalysis*, 76(4), 389–398.

Tyhurst, L. (1951). Displacement and migration. A study in social psychiatry. *The American Journal of Psychiatry*, 107(8), 561.

Chapter 2

Online therapy

There are several terms used for online counselling: online therapy, e-counselling, e-therapy, cyber therapy ... Here I use Bloom's definition of online therapy as "the practice of professional counselling that occurs when client and counsellor are in separate or remote locations and utilize electronic means to communicate with each other" (Bloom 1998: 53). My focus is on psychotherapy through videoconferencing systems, but many of the topics discussed here should be relevant to other sorts of online therapy—asynchronous through email, synchronous texting and chat, or phone.

As online counselling spread, the literature dedicated to this topic has grown in the last decade. The initial suspicions of some (Kmietowicz, 2001) were balanced by a more accepting stance of others (Hill, 2002; Lazuras & Dokou, 2016). The general opinion about the use of technology in mental health evolved: "since it is here to stay, we should study the phenomenon" (Baker & Ray, 2011: 341) and the view that "therapy can be done online, that it can be done ethically, and that online services might not be a serious threat to face-to-face therapy" (Alleman, 2002: 199).

The earlier focus in the literature on assessing the validity of the computer facilitated counselling (Alleman, 2002) and exploring the differences between the traditional in person and the online settings (Skinner & Zack, 2004; Rochlen et al., 2004) naturally shifted towards exploration of the nature of online therapy. Researchers looked at the distance therapeutic relationship (Cundy, 2015; Dunn in Weitz, 2014), consideration of ethical issues (Baker & Ray, 2011; Anthony et al., 2010; Harris & Birnbaum, 2015), or adapting computerized treatments to particular psychological issues (Overholser, 2013 and Van der Vaart et al., 2014 to depression; Moessner & Bauer, 2012 to eating disorders; Blankers et al., 2011 to addiction). One study (Simms et al., 2011) exploring counsellors' attitudes to online therapy concluded that it was positive particularly for clients in remote and/or rural locations. Sedentary vs. migrant status of therapists was not discussed.

Pre-pandemic, only a few studies directly addressed the demographics of online therapy users or explored their experience (Adebowale, 2014; DuBois, 2004; King et al., 2006; Leibert & Archer, 2006). They were mainly small-

DOI: 10.4324/9781003144588-2

scale and practice-based. DuBois looked at the characteristics of online clients who sought online therapy, but the displacement status was not addressed. In the previous decade, some authors voiced their scepticism, insisting that the limits of the therapeutic interventions bound by a screen can reduce therapy to something "less" (Carr, 2010; Russell, 2015; Turkle, 2011).

Post-pandemic recognition of digital provision of counselling propelled the profession to embrace a more open stance and start counting not only the losses, but also the gains that come with this accelerated transition (Carroll, 2021). Alongside the collective reckoning of the limits and potential dangers of our multiple screens, therapists have come to an understanding that technology is never neutral; our gadgets can also encourage ways of imagining and inhabiting our profession (Lanier, 2011; Bailey, 2016) and I can only concur with Russell who argues that "if we opt to use new tools, we need to know the nature of those tools and how those tools change us" (Russell, 2015: 6).

To contribute to the debate, I would like to further reflect on how the online delivery mode can be better adapted for helping the specific group of displaced individuals.

Why do clients choose online therapy?

This sub-chapter describes a small-scale practice-based survey that I conducted in 2017 as part of my doctoral research. A mixed methods web survey was run on 105 adult online therapy users to test the hypothesis of an affinity between the experience of displacement and online therapy use.

When we think about reasons and motivations that lead clients to online therapy, the first intuitive answer that may come to mind is about convenience: the comfort of being in your own office or home, no travel necessary, the time saved, and the possibility to have sessions during a work trip or a holiday. One pre-pandemic small-scale study explored the factors that influence an individual to choose online therapy instead of in-person therapy (Kofmehl, 2017). He looked at criteria like client's age, region, ethnicity, and introversion/extroversion. The mobility or displacement status of the participants was not assessed.

The online survey that I ran consisted in 15 questions (14 closed-ended of which 6 included a "comment" box, and 1 open-ended unstructured question) and focused primarily on the questions of whether respondents perceive an affinity between online therapy and being "displaced" and, second, on their experience of online therapy in light of their displaced status. I chose to target displaced individuals themselves. I felt that being hidden behind their screens and constantly moving, they probably rarely had an opportunity to share their peculiar experience. The data collection process confirmed that these clients were difficult to reach.

In three months, I directly contacted by email over 350 mental health practitioners based around the globe, asking them to kindly share the survey link with their former and on-going clients. These therapists had been identified on the internet through various listings and groups offering their services of remote therapy through videoconferencing. The survey was also advertised to thousands of counsellors through ads on professional groups on LinkedIn and Facebook.

I received many negative answers indicating confusion about the concept of displacement, which therefore made it difficult to proceed. The fear of interference with the therapeutic process of their client will also have eroded the relaying by therapists of my questionnaire to their clients.

I collected 105 completed questionnaires:

- Out of 105 respondents, 25 were male (24%) and 80 female (76%)
- 68 participants were 27–45 years old (65%), 19 were 46–59 (18%), 10 were 18–26 years old (9.5%), and 7 were over 60 (7 %); 1 preferred not to tick an age-bracket box.

The sample seemed representative of the general population of online therapy users that my colleagues and I have seen in our practice, but in the absence of reliable statistics in this relatively new domain, no conclusions could be drawn about representativity of the sample. It was interesting to observe that 65% of all responses were from 27–45-year-olds, suggesting that the digital natives (born after 1980) may be more inclined to use communication technologies to seek therapy compared to older groups.

If we push Prensky's point about the intrinsic differences in which digital natives process information and learn, then we can imagine that the development of online therapy was just a way for traditional therapy to adapt to this population, well before the pandemic that accelerated this process (Prensky, 2001). Mobile individuals are naturally projected at the forefront of the digital natives group, as they quickly integrate the communication technologies into their lifestyle. For them it is often a question of emotional survival.

Sherry Turkle describes the experiment run in the mid-1990s at the MIT in which participated several young researchers who called themselves "cyborgs". Their experience of being always connected to the internet through a series of elaborate devices made them "a new kind of nomad, wandering in and out of the physical real. [...] the multiplicity of worlds before them set them apart: they could be with you, but they were always somewhere else as well" (Turkle, 2011: 152). In this description of the experimental "cyborgs" there is a discernible parallel with the experience of the displaced individuals, who carry with them, even if only internally, their multiple worlds. Their fragmented identities, their familiarity with being "apart" from others, and their capacity to creatively use their parallel realities, make them naturally adopt technology-mediated therapy.

But what are the reasons that make clients opt for online therapy?

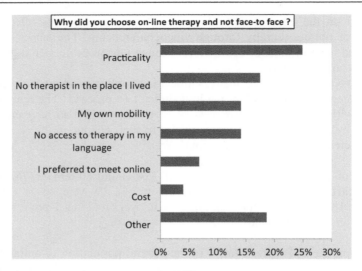

Figure 2.1 Some results from the author's 2017 survey

Practicality

Practicality came up as the most common reason for choosing online therapy (41%). Participants appreciated the comfort of being in their own "safe space", no travel necessary, the time saved, and the possibility to have sessions during a work trip or a holiday:

> *Very practical method, flexible and adaptable—well suited for global nomads.*
> *It has been positive for me and a good approach. I don't think I will ever do face to face therapy again. It is comforting to do it from home, especially after a long day at work when I am tired and when it is cold out.*
> *It is very convenient for my lifestyle, moving from one place to the next.*

The only previous study that inquired into reasons for seeking therapy online instead of in-person (DuBois, 2004) had stated that they included convenience and affordability. This study's findings echo the practicality criteria, but the cost aspect no longer seems defining (only 7% of participants). This may be linked to the fact that the DuBois study dealt with asynchronous therapy by email and chat exchanges between therapist and client that tend to be cheaper. In the case of face-to-face therapy by videoconferencing system, it seems either that the cost of online therapy is not different to in-person, or that clients tend not to use price as a factor in their decision process.

"Relatability"

- 30% of respondents were not able to find a therapist in the place where they lived
- 24% did not have access to therapy in their own language

Participants of the survey insisted that their choice was informed by "relatability" of a specific therapist:

> It was important to me to have a therapist who also had international experience.

Mobile individuals are highly adaptable. They must develop specific coping strategies to deal with their movable and changing realities. Turning towards online therapy may be one of these strategies. With the expansion of technology, distance is not an obstacle when some specific competences researched by the client are at stake (familiarity with Third Culture Kids (TCK), expats, language skills, cultural competences). Respondents looked for:

> Someone who understood my native culture
> Someone from my home country who would understand my cultural background and have no language barrier

The therapist's own experience and understanding of displacement was stated as another reason for choosing online therapy:

> Recommendation from a third party; knowledge of what expatriation means (in terms of added challenges)
> I was not able to find a therapist that had specific experience with expats and Third Culture Kids.

Online therapy often represents an opportunity for clients' expansion: they can ask for more and to reach out to a therapist who can relate to their experience of mobility or who shares with them a cultural background or a language.

Mobility

Mobility came up as one of the most common reasons for choosing therapy online (24%). The mobility of the therapist or the client himself often naturally transports therapy into the online space:

> I chose to do this due to work constraints and to maintain a regular contact with the same therapist wherever I may travel.

Participants' voices echo Reeves, who transitioned online following her mobile clients:

> My thought is that for the majority of the clients with whom I work using the phone or Skype, these media have allowed important therapy to be continued when there has been no other choice and a break in the work would have been detrimental.
>
> (Reeves in Cundy, 2015: 150)

These findings echo what is shared in the literature by therapists who took their practice online. Russell (2015) defines her own experience of expanding her practice to the online space following an international move as "sleepwalking". I suppose that her use of the term "sleepwalking" is not completely random. Sleepwalking suggests an unconscious activity driven by our inner processes. There is a degree of compulsiveness that reflects the nature of the online therapy movement. All of us, as society in general or as the professional community of online therapists in particular, are compelled to sleepwalk into the challenging and questionable world of online psychotherapy.

Beltsiou shares another example of transitioning to the online when she describes her psychoanalytic work with Sam, an Iranian emigrant to the United States. Her client moved to another city, and technology allowed him to "move and stay connected" (Beltsiou, 2015: 95). Online therapy offers indeed a simultaneous experience of moving and connectedness, paralleling the search by displaced individuals for an optimal balance between mobility and connectedness.

The feeling of shame, which in many cultures is associated with mental illness, may be one of the reasons why they felt less exposed with an online therapist who lives in a different culture and as a result able to seek therapy:

> *There is a lot of stigma attached to therapy in my home country, Russia. It is changing, but very slowly. Being able to do it from home will make it more comfortable to enter the safe place where one can talk about things one may not want to reveal otherwise.*

For many clients online therapy is the only available option for getting their mental health needs met. I have worked with refugees or expats unable to find a therapist speaking their language within reachable distance. Another displaced group consists of individuals who are constantly on the move—war journalists and photographers, employees of international non-profit organizations, or diplomats. They do not stay long enough in one place to engage in a stable therapeutic relationship (their peripatetic existence may indeed be a topic to explore in their therapy). Another distinct and vulnerable group, who may be benefiting from this globalised mental health opportunity are women from very conservative areas (e.g. the Middle East), for whom consulting a therapist outside their country is the only way they are willing to open up and explore their religious beliefs or doubts, their experience of oppression, or their sexuality, without the risk of being judged or causing potential repercussions.

In other less dramatic cases, online therapy becomes the best choice for certain deeper psychological reasons, such as shame (discussed further in Chapter 7).

The more I engage in therapy with displaced individuals, the more I distinguish a common theme in their stories, which resonate with my own peripatetic journey: our weaker roots allow us to grow more self-reliant. Often the story of a voluntary migration is a solitary one. These individuals learn how to maintain distance relationships; a romantic date or a family gathering can take place through a screen.

As for Lucy, a Canadian aid worker based in Rwanda, she was feeling disillusioned by traditional face-to-face therapy. She had never been able to trust any of her therapists. All her previous attempts to get some support had only confirmed her belief that she could only "make it on her own". This time, in the middle of an extremely unsafe environment, rigged with the weight of huge responsibilities, added to by loneliness, she decided to give it one more try and reach out to an online therapist.

Lucy's extreme self-reliance and difficulty in trusting others made the work challenging for both of us at times. But she gave it a chance. Letting a face on her screen slowly become a person, she allowed our therapeutic relationship to develop. She eventually learned how to trust again and receive external support. It is paradoxical that a virtual online therapist can facilitate the development of trust, especially when it seems nearly impossible, but turning potential obstacles into advantages is one of the creative challenges of online therapy.

Offering people who experience shame or extreme self-reliance the option of a seemingly easier way into therapy is not a trick; it is a gift to those who may otherwise never take the hand that is there to help them work on improving their lives.

In the first sessions I always invite my new client to actively explore his choice of reaching out to an online therapist. The question "Why are we meeting *here*?", irrelevant in a traditional in-person setting, becomes crucial and always gives a lot of grist to the mill, bringing therapy forward.

Therapists' transition online

The recent Covid-19 pandemic has accelerated integration of digital communication technologies into the field of mental health. For several months, psychotherapists around the globe had to engage with videoconferencing technologies that they might have considered threatening or at least foreign to their practice. Through this transition, we all became migrants, venturing into the new space for the sake of our professional survival. Each of us experienced this move in a unique way, based on our personality, displacement experience, and previous relationship with digital technology. But as a result, all practitioners around the globe were exposed to some form of remote practice, be it through phone, some video-conferencing technology, email, or chat. In order to deal with this sudden and mostly involuntary transition, many therapists engaged with peer support or supervision groups, which quickly developed online. Now that the lockdowns seem to be behind us, therapists are grasping how their practice and their way of being therapists has been challenged and transformed by the global health crisis.

My own online practice goes way further back, though. I had a choice, and, like my geographic displacement, my migration online was voluntary. When the pandemic struck, I had been already practising through video-conferencing for a decade.

Before the pandemic many mental health practitioners who were offering therapy online defined themselves as "international" and "cross-cultural". They were grouping in international directories such as the International Therapists Directory, or referenced in expatriate directories such as AngloInfo. They were often displaced and multilingual and were complementing their traditional practice with their online work.

To prepare for this book, I ran a small-scale online survey with therapists (92 respondents) to inquire into their motivations for moving their traditional practice online. Their reasons for moving online were mainly practicality, the need to expand their practice, and adapting to their or their clients' mobility. Less than half had experienced online therapy as clients. The vast majority were finding their online work rewarding.

Now that keeping or expanding the online part of their practice is a free choice for therapists, the question to ask is: why?

Compared with the post-pandemic research addressing therapists' experience of online therapy (Dunn & Wilson, 2021; Vostanis & Bell, 2020, McBeath et al., 2020), the pre-pandemic literature on this topic was limited (Dunn, 2012). The profession had to make without notice a forced major leap into the new technology-infused realm, losing some of the precious opportunity to thoroughly process this migration. This effort will nevertheless have to take place later, once the worst of the crisis is over. This delayed processing parallels what often happens in the case of involuntary or sudden displacement, when the person has no choice or little time to consider this life-changing decision. Today many therapists, displaced or not, who work with people displaced by the pandemic, wars (e.g. in Ukraine), or other dramatic circumstances, are facing a really interesting parallel process—whilst they are facilitating the mourning of losses and integration of what is found in transition with their client they are also wrestling with their own recent transition into the online.

In parallel with the process of emigration or mourning, it helps to focus on the here-and-now, the new online reality. Like the immigrant who has become "hyper-adapted" to the new world (Kelley-Lainé in Szekacs-Weisz & Ward, 2022: 8), I recognise my own displacement adaptation strategy. As I first burst out into the online therapy world, I was certainly acting in the same way as a "hyper-adapted" emigrant. When denial is our most functional defence, then looking back again and re-engaging with the loss can take considerable time and courage.

Following the pandemic crisis, the mental health profession has probably started this slow process of recognition; new and more integrated ways of practising are emerging in this transitional space, in the intimacy of dialogues between peers, be these via in-person conversations between colleagues (such as supervision or conferences), or in online peer groups. These fertile spaces are organically modelling the kind of displacement-related processing that happens in therapy with displaced clients.

Why not try it yourself?

The requirement for therapists to have an experience of personal therapy is widely recognised (King, 2011; Rake & Paley, 2009; Wheeler, 1991). For any therapist practising online, undertaking an individual therapy journey online will create an opportunity to experience the process from the other side of the screen.

One of the most meaningful therapies that I have personally experienced was online (at that time, through Skype). Having sat for hours on the other side of the screen certainly helped me offer a better service to my online clients. The sensitivity and generosity of my "virtual" therapist guided and informed my own practice, which was developing simultaneously in a fertile parallel process.

Recently more and more fellow therapists from various continents have been contacting me to seek online therapy (through video-conferencing) for themselves. How do they explain their choice?

In our first session, we systematically explore their motivation for contacting a foreign therapist based outside of their country; one of the reasons they name is the potential for increased anonymity and confidentiality: they already know socially all the good local therapists. This is particularly true for smaller towns and rural areas, but it also often becomes the case after a few years of practice in larger cities. Another reason is the broader choice of practitioners. Therapists make sophisticated clients: they usually know what they are looking for and want a particular approach that may not be available locally. With online therapy, the options are almost endless.

For trainees, online therapy can make things more affordable, especially for those training in places where fees are higher, like New York, California, or London. Additionally, more and more therapists move frequently to another state, city, or even country. Mobility naturally brings people to online therapy, because when they move they do not necessarily want to discontinue treatment and start over with a new therapist.

My own experience combined both—mobility and training needs. When I reached out to an online therapist I was in training, with personal therapy hours to accumulate for my professional accreditation. Simultaneously, I was facing an international move, and it was causing me a great deal of emotional turmoil. It was not my first expatriation, but this time it was hitting me hard—I was feeling uprooted against my will, immensely angry at the circumstances and literally sick with anxiety. I was relocating to a country where I did not speak the language well enough to reach out to a local therapist. A therapist online, with face-to-face sessions via videoconferencing, seemed like a reasonably good option. It turned out to be a bold choice that worked for me.

Beyond these practicalities there is a subtler psychological reason: the feeling of shame. There is a tacit expectation for us, as therapists, to be "all sorted" (Adams, 2013). Ironically enough, we are not immune to the shame associated with mental health struggles. Reaching out to a therapist who comes from a different cultural background and lives thousands of miles away can help us overcome the "shame barrier". Many of my clients acknowledge that online therapy allowed them to jump into it, overcoming the natural feeling of shame associated with the exposure that any therapy requires.

The online option may also foster cross-cultural exchanges beyond borders, showing us concretely how colleagues work in a different culture. I remember my own excitement as I first reached out to a therapist across the Atlantic.

As with everything new, the very idea of a therapy that is not behind closed doors of a physical office but rather through videoconferencing can be associated with some risk-taking. I used to hear cautious and even suspicious remarks, mainly from therapists who had not yet tried this new way of making therapy happen. That said, don't we expect our clients to take risks and venture into new territories for them? Therapy, by its nature, is about risk taking, and as our world changes we have to adapt, and possibly take on the role of explorers ourselves.

References

Adams, M. (2013). *The myth of the untroubled therapist: Private life, professional practice.* Abingdon: Routledge.

Adebowale, O. (2014). Disposition of students to online counselling: The Obafemi Awolowo University, Nigerian experience. *International Journal of Education and Development using Information and Communication Technology, 10*(3), 49.

Alleman, J. R. (2002). Online counseling: The internet and mental health treatment. *Psychotherapy: Theory, Research, Practice, Training, 39*(2), 199–209. doi:10.1037/0033-3204.39.2.199.

Anthony, K., Nagel, D. M., & Goss, S. (2010). *The use of technology in mental health: Applications, ethics and practice.* Springfield IL: Charles C. Thomas.

Bailey, J. (2016). The body in cyberspace: Lanier, Merleau-Ponty, and the norms of embodiment. *Christian Scholar's Review, 45*(3), 211.

Baker, K. D., & Ray, M. (2011). Online counseling: The good, the bad, and the possibilities. *Counselling Psychology Quarterly, 24*(4), 341–346. doi:10.1080/09515070.2011.632875.

Beltsiou, J. (Ed.) (2015). *Immigration in psychoanalysis. Locating ourselves.* London and New York: Routledge.

Blankers, M., Koeter, M. W. J., & Schippers, G. M. (2011). Internet therapy versus internet self-help versus no treatment for problematic alcohol use: A randomized controlled trial. *Journal of Consulting and Clinical Psychology,* 79(3), 330–341. doi:10.1037/a0023498.

Bloom, J. W. (1998). The ethical practice of WebCounseling. *British Journal of Guidance & Counselling,* 26(1), 53–59. doi:10.1080/03069889800760061.

Carr, N. G. (2010). *The shallows: What the internet is doing to our brains.* New York: W. W. Norton.

Carroll, R. (2021). Embodied intersubjectivity as online psychotherapy becomes mainstream. *Body, Movement and Dance in Psychotherapy,* 16(1), 1–8.

Cundy, L. (2015). *Love in the age of the internet: Attachment in the digital era.* London: Karnac Books.

DuBois, D. (2004). Clinical and demographic features of the online counselling client population. *Counselling and Psychotherapy Research,* 4(1), 18–22.

Dunn, K. (2012). A qualitative investigation into the online counselling relationship: To meet or not to meet, that is the question. *Counselling and Psychotherapy Research,* 12(4), 316–326. doi:10.1080/14733145.2012.669772.

Dunn, K., & Wilson, J. (2021). When online and face to face counseling work together: Assessing the impact of blended or hybrid approaches, where clients move between face-to-face and online meetings. *Null,* 20(4), 312–326. doi:10.1080/14779757.2021.1993970.

Harris, B., & Birnbaum, R. (2015). Ethical and legal implications on the use of technology in counselling. *Clinical Social Work Journal,* 43(2), 133–141. doi:10.1007/s10615-014-0515-0.

Hill, D. (2002). Computer-mediated therapy: Possibilities and possible limitations. Psy Broadcasting Corporation. Retrieved August, 23, 2002. www.psybc.com

King, G. (2011). Psychodynamic therapists' dilemmas in providing personal therapy to therapists in training: An exploratory study. *Counselling and Psychotherapy Research,* 11(3), 186–195. doi:10.1080/14733145.2010.519046.

King, R., Bambling, M., Lloyd, C., Gomurra, R., Smith, S., Reid, W. , & Wegner, K. (2006). Online counselling: The motives and experiences of young people who choose the internet instead of face to face or telephone counselling. *Counselling and Psychotherapy Research,* 6(3), 169–174.

Kmietowicz, Z. (2001). Beware online therapy, counselling association warns. *BMJ: British Medical Journal,* 322(7301), 1509. doi:10.1136/bmj.322.7301.1509/a.

Kofmehl, J. J. (2017). *Online versus in-person therapy: Effect of client demographics and personality characteristics* Available from Dissertations & Theses Europe Full Text: Health & Medicine.

Lanier, J. (2011). *You are not a gadget: A manifesto* (Updated edn). London: Penguin.

Lazuras, L., & Dokou, A. (2016). Mental health professionals' acceptance of online counseling. *Technology in Society,* 44, 10–14. doi:10.1016/j.techsoc.2015.11.002.

Leibert, T., & ArcherJr, J. (2006). An exploratory study of client perceptions of internet counseling and the therapeutic alliance. *Journal of Mental Health Counseling,* 28(1), 69–83. doi:10.17744/mehc.28.1.f0h37djrw89nv6vb.

McBeath, A. G., du Plock, S., & Bager-Charleson, S. (2020). The challenges and experiences of psychotherapists working remotely during the coronavirus pandemic. *Counselling and Psychotherapy Research,* 20(3), 394–405. doi:10.1002/capr.12326.

Moessner, M., & Bauer, S. (2012). Online counselling for eating disorders: Reaching an underserved population? *Journal of Mental Health*, 21(4), 336–345. doi:10.3109/09638237.2011.643512.

Overholser, J. C. (2013). Technology-assisted psychotherapy (TAP): Adapting computerized treatments into traditional psychotherapy for depression. *Journal of Contemporary Psychotherapy*, 43(4), 235–242. doi:10.1007/s10879-013-9241-0.

Prensky, M. (2001). Digital natives, digital immigrants part 1. *On the Horizon*, 9(5), 1–6. doi:10.1108/10748120110424816.

Rake, C., & Paley, G. (2009). Personal therapy for psychotherapists: The impact on therapeutic practice. A qualitative study using interpretative phenomenological analysis. *Psychodynamic Practice*, 15(3), 275–294. doi:10.1080/14753630903024481.

Rochlen, A. B., Zack, J. S., & Speyer, C. (2004). Online therapy: Review of relevant definitions, debates, and current empirical support. *Journal of Clinical Psychology*, 60(3), 269–283. doi:10.1002/jclp.10263.

Russell, G. I. (2015). *Screen relations: The limits of computer-mediated psychoanalysys and psychotherapy*. London: Routledge.

Simms, D., Gibson, K., & O'Donnell, S. (2011). To use or not to use: Clinicians' perceptions of telemental health. *Canadian Psychology*, 52(1), 41–51.

Skinner, A., & Zack, J. S. (2004). Counseling and the internet. *American Behavioral Scientist*, 48(4), 434–446. doi:10.1177/0002764204270280.

Szekacs-Weisz, J., & Ward, I. (Eds.) (2022). *Lost childhood and the language of exile* (2nd edn) Manila, Philippines: Phoenix Publishing House.

Turkle, S. (2011). *Alone together: Why we expect more from technology and less from each other*. New York: Basic Books.

Vaart, van der, R., Witting, M., Riper, H., Kooistra, L. C., Bohlmeijer, E. T., & Gemert-Pijnen, v., J. E. W. C. (2014). Blending online therapy into regular face-to-face therapy for depression: Content, ratio and preconditions according to patients and therapists using a Delphi study. *BMC Psychiatry*, 14(1), 355. doi:10.1186/s12888-014-0355-z.

Vostanis, P., & Bell, C. A. (2020). Counselling and psychotherapy post-COVID-19. *Counselling and Psychotherapy Research*, 20(3), 389–393. doi:10.1002/capr.12325.

Weitz, P. (Ed.) (2014). *Psychotherapy.02*. London: Karnac.

Wheeler, B. (1991). *Personal therapy: An essential aspect of counsellor training, or a distraction from focussing on the client?* New York: Kluwer Academic/Plenum Publishers.

Chapter 3

Psychology of displacement

> In my case the efforts for these years to live in the dress of Arabs, and imitate their mental foundation quitted me of my English self, and let me look at the West and its conventions with new eyes: they destroyed it all for me. At the same time, I could not sincerely take on the Arab skin; it was affectation only. [...] Sometimes these selves would converse in the void, and then madness was very near, as I could believe it would be near the man who could see things through the veils at once of two customs, two educations, two environments.

This is how Thomas Edward Lawrence, the British diplomat and writer, widely known as Lawrence of Arabia, describes his experience (Lawrence, 2002: 7). What Lawrence found awkward in the early 1920s is now the reality of many displaced individuals. Lawrence and other travellers, emigrants, and explorers of the early 20th century, had to deal on their own, or with their comrades, with the psychological fallout of their unsettled condition. They managed it in a lonely way, often through journaling, epistolary exchanges with friends or family or professional writing. Technological advances and the recent pandemic have dramatically expanded the outreach of mental health services, which are now facing the need to adapt their practice to the growing displaced population.

Looking into the psychological experience of displacement can bring us closer to grasping the particular needs of displaced clients. The question about the nature of these needs has not been widely discussed in the literature, even though the phenomenon has been recognized:

> Indeed, one cannot ignore the incidence of certain psychological problems particular to emigrants and those of their immediate entourage, in both the old and the new surroundings. These problems are difficult to evaluate because the motivations for migration and its consequences are closely intertwined.
>
> (Grinberg & Grinberg, 1984: I)

Every therapist will evaluate the particularity of each client's case, its inner and outer circumstances of migration, but understanding the universal themes

DOI: 10.4324/9781003144588-3

that come up in every singular story shaped by displacement will help them better attend to their clients' needs.

The history of psychotherapy is deeply rooted in the culture of emigration (Makari, 2008). The personal experience of displacement informed much of early psychoanalytic thought. Nevertheless, its influence was not directly addressed until recently (Phillips, 2014; Beltsiou, 2015):

> And psychoanalysis is first and foremost a psychology of, and for, immigrants (people who can never quite settle); not a Jewish science as Freud feared, but an immigrant science for a world in which, for political and economic reasons, there were to be more and more immigrants.
>
> (Phillips, 2014: 30)

The fact that the crucial role of displacement in the history of psychoanalysis was only recently acknowledged demonstrates how easily such a central facet of a life experience can be overlooked. It has taken a long time to integrate the exile-related themes into our understanding of psychoanalysis. The same can be applied to each singular therapy with a displaced individual.

During the 1980s, León and Rebeka Grinberg developed an existential view on migration (Grinberg & Grinberg, 1984). Psychoanalysis then began to explore the unconscious processes activated within an individual psyche by the challenge of leaving the familiar world (Weisz & Ward, 2004; Szekacs-Weisz & Ward, 2022). Since then, various authors have built upon the Grinbergs' classic volume and concluded that migration is a complex psychosocial process with significant and lasting effects on an individual's identity (Akhtar, 1995). Some have focused on loss and unresolved mourning (Clewell, 2004), others on the importance of offering a transitional space for working through separation (Knafo, 1998).

In particular, researchers have explored the use of different languages in therapy with bilingual emigrants (Rolland et al., 2017). Language is closely connected to emotions experienced during early psychological development. Writers from the psychoanalytical tradition have explored the potential advantages to using a second language in therapy (Weisz & Ward, 2004; Szekacs-Weisz & Ward, 2022), which may allow access to object relations of a more adult nature (Amati Mehler et al., 1990).

These themes are especially pertinent for online work with displaced individuals and will be addressed throughout this book.

Displacement as an existential condition

The psychoanalytic tradition uses migration as a metaphor for human development (Grinberg & Grinberg, 1984). Many authors extend this view to encompass exile, a condition that at some level is inscribed into the experience of every human being. As Svetlana Boym reminds us, the mourning of displacement and temporal irreversibility is at the very core of the modern condition (Boym, 1996: XVI). But I would go further and argue that the practice of therapy with the displaced would greatly benefit from an existential perspective and a willingness by therapists to address the needs of their clients arising from the basic human condition.

Existential psychotherapy was conceptualised by Irvin Yalom in his seminal textbook as "a dynamic approach to therapy which focuses on concerns that are rooted in the individual's existence" (Yalom, 1980: 5). These "ultimate concerns" are death, freedom, isolation, and meaninglessness. Yalom suggests that a deeper self-reflection, stemming from these often-unconscious concerns, is

> catalysed by certain urgent experiences. These "boundary" or "border" situations, as they are often referred to, include such experiences as a confrontation with one own's death, or some major irreversible decision, or the collapse of some fundamental meaning-providing schema.
>
> (Yalom, 1980: 8)

Based on everything seen before, displacement is a perfect example of such an "urgent" situation, or an existential crisis, as it does include all of the above elements that make it an ultimate "border" experience.

It seems intuitive that a major displacement is an existential crisis, but in my clinical observations, many expatriate or emigrant clients do not frame their experience in such a way. In many accounts from various clients about their previous therapeutic endeavours, the therapist had omitted or avoided working at this deeper existential level. Instead, they settled on dealing with other concerns—seemingly urgent and initially put forward by the client, but more superficial. Let us examine how all these major disruptive elements play out and turn displacement into a perfect existential storm.

As we cross a border to settle in an unfamiliar place, we lose most of our social connections. Emigrants are suddenly confronted with loneliness, which at a deeper level reminds us of our own finality. This major existential concern can often be successfully denied and repressed in a reality full or mundane activities and distractions. But with the loss of the original place and the attachments associated with it, displaced individuals suddenly find themselves with more space, and quickly fill it with previously repressed existential anxieties.

Voluntary displacement is often driven by the desire for a greater freedom. But the gift of freedom always comes with broadened responsibility for one's condition, and as a result, with a heightened existential anxiety. Freedom "viewed from the perspective of ultimate ground is riveted to dread" (Yalom, 1980: 8), and for many emigrants who come to therapy, this existential dread is an underlying reason for the anxieties that were previously successfully repressed. This dread can also cause powerful resistance, which clients use to escape this newly encountered responsibility for their existence.

The last, and probably major, existential concern of the human condition "stems from the dilemma of a meaning-seeking creature who is thrown into a universe that has no meaning" (Yalom, 1980: 9). To deal with this harsh reality, human beings create meaning from anything. The intricate web of this activity of meaning-creation usually relies on a social circle or/and a place. With the development of communication technologies, this situation has been changing, as we can now belong to movable place-less social groups. Nevertheless, grounded and meaningful links are often necessary to create some form of meaning that helps us maintain a strong sense of self. Migration, with its powerful disruptive potential, naturally leads to an identity crisis that is always a crisis of meaning. "Why am I here?" wondered Carla, one of my expatriate clients, as she turned up for a session after a short visit back home. She looked at me visibly distressed and disoriented. "Why *are* you?" I rephrased her question, and she instantly relaxed, with tears coming up. This simple intervention turned our conversation away from her mundane pre-occupations towards more prolific existential concerns. Carla felt that her life in her original Italian small town, well before her move to France, had been lacking meaning. She had been drifting through her otherwise-comfortable existence without much scope or direction. Her international move, super-ficially driven by her "desire to learn French" had been her only way of dis-rupting her settled life and break out from its overwhelming meaninglessness. Displacement pulled away the veil of normality from her reality. It also revealed her inner conflicts and existential struggles. This is when she turned to therapy, but her craving for meaning was still well hidden (at least from herself) behind her mundane preoccupations.

For clients like Carla, shifting the focus to the displaced condition itself, to deeper existential concerns—such as fear of loss and death, existential isola-tion, or the apparent meaningless of life—will enrich the therapeutic work and help address the roots of their psychological discomfort.

Displacement and identity

Across various views on identity, one element seems to prevail—its dynamic, fluid, and integrative quality. The integration of a personal self and social outer world is a developmental process (Erikson, 1968), which has to do with the gradual and never-ending development of a self-narrative that bears enough consistency and meaning. León and Rebeka Grinberg insist that our sense of identity is "born of the continuous interaction among spatial, temporal, and social integration links" (Grinberg & Grinberg, 1989: 132). Dowd argues that displacement disrupts all three of these links simultaneously, generating "extreme primitive states of alienating shame" (Dowd, 2019: 248) and throwing the dislocated person into a state of terrible existential anxiety and inner conflict.

The relation between displacement and identity is as intrinsic as it is para-doxical. On the one hand displacement threatens identity but on the other it redefines it. Anybody who experiences displacement is shaped by it to some extent, and simultaneously is defended against it. This paradoxical nature of displacement's impact on identity often leads to confusion, not just for emigrants themselves but also for their therapists. It can be tempting to resolve this ambivalence by embracing only one of these poles—conceptualising displacement as a traumatic rupture to be treated as such or, on the contrary—glorifying it as an identity-affirming act.

Grinberg & Grinberg describe displacement as "a change of such magnitude that it not only puts one's identity on the line but puts it at risk" (Grinberg & Grinberg, 1989: 26). Any post-emigration story can be read as an effort to adjust to this change, or to reorganise one's identity in order to survive. This survival effort often comes with the development of an individual set of defence strategies. A unique and complex identity eventually emerges, which comprises of the parts acquired in the adjustment process, but also of the parts that had to be discarded or stored away. As Boulanger argues:

> As analysts, we hope to bring understanding to our work with patients. With immigrant patients we succeed when we understand not only the selves our patients present in this new culture, but also when we find a way of addressing the selves they have alienated in their attempts to belong.
>
> (Boulanger, 2004: 370–371)

The scope of any deeper therapeutic process with a displaced client is integration of these scattered parts into one complex but whole self.

Any individual whose identity was shaped by relationships with several cultures and languages ends up with a hybrid self. The variety of cultural, geographical, and linguistic influences will be experienced in many individual ways, but a sense of fragmentation remains a common theme. The Russian-American writer Vladimir Nabokov describes himself as "a tricolor Russian, an American brought up in England, a St. Petersburger with a Parisian burr in Russian but who, in French, rolls my 'R's in the Russian manner" (Nabokov, 2019: 365). Behind the apparent ease, with which he presents himself, there is a life of writing in two languages about his own experience of exile. For many emigrants, such an integration will not come as easily and will take months of therapy.

Such a hybrid identity will be the result of endless adaptations, multiple readjustments, relentless code switching, and other metamorphoses. Working with a displaced client, the therapist must keep these processes in mind, identifying the ways in which each individual metamorphosis has taken shape, creating a unique identity blend. As suggested by Nabokov, the unique accent of each emigrant client may start guiding us through these layers of identity.

For individuals coming from mixed and highly mobile backgrounds, the question of belonging can hardly be narrowed down to a binary dilemma. The multiplicity of their attachments and the structure of their relational nets plunge them into emotionally charged waters. For these clients, who wrestle with complex identities, reconsidering belonging is an on-going, repetitive task. In Jhumpa Lahiri's words:

> Those who don't belong to any specific place can't, in fact, return any-where. The concepts of exile and return imply a point of origin, a home-land. Without a homeland and without a true mother tongue, I wander the world, even at my desk. In the end I realize that it wasn't a true exile: far from it. I am exiled even from the definition of exile.
>
> (Lahiri, 2017: 133)

This is a strong statement about an identity shaped by a displacement that happened at the earliest developmental stage and has always been there as a pre-existing condition. Patients who were born to emigrant families carry this wired-in displacement through their lifespan, and its psychological implications are vast and may lead to detachment from any traditional form of belonging. Lahiri manages, through her writing and translation work, through her passion for another language, to find other ways to attach or to belong. Similarly, clients from such emigrant and mixed backgrounds often use all forms of creativity to resolve their belonging conundrum. They may seek strong professional affiliations, create fictional realities in books they write or video games they play, in order to belong to worlds that offer them a sense of homecoming, as illusive and fleeting it may be. They have a taste for online therapy, as the virtual space with no obvious links to any particular space feels less threatening and offers a familiar illusionary quality. The therapeutic endeavour with these mostly unattached individuals is to co-develop a strong enough relational bond. It will validate their fluid ways of being in the world, and at the same time give them a sense of being more grounded, anchored somewhere (which is not home), and attach to someone (who is not a parent, but these "second bests" eventually teach them the tricky art of belonging).

Loss

For many voluntary emigrants, leaving a place to which they did not entirely belong feels like a "triumph", but the move also comes with a sense of mourning. This ambivalent tension between triumph and mourning is the essence of what Freud, after fleeing from Vienna to London at the age of 82, shares in that letter to Max Eitingon: "The feeling of triumph at liberation is mingled too strongly with mourning, for one had still very much loved the prison from which one has been released" (Freud in Gay, 2006: 9). The loss of the familiar world or home, even though home felt like a prison, is one of the central themes in many stories of voluntary migration.

Loss is the one element in the displaced condition that is impossible to ignore, and it has been widely addressed in the professional literature. The most recent edition of Szekacs-Weisz and Ward's volume asks the most important question in the opening lines of the preface:

> Are we ready to face the pictures [of lost childhood] that are going to emerge? Can one do it alone? Will anybody be present to share the stocktaking of what has been lost and what has been found while going through the passages of moving from one country, language, and culture to another?
>
> (Szekacs-Weisz & Ward, 2022: 1)

Any displacement-sensitive therapy can only be acutely tuned to loss, and its task is often about creating a space in which the losses can be witnessed, recognised, and counted in a shared relational effort. The painful truth of the emigrant condition is that there is no leaving without loss, no matter how urgent and necessary that leaving was. Many displaced individuals deny the real extent of their loss for years. Facing it seems too painful or even life-threatening to them. In my own personal displacement story, it has been a confusing emotional reality to grieve a place that had felt alienating in many ways, and has kept feeling so from a distance, even after my migration.

Loss often comes disguised, as emigrants feel that their life in the new place is compromised by their mourning. Clients use multiple defence strategies to escape into a safer emotional space free of loss. The emotional cover-ups and escape routes vary. Therapists should listen carefully to their clients' emotional themes, keeping in mind the underlying loss. Many displaced clients do not bring up the migration-related loss, especially those who do not visit their original country often and have cut ties with their families. They have efficient defences and will cite good reasons for that. This is where the displacement rabbit ears come useful again, attuned as they are to loss in all its stunning variety: from the loss of one's mother tongue to the mourning of a familiar landscape.

Some losses may seem mundane, such as the loss of an object thrown away by our parents when selling the house in which we had grown up. Other losses can be dramatic and too overwhelming to even consider—like the loss of one's country all together. There are many examples in the history of humanity when the country that was left behind crumbles, at least for us. Think about the Jews forced out of Spain in the XVth century. Nearer to us, many Indian emigrants consider that their country has turned into a place of division and persecution. I have my share of this slow and painful mourning process, as have most Russians outside and even inside Russia. The war in Ukraine has put a definite end to any hopes for my original country to be a kinder, more humane place. Lately this collective experience that is also very personal as far as I am concerned has been resonating through my practice. With my Russian emigrant clients, no matter when they left or what the central preoccupation in their current life is, this loss of our shared hope is lurking in each of the four corners of our screens. Often, we will simply acknowledge its ghostly presence, not ready yet to embrace all the consequences of this new loss that was thrown at us by history. The recognition of this shared loss strengthens further the therapeutic alliance—it brings us closer in face of the unavoidable impact this will have on our lives and even our identities.

When Kelley-Lainé refers to the experience of refugees fleeing Stalin's repressions after the Second World War, she insists that "The loss of place soon became loss of identity and the question: 'where am I?' was confused with 'who am I?' This is the beginning of the language of exile. Those who have never been displaced can continue to ask 'who am I?' from their place of origin, the shame and guilt involved in loss is not the same" (Kelley-Lainé in Szekacs-Weisz & Ward, 2022: 4). This is the key point, from which the need for a displacement-sensitive practice stems out. For emigrants, the bitter taste of loss comes with an underlying shame and guilt, shaping any identity challenged and forged by dislocation.

As we address loss in therapy, no matter how big or small, it always gives us an opportunity to elevate therapy to its more existential layer, as every additional loss brings us closer to our own death. Displaced clients are particularly sensitive to existential anxiety, since they encounter loss more often, and in circumstances that make it difficult to ignore.

Loss of one's original place is not dissimilar to the loss of one's parent. Some emigrants find it easier to mourn and engage fully with their new realities; others may be haunted by the ghosts of their home, never finding peace in the new place. A 2010 systematic review of the literature on predictors of complicated grief suggests the importance of previous loss, exposure to trauma, a previous psychiatric history, attachment style, and the relationship to the deceased (Lobb et al., 2010). For an individual who experienced displacement, especially a repetitive one, the majority of these factors are most probably present, since the nature of displacement is traumatic, and any previous displacement will have created enough loss and rupture to impact the consecutive grieving process. As will be further discussed in Chapter 5, insecure attachment may be associated with voluntary dislocation, one of the predictors of complicated grief. The last element—the relationship to the deceased—may be of a particular relevance. Voluntary migration is often the result of a problematic relationship with one's home. Research suggests that the relationship quality with the lost significant other is one of the factors associated with greater grief misery (Easterling et al., 1998; Gamino & Sewell, 2004). Those mourners who had a conflictual, ambivalent, or overly dependent relationship with their deceased are more at risk of a prolonged and complicated grieving process. Emigrants who have a history of a problematic or highly conflictual relationship with their place of origin, like those who felt rejected because of their intrinsic individual characteristics or beliefs and who were alienated or forced out by the political regime, are probably more likely to find it difficult to mourn their loss.

A Russian client of mine, Elena, was a published writer married to a Spaniard who had brought her to Madrid. After years of learning the language, adapting to the new place, and raising their children there, she was still unhappy about her new place, as welcoming and warm as it might have been. She was constantly irritated by the local ways, and often felt depressed. When she first came to see me, she was confused and bewildered by her own inability to "be more positive". Her judgemental attitude towards all things Spanish was putting a strain on her otherwise happy marriage. Her avoidance of any situation that might prove her wrong in her rejection of Spain led to her isolation and alienation from her own children, who were growing up happily Spanish and loved Madrid. "Why do I keep feeling so nostalgic? I was not even happy in Moscow", Elena would often wonder, puzzled by her own feelings. She was paranoid about losing her Russian language, which she was using for her rather successful writing career. She was aware that I spoke Spanish but made sure to avoid any Spanish words. As our work moved forward, we learnt how to look back to her past with curiosity, and with time more elements of that lost life started to emerge. She spoke about her childhood: she never knew her father. Her mother married when Elena was eight, so she felt unwanted and "superfluous" in the new family. Things got much worse when the couple had twins, and her stepfather was offered a job in a different city. The family moved. Elena lost her familiar world and became immersed in a reality she hated. She constantly felt that her stepfather disliked her, as kind as he might seem on the surface. Her mother was avoiding spending too much time alone with her, and had her own version of their reality: Elena had been "given a wonderful new home and a family to grow in". No matter how actually "good" this family seemed, Elena felt only resentment and was always resistant to showing any positive feelings in the presence of her mother and stepfather. "I was so furious with them that I simply could not give them the satisfaction of being happy", she told me once. Stuck in the role of the poor unloved firstborn, Elena's negative and paranoid attitude to her parents ended up extending to the rest of the world. "Is this how you now feel towards Madrid?" I asked. Elena stayed silent, considering this hypothesis. Then she nodded and for the first time, we both felt an overwhelming sadness. Our silence gave her space to mourn all the joy she had lost. "They were actually good parents, I was always included in everything they were doing", she added almost inaudibly. This session led Elena to reconsider the "new family" forced onto her by her mother. And, in a fascinating parallel process, she started reconsidering her own family situation, and Madrid started to look like a gift. Freed from the childish resentment towards her mother, she managed to re-engage more openly with Madrid. Some Spanish words started to pop up in our Russian conversations.

Elena had not processed the loss of her original idealised family before moving cities with her second family. As a result, her grievance had been re-enacted back then. As we talked about what she had lost in that first move—a best friend, a beloved music teacher, and her first bedroom—Elena could finally count her losses. As a result, she could separate those early emotional experiences from her later adult migration. Of course, she did not suddenly love everything Spanish, but she shifted to a more open, curious, and optimistic attitude.

Nostalgia: the importance of looking back

Nostalgia. All humans, emigrants or not, can easily recognise this sweet and sour feeling, so well transmitted by a fado song, an old Ashkenazi melody played by a lonely violin, or a pre-war black-and-white picture of kids playing in the sunny street of a southern town. Neither the street nor the kids of that picture exist any longer. Svetlana Boym, in her unique inquiry on nostalgia, gives this definition of the phenomenon:

> Nostalgia (from nostos—return home, and algia—longing) is a longing for a home that no longer exists or has never existed. Nostalgia is a sentiment of loss and displacement, but it is also a romance with one's own fantasy [...] Nostalgic love can only survive in a long-distance relationship. A cinematic image of nostalgia is a double exposure, or a superimposition of two images—of home and abroad, past and present, dream and everyday life. The moment we try to force it into a single image, it breaks the frame or burns the surface.
>
> (Boym, S., 2001)

The word nostalgia sounds Greek but is actually pseudo-Greek. The word was coined by a Swiss doctor, Johannes Hofer, in 1688. It came from medicine and not poetry. Among the first sufferers diagnosed by Hofer were all kind of displaced individuals of the 17th century—domestic servants, soldiers, students (Boym, 1996). In Hofer's time, displacement was an unescapable condition, a person ended up locked in, with an unbridgeable distance between the individual and their original land and language. In modern displacement on the other hand, photography, video, telephone, messaging and ever emerging communication technologies are somehow keeping nostalgia alive. Old places and people can be brought back into our present moment or space.

Nostalgia will not disappear any time soon. As I work with all kinds of modern nomads—expats, emigrants, globe-trotters—I am in touch with nostalgia-related feelings on a daily basis. Akhtar suggests that analysts should be prepared for much nostalgic rumination in the treatment of the immigrant, and little in the treatment of the exiled clients (Akhtar, 1995). But in my practice this is not as clear cut, and feelings of nostalgia have more to do with the nature of the relationship one has with one's home country rather than with the particular nature of one's displacement condition.

Oliver Sacks, another immigrant, adapted a telling epigraph from Kierkegaard for his memoir: "Life must be lived forwards but can only be understood backwards" (Sacks, 2019). In any kind of psychodynamic therapy, we work in-between the past and the present. In therapy with emigrants, this duality is easily represented by home and abroad. Nostalgia becomes a therapist's best ally, a guide into that lost world which usually does not disappear from our dreams or our nightmares that easily. Akhtar summarises the three intrinsic facets of the analytic treatment of refugees and exiles as "(1) empathy with the bitter side of the patient's negative nostalgia, (2) interpretative resolutions of the defences against nostalgia, and (3) bridging interventions to link up the sweet with the bitter memories of the homeland" (Akhtar, 1995: 130). Any therapist, no matter her school of thought, will probably recognise in this summary the work that we usually perform with our patients around their problematic carers. The defensive split that often separates the good parent from the bad one, or the warm motherland from the rejecting one, must be understood and repaired, which can eventually lead to an integration of these two contradictory facets of the same attachment figure.

Exploring the phenomenon of post-communist nostalgia, Maria Todorova emphasises: "If nostalgia is about, loosely, some form of remembrance, our task is to analyse all of this—in short, to put thoughts to memories" (Todorova & Gille, 2010). This could be applied to therapy with displaced individuals. The process of putting together the pieces of our clients' stories, integrating their emotional experience with their cognitive reality, makes them more whole. Life stories involving dislocation often feel messy and fragmented; it is critical to bring their threads together and make a more meaningful outline out of them. Therapy then becomes a safe transitional space (Knafo, 1998), where one can look at the chaotic material of one's movable worlds and appreciate its diverse quality, its richness, before using its spread parts to construct a more integrated self.

Here again, the emigrant writers have put into words an emotional experience of nostalgia that can be too confusing to be verbalised by displaced clients. Eva Hoffman, an American writer whose family fled Poland to escape the Holocaust, describes nostalgia as:

> a feeling whose shades and degrees I am destined to know intimately, but at this hovering moment, it comes upon me like a visitation from a whole new geography of emotions, an annunciation of how much an absence can hurt.
>
> (Hoffman, 1998)

Olga Tokarczuk, an acclaimed Polish writer with displacement history in her family, is a psychologist and a self-described disciple of Carl Gustav Jung. This background makes her writings particularly interesting to consider when reflecting on nostalgia. This is how she describes one of her character's nostalgic feelings:

> Just before she'd come here she'd suddenly been battered by waves of a strange nostalgia. Strange because it had to do with things that were too trivial to really be missed: the water that collects in puddles in the holes in the pavements, the shades of neon left in that water by stray drops of petrol; the heavy creaky old doors to the dark stairwells. She also missed the glazed earthenware plates with the brown band with the Społem co-op logo on it that they used at the cafeteria to serve lazy pierogi with melted butter and sugar sprinkled on top. But then with time nostalgia had seeped into the new land like spilled milk, not leaving any trace.
>
> (Tokarczuk, 2018: 295)

The bewilderment that emanates from these lines reflects what many displaced clients feel when they stumble on nostalgic feelings. Why should I miss these simple things from home that had no particular meaning or even felt annoying back then? Loss of the familiar puts a nostalgic veil onto old familiar objects, making them somehow more meaningful, bringing them into the foreground of our awareness. The metaphor of the spilled milk naturally alludes to the English proverb about the uselessness of crying over spilled milk, which can be interpreted here as "one should not mourn the loss of an object". But milk, on an unconscious level, is what humans, like other mammals, need for their early survival. This makes the interdiction even stronger. When Tokarczuk choses to use this idiom, she also reminds us of the resistance that one feels against embracing the loss when experiencing nostalgia.

Nostomania is another fascinating facet of nostalgia. It is usually seen as a rare medical condition that describes a person with an abnormal desire to go back and relive moments in the past. Somebody suffering from nostomania displays an obsessive interest in nostalgia, especially as an extreme manifestation of homesickness. The Russian poet Joseph Brodsky, who spent half his life in exile, reflected at length on this condition:

> a writer in exile is, by and large, a retrospective and retroactive being. In other words, retrospection plays an excessive (compared with other people's lives) role in his existence, overshadowing his reality and dimming the future into something thicker than its usual pea soup. Like the false prophets in Dante's Inferno, his head is forever turned backward and his tears, or saliva, are running down between his shoulder blades.
>
> (Brodsky, 2011)

Whilst many emigrants organically develop these peculiar backward-looking parts within them, all therapists naturally "suffer" from nostomania, as they constantly investigate their clients' past. Both, nostalgia and nostomania are ultimately about loss and pain we experience whilst considering what we had in the past and what is missing in our present. Displaced individuals have left behind, and possibly lost forever, people, houses, furniture, landscapes, and books. The fact that they keep existing somewhere without them makes the whole experience even more painful. In that Haraucourt's line, "partir c'est mourir un peu" (to leave is to die a little), there is a deep truth that any expatriate is familiar with: every time we leave a place, we leave some parts of ourselves behind. And this partial death is scary. In her novel *Latecomers* Anita Brookner, a British writer who was born to a Jewish emigrant family, states that "Nostalgia is only for the securely based" (Brookner, 2010: 196). The two main characters of the novel were brought to England as children from the Nazi Germany. As adults, they both struggle with the psychological consequences of this early displacement and looking back seems like a life-threatening activity. Only one of them, and only as an ageing man, will be able to afford the luxury of returning to his original city, and eventually recover some lost part of his own identity.

For many emigrants, fear of facing the loss often results in an aversion to therapy. This common resistance is often linked to the belief that if we do look back, something catastrophic could befall us, exactly as happened to Lot's wife who turned into a pillar of salt (Genesis XIX, 1–29). She literally became frozen, illustrating the frigidity and desensitisation of some trauma-tised patients. This powerful biblical injunction to not look back, or be pun-ished, responds to this often-unconscious fear. But can we look back without getting stuck in the past? Many emigrants turn up for their initial therapy session with this question in mind.

Maybe there are different ways of looking back: either from a nostalgic or from a nostomanic positions. If nostalgia is located at one end of the rela-tionship-to-the-past continuum, nostomania would be at its opposite end. In exploring one's nostalgic feelings, they are often imbued with sadness but also with joy. In the nostalgic mourning there is the potential for acceptance of loss and the subsequent integration of the past experience into the present inevitably shaped by displacement.

In contrast, a nostomanic person is stuck in regret about the loss, and unable to go on with his life. In the safety of the therapeutic relationship, we attempt to make bridges between the past and the present. After all, in this specific setting we are not expected to look back and count losses in solitude. The pre-displacement past is often inhabited by ghosts, which seem scarier when the lights are off. On entering a dark room lonely, to have at one's side somebody who knows where the light switch is makes a real difference.

With optimistic élan, Svetlana Boym defines nostalgia as "both a social disease and a creative emotion, a poison and a cure" (Boym, 2001: 354). The therapy of displacement has this exact scope—in integrating the disowned parts of our clients' narratives, together we exercise the power of turning the disease into its cure.

Lostness, derealisation, depersonalisation

"I remember arriving at Victoria to set out for Lowell's, and when I saw the train schedule, I suddenly lost it completely. I stopped being able to process information. It wasn't that I was frightened by the thought that here was somewhere else I had to go but ... My retina was overworked, probably, and I thought with some horror about the notion of space unfolding before me right then. You can probably imagine what it is like."

"Oh, yes! It's a sensation of horror and uncertainty about what ..."

"About what's happening just around the corner, right?"

This dialogue between two Russian emigrant writers, Joseph Brodsky and Solomon Volkov, captures the sudden experience that is familiar for many displaced clients (Volkov, 1998: 134). Brodsky, who lived more than half of his life in exile, recognises this disconnection from reality, lostness, and inability to re-engage with the new surroundings that feel overwhelming. The scenery that prompts Brodsky to experience derealisation is far from coincidental—Victoria, a busy London train station, an island of transience in the middle of a big foreign city—a perfect metaphor that illustrates the confusion that is the life of a freshly arrived emigrant.

Derealisation and depersonalisation are dissociative phenomena that are typically associated with some severe neurological conditions such as epilepsy and various psychiatric disorders such as depersonalisation disorder, borderline personality disorder, bipolar disorder, schizophrenia, dissociative identity disorder, and other mental conditions (Spiegel et al., 2011; Stein et al., 2014). Derealisation is a state in which the environment is experienced as unreal or dreamlike (Spiegel & Cardeña, 1991). Depersonalisation is an experience of feeling detached, or as if one is an outside observer of one's own mental process or body, or feeling like an automaton (Spiegel & Cardeña, 1991). Both of these dissociative phenomena are "quintessential responses to acute trauma; they are highly prevalent in those subjected to motor vehicle accidents, emotional/verbal abuse, and imprisonment, among others" (Spiegel et al., 2011: 830), but in my own clinical observations, these phenomena are also widely experienced by clients experiencing displacement.

The presence of dissociative symptoms of this kind amongst emigrants is not widely researched. The rare exception is the recent paper by Dowd in which she discusses the case of Jane, a young woman whose family fled the Balkan wars, who walked into her therapy room in a highly dissociative state. "I recognised the dissociation and uncanny out-of-place feeling as extreme displacement anxiety and knew therefore that matters of 'place' were paramount" (Dowd, 2019: 255). Dowd is a British emigrant in Australia and recognises something that often gets overlooked—"the acute displacement anxiety", demonstrating an inspiring example of a sophisticated pair of displacement rabbit ears.

Reflecting on these symptoms, Anna Lembke, an American psychiatrist who specialises in working with addiction, points out the deeper psychological mechanisms that underlie derealisation and depersonalisation:

> When our lived experience diverges from our projected image, we are prone to feel detached and unreal, as fake as false images that we created. [...] It is a terrifying feeling, which commonly contributes to thoughts of suicide; after all if we don't feel real, ending our lives feels inconsequential.
>
> (Lembke, 2021: 192)

This divergence is even more acute for those emigrants, like Brodsky, who have not had the chance to prepare for their displacement and have been thrown into the new alienating reality. These feelings can be momentaneous and brief but can also linger if the emigrant does not feel welcomed or is unable to find his mark in the new place. In some extreme cases, this can lead to suicide, which is then perceived as the only way to escape this seemingly unresolvable existential confusion. Suicide rates amongst immigrants are higher than in the general population (Bursztein Lipsicas et al., 2012; Forte et al., 2018; Spallek et al., 2015). This is hardly surprising if we keep in mind that displacement is a traumatic and stressful event that happens in the context of increased isolation and loss of the usual support system. When clients bring such symptoms as derealisation and depersonalisation to therapy, they usually are not able to identify them as a defence and feel utterly confused about this scary emotional experience. Paying close attention to the reporting of these symptoms, even if the latter is done timidly, can help to identify clients who may be at a risk of suicidal behaviour earlier on.

The concept of "Home"

The notion of "home" is both confusing and crucial for those who have left their original place and made a life elsewhere. In therapy with displaced and highly mobile individuals, it also turns into a vulnerable and emotionally charged topic. Each time one of my clients goes back to their original home for a visit, I think twice before uttering the otherwise common "Enjoy your stay back home"; it is far too complex an objective for those who are constantly experimenting with physical separation from their original place and significant others.

Geographers routinely recognise the importance of the homeland as universal:

> The profound attachment to the homeland appears to be a worldwide phenomenon. It is not limited to any particular culture and economy. It is known to literate and nonliterate people, hunter-gatherers, and sedentary farmers, as well as city dwellers. The city or land is viewed as mother, and it nourishes; place is an archive of fond memories and splendid

achievements that inspires the present; place is permanent and hence reassuring to man, who sees frailty in himself and chance and flux everywhere.

(Tuan, 1977)

With this reassuring quality of homeland disrupted, displaced individuals' concept of home is challenged by their detachment from it, and eventually transformed accordingly into their new uprooted existence.

If mythological home is a place where we should feel safe and protected, for some expatriates the original place felt neither safe nor nourishing. When the original home is experienced as oppressive or rejecting, leaving becomes a matter of self-protection or even survival; the only way to allow the necessary self-development to take place. I remember clearly my departure from Russia: my first steps on Italian soil, discovering the palm trees, the smell of coffee, and the sun-tanned people smiling, gesticulating, and talking loudly all around me ... I was instantly overwhelmed by a feeling of familiarity; I felt safe and at peace. I had not yet mastered the language, I didn't know many people there, yet I felt at home. Years later, returning to my native town, I didn't experience anything similar to this warm feeling of homecoming.

For the more settled, "home" comes down to a house or a suburb or a town, for others it is a country. For many of the clients I meet online, home is more of a multiple and dynamic object. They often struggle to answer the question: "Where is your home?" This question, simple for some less uprooted individuals, has no simple answer for those who are displaced. In therapy with an emigrant client, searching for the answer to this particular question can become a guiding theme of the therapeutic journey.

Recently a client of mine, Rachel, an American expat in Paris, shared an incident that was causing her a lot of turmoil. She was having a French lesson, and as she was talking about her plans for travelling back to the USA, she was unsure about which verb to use. "What stands for 'return'"? she asked. "It really depends on which place you consider home", her teacher answered placidly. In French, there are two verbs that mean to "return" (rentrer/retourner), and their use is informed by what one considers "home" at that particular moment. "Am I an emigrant then?" Rachel asked me in bewilderment, as we pondered on what "home" was for her. Paying close attention to her quandary allowed us to open a new, fascinating, chapter in her therapy work. Rachel recognised that as she was thinking about "home", her original place—a small town in rural California—was simply not popping up in her mind. What she was actually thinking about was her husband and the dog that they had adopted in Paris, her few friends scattered around the globe ... all these objects, seemingly unrelated to the place that she was brought up in, constituted the concept of "home" at that moment. As we kept reflecting on this topic, she looked around and added "your room also feels like home", and I instantly knew what she was talking about; for emigrants the evolution from place to people is natural and necessary, as one can hardly rely on the stability of places when leading a peripatetic life. As Pico Iyer, a British-born essayist mainly known for his travel writings, sums up in his viral 2013 TED talk, "Where Is Home?":

> For more and more of us, home has really less to do with a piece of soil, than you could say, with a piece of soul. If somebody suddenly asks me, "Where's your home?" I think about my sweetheart or my closest friends or the songs that travel with me wherever I happen to be.

When pondering on the meaning of such a primary object as "home", it is refreshing to go back to the definition used by biologists: "area traversed by the individual in its normal activities of food gathering, mating, and caring for young" (Burt, 1943). If I go with this definition, then my "home" is the 16th arrondissement in Paris, as I rarely venture out of this neighbourhood to complete these survival tasks. On the other hand, I strongly rely on the internet, which is a rather place-less space, in order to meet many of my relational and other needs—this is where I mostly shop for books, meet with my clients, engage with peers, friends, and family. Of course, since this definition was put forward 80 years ago, human society has evolved greatly and is now challenged by its own technological advances. For some of my clients, especially the young ones, the virtual spaces, such as an online game they obsessively play, or an internet community they belong to, can feel as "homely" as any physical place in which their lives evolve. Inviting them to reflect on what actually feels like home leads to a better understanding of their emotional and relational landscapes.

From environmental psychology, preoccupied with the notion of place and place-identity, comes a definition of "home" as places that "are organized and represented in ways that help individuals to maintain self-coherence and self-esteem, to realize self-regulation principles" (Dixon & Durrheim, 2000: 29). This opens a developmental dimension that strongly links our identity and our emotional wellbeing to the place we associate ourselves with. The experience of home, if disruptive or unreliable, can easily lead to a sense of fragmentation and confusion. Well before I started any personal therapy, I found myself for the very first time in the group of my fellow trainees. It was the first day of our therapy training, and I was one of the two people for whom English was not a first language. When we had to introduce ourselves and share how we felt at that particular moment, I could not utter anything but "confused". Not only in my home culture was talking about feelings a no-go area, but also my then experience of dislocation was causing me a complete sense of confusion not only about *where* my home was but also about *who* I was. I was only able to figure this out in retrospect; it took me years of personal therapy, and countless hours spent with my displaced clients, in whom I recognise the same confusion again and again. In many cases, in order to address and eventually resolve displacement-related identity dis-orientation, we have to look at what constitutes "home" and inquire through deep layers of this historical concept.

A certain level of ambivalence is always part of a displacement experience: "every immigrant carries with him a mixture of anxiety, sadness, pain, and nostalgia, on one side, and expectations and hopes on the other" (Grinberg & Grinberg, 1984: 9). We ought to use our displacement rabbit ears and identify when this ambivalence is strong enough to bring up a defence mechanism. As a typical illustration, one of my clients started our first therapy session with a strong statement: "I hate my hometown". Those striking words became the beginning of her journey back to that place which haunted her.

A child may end up feeling angry when his carers who are associated with the original home become emotionally challenging or unresponsive. This anger (or even hatred of an object that they are supposed to love for my client mentioned above) seems so unacceptable that we look for ways to deal with the ambivalence. Hating one's home place often seems more acceptable than hating one's parents. But for some even this is out of reach. In this case one may try to resolve the tension by splitting home into Bad and Good, separat-ing two conflicting parts. Then we can hate one of the two and ignore the second. Or, alternatively, adore the "good home" and ignore the "bad" one. In both cases, we lose touch with some parts of our culture and ourselves. To re-integrate these parts becomes one of the aims of a therapy.

Examples of emigrants adjusting to their dislocated realities abound in both strategies. Many, craving for inclusion, try hard to melt into the new culture. In order to do so they often have to deny the "good" home and reject the remaining part as "bad". The cost of such defence can involve losing their first language or links to those who stayed back home. Another, opposite, strategy involves the idealisation of the "good" home; those who choose it prefer to evolve in their restricted social circle, to eat the traditional food of their original home country, and keep speaking their native language, segre-gating themselves from the local community.

It is always fruitful to pay close attention to the personal defence strategies used by our displaced clients to resolve their ambivalent feelings about home. It can open fruitful avenues for exploring their broader coping mechanisms, and eventually lead to the integration of the rejected or alienated parts asso-ciated with their past homes.

Displaced therapists

"I feel a kind of great privilege in the coincidence of my existential condition and my occupation," writes Brodsky, who experienced his exile not as a political condition, but as an existential one (Patterson, 1993). This is a rela-table situation for many displaced therapists practising around the world, for whom the personal wrestling with their dislocation creates a fertile ground for the meaning-making work they perform daily with their clients. The number of such therapists grows constantly, mirroring the increase of mobility in the general population. In many ways their task is similar to that of exiled writers—processing the collective experience of displacement-related trauma, to alleviate the individual struggles of their clients.

The awareness a therapist may or may not have of her personal experience of displacement impacts her identity and work. Yet, personal accounts of emigrant therapists in the professional literature are scarce, especially when you consider the number of displaced practitioners. This literature gap has been slowly filling, and a few more recent volumes have arrived to enrich this necessary conversation (Beltsiou, 2015; Szekacs-Weisz & Ward, 2004; Szekacs-Weisz & Ward, 2022; Nayar-Akhtar, 2015). The contributors, all emigrant psychoanalysts or therapists, dig into their personal displacement and its impact on their identity and work.

The most candid reflection comes from an Indian-American psychoanalyst, Salman Akhtar (Akhtar, 1995; Akhtar, 2006). In his 2006 paper, Akhtar ponders on the "technical challenges" an immigrant psychoanalyst may face in his work. And yet, the term "technical" puts an unusual distance between this otherwise-warm analyst and his topic. In the opening lines of his paper, Akhtar refers to Freud's personal experience of emigration, noting that because Freud's two personal displacements occurred early and late in life, "the inner world of an immigrant analyst, therefore, did not capture his attention" (Akhtar, 2006: 22). Akhtar attributes the reluctance of early psychoanalytical thinkers to dwell on their emigrant condition to "the reluctance of main-stream psychoanalysis to deal with sociological, historical, and cultural factors in adult life, in favor of an exclusive focus upon the intrapsychic residues of early childhood" (Akhtar, 2006: 22). Akhtar makes another guess about the underlying reasons for their silence on this topic, and it is probably a relatable one for many emigrant therapists, myself included: it is our avoidance of trauma. We may fear that this trauma, which is part of any displacement, will prevent us from making a better life in the new place:

> Wanting to forget their traumatic departures from their countries of origin, to deny cultural differences between themselves and their patients, and to become rapidly assimilated at a professional level, they had no desire to draw others' (and their own) attention to their ethnic and national origins. Hence, they wrote little about their experiences in practicing analysis as "foreigners"
>
> (Akhtar, 2006: 23)

The therapist's failure to fully recognise their own displaced condition—their "foreignness" in front of their clients—often stems from the shame that displacement brings up. In my own work with dislocated clients, I am constantly reminded of the therapeutic power of recognising and addressing the shared experience of shame in the "here-and-now" of the session. In a striking example from her work with an emigrant client, Sam, Beltsiou demonstrates how being aware of her own experience of displacement-related shame helped her better connect with his struggle: "Alongside my shame, I am determined to understand him" (Beltsiou, 2015: 94). Another interesting account comes from the same volume (Ipp, in Beltsiou, 2015). Ipp, a white English-speaking South African emigrant in Canada shares her work with Nell—a South African who speaks Afrikaans. Working with her fellow South African who came from a different, opposing camp of their torn and divided home country, triggered an unsettling emotional response—a feeling of shame, which allowed her to connect at a deeper level with the mutual pain and dissatisfaction with their original environment, which had led them both to the decision to emigrate.

Akhtar calls on emigrant analysts to "wonder about the patient's choice of him in particular as the analyst" (Akhtar, 2006: 23). Inquiring into a client's choice of us as their therapist is important in any case, but when the client has researched their suitable therapist on the Internet, it is even more so. When, given almost an endless choice of online therapists, they go for somebody whose name sounds different from their own and who practises in a second language, this question takes on an additional weight. "Why me?" I repeatedly ask such clients, and the array of responses always brings some precious grist to the therapy mill.

Michael, one of my online clients, was referred to me by an American colleague, who could not see him at the time. A white, middle-aged Minnesota man, Michael had rarely ventured outside of his state, and had never left the US. In addition, I knew that his initial choice had been for an older American male therapist. "How would you feel about ending up with a Russian-born therapist who lives across the ocean?" I asked him at the end of our first session. He kept silent for some time, pondering on my question. "Actually relieved", he finally said. His surprising answer opened a wide path for our further exploration of his constant self-doubt and deep shame. Later on, he recognised that it would probably have taken him longer to share some of his fantasies, that he thought shameful, with a more "conventional" therapist from his own conservative and religious background. Conscious and unconscious reasons for which clients may choose an emigrant therapist from a cultural background different from their own are endless but maintaining a curious stance about their underlying motivations is always a fruitful path.

When working with displaced clients, our ability to recognise our own displaced condition (when that is the case of course), gives us a powerful tool that facilitates the connection—the kinship that results from a shared emigrant background can be turned into a reliable relational glue. My own work with emigrants constantly reminds me that leaving my own displaced condition outside my therapy room is not an option. After all, both my name and my accent, no matter which language I use, give it away. The warm feeling of kinship I feel when listening to an emigrant client speak, is a solid and steady ground on which we can build a therapeutic alliance, even with the most avoidant online clients, who tend to hide behind the reassuring boundary of their screen or the comforting limits of their second language.

Internal emigration: a particular form of displacement

Among my online clients, there is a group that does not fit the exact definition of displacement as discussed so far. They remained in their country of origin but seem frozen in space and time, often displaying recurrent symptoms such as depression, anxiety, low self-esteem, and constant self-doubt. They often grew up feeling that they did not belong in their country, but for various reasons (e.g. an "iron curtain" of any kind, family situation, physical handicap, etc.) they cannot emigrate. They feel trapped and disempowered in the face of the unresolvable conflict that this situation represents. Their inability to escape the place that is rejecting them only reinforces the feeling of shame triggered by a constant experience of being different and rejected by the place itself. Such internal exile is often even more poignant than exile to or from a particular place (Bevan, 1990). Exile within a place called "home" results in a feeling of shame about not being a "good enough" son or daughter of that homeland.

My own Russian culture offers abundant examples of such a psychological strategy for subsisting in an unfriendly reality. The Soviet history gave us not only the concept of internal migration, but also a rich cultural heritage, which survived "underground" despite the intermittently tyrannical regime. Many artists—Shostakovich being probably the most striking example—were living a paradoxical experience of inner freedom in the middle of an oppressive outer reality (Volkov, 2004).

When I meet with clients who have evolved under an authoritarian regime, I recognise the strength of this coping strategy. Our sessions happen online through videoconferencing systems, as they are often unable to find suitable support in their own place. These regimes have no love of therapy, which aims at empowering the individual; they usually opt for a kind of punitive psychiatry, which was so well developed in Soviet Russia. Its aim was, in Brodsky's words, "to slow you down, to stop you, so that you can do absolutely nothing ..." (Volkov, 1998).

Online therapy offers these inward emigrants a third space, outside of their unfriendly environment and somewhat on the outskirts of their inner reality. In the virtual space of therapy, they find a friendly person before them, open and curious to learn about their worlds. The online reality shared with their transcultural therapist beyond the curtain eventually becomes a safe space in which to reflect upon the painful discordance between their inner and outer worlds.

"I was born in the wrong place", one of my online clients told me once. Someone with fidgety feet and a knotty relationship with their home place.

Growing up she had felt out of place in her native town, tucked away in the middle of Pennsylvania. I keep hearing different versions of this hard-sounding statement, from clients from various cultures and social backgrounds. The feeling of not fitting in, not belonging to their original environment, is widely shared by emigrant writers. Edward Said's account of this experience is probably the most quintessential:

> There was always something wrong with how I was invented and meant to fit in with the world of my parents and four sisters. Whether this was because I constantly misread my part or because of some deep flaw in my being I could not tell for most of my early life. Sometimes I was intransigent and proud of it. At other times I seemed to myself to be neatly devoid of any character at all, timid, uncertain, without will. Yet the over-riding sensation I had was of always being out of place.
>
> (Said, 1999: 3)

Said's experience of being deeply flawed, his constant uncertainty and confusion about his own worth are all indicators of various degrees of feeling shame. Joe Burgo, a psychotherapist and author of *Shame*, insists that

> Unreciprocated affection or interest will always stir emotions from the shame family. As part of our genetic inheritance, we want to connect with a loved one who will love us in return; when our longing is disappointed, when we fail to connect, we inevitably experience shame, however we name the feeling.
>
> (Burgo, 2018)

The motherland that does not love us in return is similar to a parent that fails to meet our expectations of love. Both of these unfortunate situations naturally result in feeling that something is deeply wrong with us. One of the ways we can cope with such circumstances is by leaving our original place altogether. For some, the decision to emigrate, often a difficult one, is unconsciously driven by the need to avoid the shame provoked by the discordance between who we are and who we are expected to be in order to fit in. Many of my clients' stories confirm that their choice to leave home was the best survival strategy. The most obvious examples are those of queer individuals from countries that pathologise and punish homosexuality: they flee their homes to be able to freely live their lives in the way that feels right to them.

Russian emigrant writers give us a powerful lesson of resilience in dealing with hostile but inescapable realities. Through their art they create inner bubbles of freedom, and have often had to evolve in parallel realities like Joseph Brodsky, who, decades before emigrating, introduced the notion of an "indifferent homeland" in his early poem *Stanzas* (1962) inspired by the quintessential poet in exile, Ovid.

The use of a foreign language in their writing by emigrant writers such as Brodsky or Nabokov is emblematic and has a deeper meaning: they claim a new freedom from constrains imposed by their culture. Committing to a chosen second language, despite the difficulties and losses that this choice implies, is a powerful affirmation of the individual freedom (Kellman, 2003). This second language becomes the tongue of the parallel inner world and a language of freedom. The same is true for some of my clients living in the state of internal exile. They often reach out to a therapist who speaks English even though it is not their mother tongue. This choice complicates their therapeutic journey but also allows some unexpected depth, and an escape from the shame that binds them.

Evolving in the self-created bubbles of parallel realities drives them further away from reality. This further isolation can only deepen the shame that they already feel about being deeply flawed and not fitting in. Those constricted into these self-created inner worlds will often display recurrent symptoms, such as depression, anxiety, low self-esteem, and constant self-doubt, as described by Said. What online therapy can offer to these inward emigrants is a third space, located outside of their unfriendly environment, on the outskirts of their inner reality. In their conflicting inner and outer worlds, they are alone, but in the virtual space of therapy, they find a friendly ally in front of them, open and curious to learn about them and their worlds.

The media of communication used for therapy online often play an important role in dealing with life in unfriendly, inescapable surroundings. Many of my clients living in a state of internal immigration turn to the internet to find likeminded peers and feel less alienated.

There is an intriguing parallel between the "voices" of the free radio that had offered, during the Soviet era, an opening towards the other side of the curtain, and the social media of today. The latter are more interactive by nature. During the Soviet times one was only able to listen and feel connected by a stranger's voice talking in one's own language but from the other side of the divisive wall, whilst the modern technologies offer a possibility for a dialogue, often in English, the current lingua franca.

I have witnessed many situations in which a bubble of freedom offered by the internet kept individuals sane: Saudi women who would connect with each other in the ethereal space of virtual freedom; a gay man from Siberia finding a connection with those just like him and acquiring some form of validation of his own experience; a queer young woman in Putin's Russia working for a liberal online news platform and through her work connecting with those whose thinking she can share.

Online therapy with a transcultural therapist, who evolved on the other side of the wall, in a different and often freer reality, thus becomes an ultimate opening for individuals who experience their realities as oppressive. In some fortunate cases, it will shake up the juxtaposition of the two incompatible

realities, into which the individual has got locked, and offer something else—
a less lonely space in which one can experiment with fitting in, belonging and
imagining other, less lonely, and freer possibilities.

References

Akhtar, S. (1995). A third individuation: Immigration, identity, and the psychoanalytic
process. *Journal of the American Psychoanalytic Association*, 43(4), 1051–1084.
doi:10.1177/000306519504300406.

Akhtar, S. (2006). Technical challenges faced by the immigrant psychoanalyst. *The
Psychoanalytic Quarterly*, 75(1), 21–43. doi:10.1002/j.2167-4086.2006.tb00031.x.

Amati Mehler, J., Argentieri, S., & Canestri, J. (1990). The babel of the unconscious.
International Journal of Psycho-Analysis, 71 (Pt 4), 569.

Beltsiou, J. (Ed.) (2015). *Immigration in psychoanalysis: Locating ourselves*. London
and New York: Routledge.

Bevan, D. (1990). *Literature and exile*. Amsterdam/Atlanta GA: Rodopi.

Boulanger, G. (2004). Lot's wife, Cary Grant, and the American dream: Psychoanalysis with immigrants. *Contemporary Psychoanalysis*, 40(3), 353–372.
doi:10.1080/00107530.2004.10745836.

Boym, S. (1996). Estrangement as a lifestyle: Shklovsky and Brodsky. *Poetics Today*,
17(4), 511–530. doi:10.2307/1773211.

Boym, S. (2001). *The future of nostalgia*. New York: Basic Books.

Brodsky, J. (2011). *Less than one: Selected essays*. London: Penguin Books.

Brookner, A. (2010). *Latecomers*. London: Penguin Books.

Burgo, J. (2018). *Shame: Free yourself, find joy, and build true self-esteem*. New York:
St. Martin's Press.

Bursztein Lipsicas, C., Mäkinen, I. H., Apter, A., De Leo, D., Kerkhof, A., Lönnq-
vist, J., & Schmidtke, A. (2012). Attempted suicide among immigrants in European
countries: An international perspective. *Social Psychiatry and Psychiatric Epide-
miology*, 47(2), 241–251.

Burt, W. H. (1943). Territoriality and home range concepts as applied to mammals.
Journal of Mammalogy, 24(3), 346–352.

Clewell, T. (2004). Mourning beyond melancholia: Freud's psychoanalysis of loss.
Journal of the American Psychoanalytic Association, 52(1), 43–67. doi:10.1177/
00030651040520010601.

Dixon, J., & Durrheim, R. (2000). Displacing place-identity: A discursive approach to
locating self and other. *British Journal of Social Psychology*, 39, 27–44.

Dowd, A. (2019). Uprooted minds: Displacement, trauma and dissociation: Uprooted
minds. *Journal of Analytical Psychology*, 64(2), 244–269. doi:10.1111/1468-
5922.12481.

Erikson, E. (1968). *Identity: Youth and crisis*. New York: W. W. Norton.

Forte, A., Trobia, F., Gualtieri, F., Lamis, D. A., Cardamone, G., Giallonardo, V., … Pom-
pili, M. (2018). Suicide risk among immigrants and ethnic minorities: A literature over-
view. *International Journal of Environmental Research and Public Health*, 15(7), 1438.

Gamino, L. A., Sewell, K. W., & Easterling, L. W. (1998). Scott & White grief study: An
empirical test of predictors of intensified mourning. *Death Studies*, 22(4), 333–355.
doi:10.1080/074811898201524.

Gamino, L. A., Sewell, K. W., & Easterling, L. W. (2000). Scott and White grief study phase 2: Toward an adaptive model of grief. *Death Studies*, 24(7), 633–660. doi:10.1080/07481180050132820.

Gamino, L. A., & Sewell, K. W. (2004). Meaning constructs as predictors of bereavement adjustment: A report from the Scott & White grief study. *Death Studies*, 28(5), 397–421. doi:10.1080/07481180490437536.

Gay, P. (2006). *Freud: A life for our time*. New York: W. W. Norton.

Gopnik, A. (2000). *Paris to the moon*. New York: Random House.

Grinberg, L., & Grinberg, R. (1989). *Psychoanalytic perspectives on migration and exile*. New Haven CT & London: Yale University Press.

Hoffman, E. (1998). *Lost in translation: A life in a new language*. London: Vintage Books.

Kellman, S. G. (Ed.) (2003). *Switching languages: Translingual writers reflect on their craft*. Lincoln NE and London: University of Nebraska Press.

Knafo, D. (1998). Transitional space in the treatment of immigrants. *Israel Journal of Psychiatry and Related Sciences*, 35, 48–55.

Lahiri, J. (2017). *In other words*. London: Bloomsbury Paperbacks.

Lawrence, T. H. (2002). *Seven pillars of wisdom*. London: Penguin.

Lembke, A. (2021). *Dopamine nation: Finding balance in the age of indulgence*. London: Headline.

Lobb, E. A., Kristjanson, L. J., Aoun, S. M., Monterosso, L., Halkett, G. K. B., & Davies, A. (2010). Predictors of complicated grief: A systematic review of empirical studies. *Death Studies*, 34(8), 673–698. doi:10.1080/07481187.2010.496686.

Makari, G. (2008). *Revolution in mind*. New York: HarperCollins.

Nabokov, V. (2019). *Think, write, speak*. London: Penguin Books.

Nathanson, D. L. (1992). *Shame and pride: Affect, sex, and the birth of the self*. New York and London: W. W. Norton.

Nayar-Akhtar, M. (2015). *Identities in transition: The growth and development of a multicultural therapist*. London: Karnac Books.

Patterson, D. (1993). From exile to affirmation: The poetry of Joseph Brodsky. *Studies in 20th & 21st Century Literature*, 17(2), 365. doi:10.4148/2334-4415.1330.

Phillips, A. (2014). *Becoming Freud: The making of a psychoanalyst*. New Haven CT: Yale University Press.

Rolland, L., Dewaele, J., & Costa, B. (2017). Multilingualism and psychotherapy: Exploring multilingual clients' experiences of language practices in psychotherapy. *International Journal of Multilingualism*, 14(1), 69–85. doi:10.1080/14790718.2017.1259009.

Sacks, O. (2019). *Everything in its place: First loves and last tales*. London: Picador.

Said, E. W. (1999). *Out of place: A memoir* (1st edn). New York: Knopf.

Shostakovich, D. D., & Volkov, S. (2004). *Testimony: The memoirs of Dmitri Shostakovich* (25th edn). New York: Limelight.

Spallek, J., Reeske, A., Norredam, M., Nielsen, S. S., Lehnhardt, J., & Razum, O. (2015). Suicide among immigrants in Europe: A systematic literature review. *The European Journal of Public Health*, 25(1), 63–71.

Spiegel, D., & Cardeña, E. (1991). Disintegrated experience: The dissociative disorders revisited. *Journal of Abnormal Psychology*, 100(3), 366–378. doi:10.1037/0021-843X.100.3.366.

Spiegel, D., Loewenstein, R. J., Lewis-Fernández, R., Sar, V., Simeon, D., Vermetten, E., ... Dell, P. F. (2011). Dissociative disorders in DSM-5. *Depression and Anxiety*, 28(9), 824–852. doi:10.1002/da.20874.

Stein, D. J., Craske, M. A., Friedman, M. J., & Phillips, K. A. (2014). Anxiety disorders, obsessive-compulsive and related disorders, trauma- and stressor-related disorders, and dissociative disorders in DSM-5. *The American Journal of Psychiatry*, 171(6), 611–613. doi:10.1176/appi.ajp.2014.14010003.

Szekacs-Weisz, J. (2004). How to be a bi-lingual psychotherapist. *Lost childhood and the language of exile*, pp. 21–28. London: Imago East-West.

Szekacs-Weisz, J. (2016). Emigration from within. *American Journal of Psychoanalysis*, 76(4), 389–398.

Szekacs-Weisz, J., & Ward, I. (Eds.) (2022). *Lost childhood and the language of exile* (2nd edn). Manila, Philippines: Phoenix Publishing House.

Todorova, M., & Gille, Z. (2010). *Post-communist nostalgia* (1st edn). New York: Berghahn Books.

Tokarczuk, O. (2018). *Flights*. London: Fitzcarraldo Editions.

Tuan, M. (1977). *Space and place: The perspective of experience*. Minneapolis: University of Minnesota Press.

Volkov, S. (1998). *Conversations with Joseph Brodsky*. New York: The Free Press.

Volkov, S. (2004). *Testimony: The memoirs of Dmitri Shostakovich* (25th edn). New York: Limelight.

Yalom, D. I. (1980). *Existential psychotherapy*. New York: Basic Books.

Yalom, I. D. (2002). *The gift of therapy: Reflections on being a therapist*. London: Piatkus.

Chapter 4

Addressing displacement

Displacement rabbit ears

In his address to young therapists, Irvin Yalom advises them to grow "rabbit ears" for the "here-and-now" equivalents of their patient's interpersonal problems (Yalom, 2009). For an online therapist, such ears should also be developed for a variety of displacement-related issues. As a way of modelling a displacement-sensitive practice, all vignettes in this book are written with such ears on.

Despite Grinberg and Grinberg's definition of migration as a trauma and a crisis (Grinberg & Grinberg, 1984), this view has been slow to penetrate the mental health field. Unless the circumstances of migration are strikingly dramatic, as in the case of refugees crossing the sea on a rickety boat and fighting for immediate survival, the traumatic elements of a more mundane displacement life story are often overlooked, not only by emigrants themselves, but also by those who attend to their mental health.

The underlying reasons for this displacement blindness vary. Dowd puts forward one possible interpretation:

> However in my experience, the loss and peculiar nature of the pain that underpins the displacement experience is rarely emotionally processed, not only because pressing life matters and often explicit post-traumatic stress require attention, but more specifically because it is generally not understood as trauma, that is as psychic rupture, and trauma, by its nature, is unthinkable.
>
> (Dowd, 2019)

Another reason for overlooking displacement trauma can be linked to the emotion of shame. Psychological experience of displacement is closely associated with shame (more in Chapter 7), and one of the most natural defences of shame is the compulsive desire to avoid being seen, to find a refuge in the perceived safety of isolation (Nathanson, 1992). Therefore, a displaced individual who seeks online therapy may be dealing with an additional burden of

DOI: 10.4324/9781003144588-4

shame (comparing to a non-displaced client), and the online mode of delivery, be it videoconferencing technologies, email, or chat, is rich in opportunities to hide. As a result, many clients do not bring up their displacement-related issues easily. They may never even talk about their displacement condition if not prompted by their therapist. Many, especially the well-settled emigrants, are unconscious about how their history of displacement resonates with their current life situation, impacting their behaviours and the decisions they make. It is their therapist's responsibility to detect and attend to this hidden part of a client's painful experience. Add to this the human tendency for therapists to avoid and deny shame (Burgo, 2018), and, in such a shame-infused field, clients' displacement-related issues can get overlooked or even completely missed. When an emigrant therapist meets with a displaced client, they can unconsciously collude in "looking away" and avoiding their "untouchable issues" (Szekacs-Weisz, 2016). This hide-and-seek game unconsciously played by the therapeutic dyad can result in a displacement blind spot. The only way to break this vicious cycle of shame and avoidance is for therapists to develop a higher sensitivity and awareness for issues surrounding displacement. Hence the need for this peculiar set of "rabbit ears". As often, when answers are scarce or simply not straightforward, it is all about asking the right questions. A pair of reasonably sized rabbit ears leads to formulating the right questions. The process discussed in this book is one of talking through the displacement-related topics, and it shapes a therapy, giving it a precious thread.

Displacement history can go back generations. For example, let us take a client with the perfect American look, name, and accent walking into a therapy room. This hypothetical client can even be conservative, actively supporting anti-immigration policies. I argue that in any deep-enough therapy, his family's emigrant background will resurface at some point, but the therapist has to be ready to seize the opportunity, to intuit the hidden narrative, and of course, to ask the right questions.

When a second- or third generation emigrant comes into a therapy room, it may be relevant to inquire about his family displacement history and cultural background. This kind of displacement material can be especially well hidden away when, for example, only one of his ancestors was displaced.

The proximity of an emigrant relative can play an important role in how a child constructs his worldview—such an early exposure to displacement will probably impact his own expatriation later on as an adult. For example, if this emigrant relative had disappeared from the family system after leaving home, what kind of stories were told about him? Were these stories filled with anxious projections and a punitive stance, or was the family attitude to this member who broke off, a more positive and curious one? Children are very sensitive to such stories because they play out in their imagination, adding to the construction of their inner world and the story they develop about themselves.

The case of Natasha illustrates how a good use of displacement rabbit ears lead me to realise how her earlier experience of displacement, previously unaddressed, was impacting her current exposure to a new culture and place.

Natasha looked like a perfectly groomed Barbie girl, or at least, this thought crossed my mind as I opened the door and welcomed her into my office. I felt bad; a spark of shame made me smile a bit more broadly at her than I would usually do ... How could I have reduced this person to a soul-less doll? Natasha was probably suffering—otherwise why would she be here?

She introduced herself as an American expat living in Paris; she moved here to follow her French boyfriend met in college.

"I hate everything here!" was her opening line.

This was an interesting beginning. My American clients more commonly fall in love with Paris.

"Everything?"

"Yes, I hate French people, I hate French food ..."

"Is there anything you might like about Paris?"

"Nope".

She sounded certain; the frozen frown on her perfect face confirmed this commitment to disgust. I believed her feeling. She looked exhausted from trying to fit into a place where she did not belong. What caused her distress was the confusion she felt about her inability to like Paris. Before moving she had been so excited about this year abroad. Her Texan girlfriends could not hide their envy. This had sat well with her—she was into fashion, and Paris was the place. She could picture herself working for one of the luxury brands, wearing a Chanel jacket and fine jewellery ...

But Natasha was a very practical person. She made it clear—she just wanted me to help her figure out whether she should stay and give France another chance or return home.

Initially she stubbornly resisted my attempts to explore her past; she wanted a quick, pragmatic help. During the best part of that first session, I felt stuck and unable to support her. Out of desperation, I finally asked her about her origins. Her name sounded Russian, I said.

This question changed everything.

First, she frowned and stayed silent for a second. Then unwillingly filled me in: her parents had emigrated to Texas and this is where she had grown up. She felt American and preferred to keep speaking English with me if I did not mind.

Initially Natasha stubbornly rebuked my attempts to enquire into her relationship with her parents' original home, Russia. She did not have much recollection of her first years of life there and had never given it much thought. She insisted on being happily American. Could it be that her current exposure to another strong culture was threatening her American identity?

It took us time to get to a point when she trusted me enough to admit that she felt embarrassed about her emigrant background. As she was able to acknowledge her shame, a different narrative emerged: a completely new character slowly replaced the initial Barbie persona. I could now see the young Russian girl brought by her parents to a new and alienating place. Her first American year had been hard: children at school mocked her for her odd clothes and her rudimentary English. But she was a tough kid, and soon enough she had joined the camp of the popular girls. This visibly successful adaptation came with a cost—with every pound that she lost in order to join the netball team, with every Russian sound chased out of her quickly improving English, Natasha developed a strong dislike for her own foreignness and her Russian parts slowly died off, and what remained of her was the doll-like American girl whom I first met.

Here in Paris the adult Natasha was certainly feeling as inadequate as the younger Natasha during her first years in America.

Since Natasha got in touch with the shame she felt about her unperfected origins, her experience in Paris started to make more sense. She decided to stay in Paris until the end of the year. At some point we discussed her initial choice of a therapist—a Russian turned French, rather than one of the many Paris-based Americans. She admitted that maybe a well-hidden part of her had wanted to connect with her "shameful" roots.

Her therapy was not about the Parisian dilemma after all; she had another, deeper task—she was after re-integrating the discarded pieces of her emigrant past. The narrative that Natasha had constructed and found easier to live with was incomplete; a huge chunk of her pre-emigration self was well hidden and out of sight. The shame she felt about this part of her life played as a safeguard, which was not allowing an easy access to this early displacement material. Intuitively Natasha had sensed that her unexpected and unexplained inability to enjoy Paris had to be addressed but it took us both some hard emotional labour to put back together the missing bits of her life story. With the pieces of her emigrant puzzle in place, Natasha felt freer to engage with Paris. A few years after we had ended our work, she reached out again, to let me know that she was marrying her French boyfriend and staying in France after all. This last email was written in a good French, and a short note in Russian said "Thank you" at the end. This was probably Natasha's subtle way of letting me know that the little Russian girl was now out of the closet and allowed to talk again.

I often meet with clients who have already had a previous therapy, but one in which their displacement experience was left unaddressed. This unexplored displacement-related burdensome material then stays with the person, provoking distress in his every-day functioning, or can turn into a relational crisis, as illustrated by the following couples therapy vignette.

Anna and Andrew reached out to me in deep distress, as their family was falling to pieces. The crisis had been triggered by an impending move to Hong Kong due to a new work assignment for Andrew. They had arrived in France, after meeting and living for a few years together in the US, Andrew's country, to where Anna had emigrated from Russia as a teenager.

At the first session, Anna was boiling with anger as she talked about the upcoming relocation; she felt dragged into this against her will. Since they had extensively discussed the move before Andrew accepted the job offer, and this decision made complete sense, Andrew was confused and shaken by her attitude. He believed she was overreacting; after all, she had moved before, and dealt with it simply.

She had seen a local therapist in Paris a few years ago; her previous experience of moving internationally had not been discussed though. I asked her about the story of her family's emigration from Russia to the US. She was a teenager then, and the decision to emigrate was taken without consulting her. In that first move she had lost her friends, her beloved city, and her language.

"I was transported like a package", she said, her anger finally giving way to pain.

This time again, years later, the original experience of loss was resonating. The anger she had felt as a teenager had never really expressed itself, nor been acknowledged by her stoic parents who had grown up in the Soviet world. It was coming to the surface now, threatening to destroy the family she had built.

Anna's main concern was with their teenage daughter, who—she thought— was at risk of losing her friends and her newly acquired roots. Anna was terrified for her, and ready to fight to protect her from this "unnecessary trauma".

As our dialogue developed, Anna started to realise that she was still enraged with her mother who had put her through emigration, motivated by her own reasons, and without even considering the impact on her teenage daughter.

The unfortunate coincidence (their daughter was roughly the same age now as Anna was when her family emigrated) turned out to be a real therapy gift. Witnessing her daughter having to deal with the upheaval of the international move, she was re-experiencing her own trauma. This gave us access to her earlier emotional experience. This time again, she felt that she had no choice but to move as imposed by her family circumstances. Their livelihood largely depended on Andrew's income; and the offer could not be declined without risk. On the other hand, Anna did have a choice about what kind of relocation experience her daughter would have. With more clarity now about her own displacement history, she was empowered to do things differently and simply put, to have a better move.

As a result of the work we did, Anna was not only able to express her distress more clearly to her husband, but also to make sure that this time her needs would not get overlooked as the family was mobilising for the move. She was able to negotiate with her husband the conditions that would make this move more valuable for her own development: she engaged in a Ph.D. programme that she had not been able to afford before. They also made sure their daughter could be associated with the decision process early on. They gave her an opportunity to express her fears and concerns, and both parents took these seriously—something that Anna had not had at the time of her own emigration.

This example gives an idea of how crucial it can be for a therapist to have his displacement rabbit ears always ready and out. Had Anna's childhood emigration experience not been part of our sessions, the outcome of the therapy would probably have been very different. For highly mobile clients whose displacement trauma is cumulative and dynamic, every consecutive move has the potential either to reinforce the earlier traumatic experience, or to turn into a powerful reparative experience facilitated by therapy.

Had online therapy not been an option at the time of Anna and Andrew's relocation, we would not have worked through this crisis together, as close allies. As often in cases of family relocation following a work assignment taken by one of the partners, the family members do not move all at the same time. The person who drives or initiates the move relocates first, and as a result the already shaken and destabilised family is separated. This additional challenge—the temporary distant status of the relationship—happens at a pivotal and stressful time. In the case of Anna and Andrew, we were first meeting in my Paris office, then online through a videoconferencing platform as they went on a reconnaissance trip to Hong Kong. Andrew then lived there on his own for a few months. In Paris Anna was preparing for the move and their daughter was finishing the school year. An online session was the only possible way to continue our work.

The mixed medium work (in person and online) also helped create a functional model of adaptation, giving Anna and Andrew an example of how a relationship (our therapeutic alliance in this case) could survive a displacement crisis, and even get stronger as a result.

In their case the unaddressed displacement material was sitting on both sides. Both partners had emigrant roots. But this apparent commonality was playing against them, because the respective outcomes of this experience had been different for their respective families: Anna's family had been torn by their move and their relationships deteriorated; whereas for Andrew's parents, the move had allowed them to move up the social ladder, with a better social integration. These differing histories had been shaping their unconscious stances towards migration and mobility. We worked together on raising their awareness of these different background histories, reaching a more integrated version of their emigrant identities. As a result, their daughter's experience of displacement turned out to be a more balanced and resilient one.

Working with cross-cultural displaced couples is a topic for another book, but as couples therapy is an important area of caring for the mental health of displaced individuals, it seems relevant here to clarify what I mean by a "displaced couple". It is a couple dealing with life circumstances that are a result of one or both partners living in a country that is different from his or her original home. These circumstances usually include some form of multilingualism and strong cross-cultural elements.

Another often overlooked area of displacement, which impacts many couples, is repatriation. Many cross-cultural couples who have met during their respective expatriation, decide later to settle in one of the partner's original places. This decision is often discussed and negotiated before the move.

Reasons vary—better childcare conditions, proximity of aging parents, better job opportunities for one or both partners are among those often quoted. No matter how well the partners have prepared for their relocation, the uneven circumstances from the start usually result in additional stress and may stir up difficult emotions. This was the case with François and Emily, a French man and a British woman, who initially met in London and moved to the South of France when their son was born and François was offered a tenure track teaching French literature at the University of Toulouse. Emily, who back in England taught French in a prestigious boarding school, found herself unable to find a similar job. What used to constitute her professional identity and her pride became redundant. Her mastery of French, admired at home, was downgraded to an interesting accent for the locals.

"Here any baker speaks better French than me", she complained. Emily struggled to make friends, and the culture that she used to admire from afar now alienated her. François felt responsible for Emily's happiness, or in this case her unhappiness. Her shame, triggered by this expatriation and his exacerbated guilt about putting her through this struggle, was stretching their relationship thin.

In our online sessions, as we talked about the multiple ways the move to France had impacted them individually and as a couple, we managed to shift the focus to a more balanced reality. We soon realised that the burden of Emily's expatriation was shared by both of them, even though, technically speaking, she was the displaced one, and François was just repatriating to his original place. The displacement was affecting each of them in different ways but belonged to them both as their relationship carried its burden. This change of stance helped them get out of their respective emotional corners—Emily felt more compassionate towards François, and he reviewed his perception about the amount of responsibility he was carrying here. For François, returning to his homeland came with an exciting professional move, and his original family offered him additional support. These lucky circumstances added to the imbalance and were experienced as "unfair" by his partner, but once the balance was restored (Emily eventually found an alternative career path, which expanded her social circle), their re-rooted relationship blossomed again.

For many other individuals who come back home with their foreign partner, this experience can be an even bumpier ride. Repatriation, especially after a long and/or impactful expatriation, puts an additional strain on the individual psyche. Not only is it often experienced as a "failure" for not making a better life elsewhere, but also it demands from the person another effort to re-engage with realities of the place and people once left behind. In individual therapy, this logically becomes the focus of the therapeutic work, but in couples therapy, the focus naturally shifts towards the expatriate partner, and the repatriated one can be easily overlooked. Exploring this experience for the one that has come back home, and how it is affecting both partners will help them recognise another important facet of the couple's broader experience of displacement.

Use of narrative in addressing displacement

Humans have told stories about their own lives since antiquity (Baldick, 2015). Any autobiographical narration is about understanding oneself; the retrospection is the main quality of this kind of storytelling. The need to clarify one's story, to keep the thread, is the underlying force of any auto-biographical endeavour.

Autobiography is a narrative account of an extended period of a person's life, written by that person (Baldick, 2015). The preface to almost any auto-biographical book usually includes some reflection on why the author under-takes such a humbling task of an uncertain commercial value. The answers vary of course but recognising the therapeutic value of such writing is a common theme. A most striking reflection on what self-narration involves comes from the American novelist Philip Roth. His reflection on the implication of his Jewish emigrant roots is an intrinsic part of his self-discovery endeavour. In his memoir *The Facts* Roth demonstrates how such autobiographic writing saved him at a time of major mental crisis, or "dissolution" as he puts it. Roth turns to auto-biography with his hope to "repossess life", "to retrieve my vitality, to transform myself into myself" (Roth, 1997). Irvin Yalom echoes Roth, choosing "Becom-ing myself" for a title to his memoir (Yalom, 2017), stressing the identity-rein-forcing potential of the genre. Through writing about oneself, one may come closer to the version of oneself that one aspires to be. As Anna Lembke insists: "Truthful autobiographies create accountability. [...] Autobiographical narra-tives are an essential measure of lived time. The stories we narrate about our lives not only serve as a measure of our past but can also shape the future behaviour" (Lembke, 2021). This potential of a witnessed self-narrative is broadly exploited in any talking therapy.

Autobiographical storytelling can take many different shapes or forms—from writing an intimate journal, to composing a curriculum vitae (de Grève, 2008), but therapeutic self-narration, composed as a part of a talking therapy, in front of a therapist, is a specific version of this genre. One of the reasons for the enduring popularity of autobiographies may lie in the empowering potential they represent: "If this manuscript conveys anything, it's my exhaustion with masks, disguises, distortions, and lies" (Roth, 1997: 6). Tell-ing one's own story in one's own words provides a chance to give one's own account of the events; for a person whose life evolves away from a writing desk, therapy can be the only space where this version of the story can be told, listened, and ultimately exist.

"Looking back at my life from my eighties is daunting and sometimes lonely", Yalom recognises (Yalom, 2017: 17). He tries to conjure this lone-liness by sharing his memories with his anonymous readers. For therapy cli-ents as well, sharing their fragmented stories and co-reconstructing themselves with their therapist is a way to make this endeavour less lonely, and ideally less daunting.

Retelling one's own life facts in therapy is a dialogical process (Ferro, 2006). By sharing the intimate, often previously untold, and sometimes embarrassing details of one's life with another person, who is by nature open for connection and ready to listen, clients co-create a meaningful account of themselves and their lives. The therapist bears witness to their story, and unlike an anonymous reader for a solely written autobiography, she has a chance to react in the "here-and-now" of the session to what she hears, actively creating in this way a reparative emotional experience for her client. This collaborative or relational benefit takes self-narration to a different level, turning it into a talking cure.

Many fascinating autobiographies are composed by writers who came from an emigrant background (Vladimir Nabokov, Eva Hoffman, Jhumpa Lahiri, Gabriel Byrne, Philip Roth, Irvin Yalom, etc.). This is probably not a pure coincidence—stories shaped by displacement naturally call for retrospection; looking back becomes a necessity, or even a question of survival. Freedom in this case is not a freedom from memory but a freedom to remember, to choose the narratives of the past and remake them (Boym, 2001). This sums up the potential of therapy in displacement; for those who are uprooted and dislocated, the gift of therapy is a hope for redemption.

Displacement unavoidably results in a certain level of identity confusion, especially if it has been happening repeatedly or started at an early age, before the person could deal with its emotional complexity. Reorganising one's life timeline and re-organising its facts helps to make sense of the existential disorientation that is often a side effect of displacement. Life stories involving elements of displacement often feel messy and fragmented. Yalom assigns the fragmented quality of his childhood memories to his early unhappiness and the poverty in which his family lived, but there is probably another dimension to it, as his parents had arrived in America as emigrants, "penniless, without an education, without a word of English" (Yalom, 2017: 17). Yalom's growing up "always out of place—the only white kid in a black neighbourhood, the only Jew in a Christian world" had probably contributed to the fragmentation of his early memories. Shame is a natural emotional response to being different, to squalor, and to emotional neglect. Confusion about the surrounding world and one's place in it often results from the shame one is unable to recognize or share.

The American bestselling writer Stephen King was brought up by a single mother who moved around a lot; he describes his childhood as "jerky-jerky", and his early experience as

> a fogged-out landscape from which occasional memories appear like isolated trees … the kind that look as if they might like to grab and eat you … This is how it was for me, that's all—a disjointed growth process in which ambition, desire, luck, and a little talent all played a part. Don't bother trying to read between the lines, and don't look for a through-line. There are no lines—only snapshots, most out of focus.
>
> (King, 2000: 4)

This may sound familiar to many of my clients who had childhoods disrupted by repetitive dislocation. By writing his autobiography King redefines a storyline that holds these disjointed parts together, and ultimately creates a meaning (King, 2000), but for most displaced clients it is the therapeutic dialogue that facilitates this process of turning the scattered themes of their peripatetic childhood into a story with a more meaningful outline. Highly mobile clients struggle with inconsistency in their environments and relationships. They are organically wired for interruptions, as their narratives abound in them (which could explain why they generally feel comfortable with videoconferencing). When these individuals stay in therapy for long enough, they gain a chance to experience a consistent relationship that survives their mobility and becomes a buoy of stability.

Narrative elements are naturally present in any talking therapy. This storytelling element is particularly valuable when the client's story has been disrupted in some major way—be it a sudden illness, a divorce or a dislocation. Integrating narrative-focused elements into therapy, such as by McAdams' life-story method (McAdams, 1996), can help therapists who do not practice narrative therapy as their main approach to better assist displaced clients with their identity integration, and take them to a more integrated version of their self.

In early stages of therapy with highly peripatetic clients, I often suggest a practical experiment, and ask them to draw a timeline of their transitions, from one place to another, associating important life events with their mobility history. This is particularly useful for those who have had to move continuously or were uprooted as children. Afterwards I invite them to reflect on their experience of engaging with this experiment; this makes us travel together, not only back in time but also through places significant to the client. As they bring me to the significant places of their past, Irvin Yalom's definition of the dyad as "fellow travellers" takes on an even deeper meaning (Yalom, 2009). As a result of travelling together across this kind of mapping, the therapist gets a better picture of her client's inner and outer landscapes, and therapy acquires a sense of direction at an early stage.

The online setting seems to ease this sort of narrative inquiry. Witnessing my clients' stories unfold on my computer screen, I am aware of the filmic quality of the process. Somehow the use of the screen medium on both sides of the communication line enhances the storytelling. We are all familiar with dramas unfolding on a screen, and it organically enhances the therapy's narrative quality. With its "long run" aspect, therapy, cut into sessions—episodes— turns into a kind of TV drama, co-created and co-watched by the client and the therapist. Whereas traditional in-person psychotherapy is an oral art of telling a story, practising through videoconferencing brings us back to a more visual and imaginative way of perceiving the clients' life stories unfolding. As a compensation for the possible frustration with the lack of physical contact, therapists can become more inventive in using their sudden capacity for travelling alongside their highly mobile clients.[1]

Another precious tool for therapeutic work with displaced clients is journaling. The emotional benefits of writing have been widely recognised not only by writers themselves but also by therapists and their clients who use various forms of writing as part of their therapy work (Bolton et al., 2006). Without necessarily practising bibliotherapy, therapists from any theoretical background can integrate writing into their practice to facilitate change and growth. For those working with displaced clients online this integration offers some particularly welcome benefits.

One of the appeals of a technology-mediated therapy is its practicality. In opting for an online therapist, clients avoid traffic or long-distance commuting, and gain a much wider choice of practitioners adapted to their particular needs and circumstances. These obvious benefits come with some less obvious pitfalls. In online therapy, beginnings and endings may feel abrupt, clients often have no transitional space and time to mentally prepare for the session or to re-emerge into the world after. I often see clients jumping into the session immediately after a workout or a business lunch or leaving the session a minute before reconnecting for an online work meeting. They use the same device for their therapy that they use for other, more mundane activities; they sit in the same chair, at the same desk, and literally do not move between these very different interactions. This, of course, is also true for therapists working online. Taking a few minutes after each session to ponder, with a pen or a keyboard at hand, on what has come up in the session can help to mitigate the volatility of the medium. The lost transitional space can be regained in the form of a therapy journal. Moving the pen across the paper cannot entirely replace the movements needed to walk or drive to one's therapist's office, but it can allow some buffer space and time for reflection. Some of the work done often sinks in then, at least for me as I take reflexive notes or write a book or blog entry after a session with my online clients. Writing a journal alongside therapy is an opportunity for clients to engage actively with their inner process between the sessions, to pay attention to their dreams, and eventually take more charge of their therapy. This always deepens their therapeutic inquiry.

Bolton, Field, and Thompson (2006) stress the self-reflective value of journaling as an integrative part of talking therapy:

> in journal therapy the primary focus is on developing intimacy with the self. This can be a powerful way of dealing with feelings of shame which can be at the root of much resistance to doing therapeutic work. Writing can be a way of uncovering the unacknowledged or recovering the repressed. For some people writing will be the first stage in therapeutic work and will allow them then to speak about things which are too painful or too shameful to be addressed directly even in the safe space of the therapeutic relationship.
>
> (Bolton, Field & Thompson, 2006: 27)

As explored in other chapters (especially Chapter 7), shame is a big part of any emotional life impacted by displacement, which makes journaling a particularly valuable therapeutic tool. The stories written down in a journal may remain hidden for some time, along with the shame they convey for the client, but usually, after a while, clients feel ready to share their writings with their therapist, and sometimes these intimate writings can grow into something even more visible—they may lead to some important self-disclosure with their significant others or even supply material for a personal blog or a book.

For multilingual clients, their journaling can open wider paths for exploration of their relationship with the often-fragmented self-parts that are associated with their different languages. "What language are you writing in?" can be an obvious question to ask to such clients at the beginning of their journaling practice. This simple question can lead to some fascinating reflections about their use of languages, and, eventually, to some beautiful integration of the scattered parts of their multilingual identities. For example, when in our therapy room we use the client's second language, but for their journaling they choose their first language, or a blend of the two (or three …), then inquiring into this set-up with shared curiosity will facilitate the self-integration process.

The notebook which hosts the client's therapy journal often turns into a precious object, which has an important transitional value. They choose it with care, some carry it everywhere with them, through the foreign city they are living in; some bring it consistently to the sessions. Freshly expatriate clients often feel lonely in the foreign place, and this notebook becomes their reliable companion. Journaling between the sessions helps them feel more connected to themselves or to their therapist; this is particularly valuable for those who travel extensively for their work. When therapy takes place in the somewhat flimsy and intangible online space, having this very real, physical object provides additional weight to what happens in that space.

Cathy, a British expatriate in Paris from a mixed background, developed a strong attachment to her journals. Throughout the months of her therapy, they had expanded into several colourful pocket-sized notebooks. She would carry all of them around with her, turning to their pages daily—writing, doodling, glueing in pictures and images of the city she was painfully trying to connect with. Suffering with deeply ingrained shame due to a long history of alcohol addiction in her family and an overwhelming social anxiety, she needed these tightly filled pages to put herself together and keep her safe between our therapy sessions. One day, at short notice, Cathy texted me asking to have our session online rather than in my office. When her camera switched on, I could instantly sense her anxiety; she was on the brink of tears: "My bag was stolen from me", she announced and burst into tears. The most precious objects that the bag contained were her therapy journals. Pondering on this unfortunate event led us to acknowledge an even more significant earlier loss that had remained unprocessed—that of her grandmother who had raised her, stepping in when her mother's drinking had spiralled out of control. Exploring Cathy's obsession with these notebooks, her anxious attachment to them brought us closer to understanding her social anxiety—her fear of others was nothing more than a dread of eventually losing the people she might attach to. Before we started therapy, Cathy had successfully avoided any deep attachment, had no close friends nor romantic partners. In letting a therapeutic bond develop, she was taking a risk, and her notebooks embodied this attachment. Losing them, she experienced a major loss without disintegrating completely, nor turning to drink. She resumed journaling. My hope was that she would eventually expand her risk-taking to other people, and she progressively did.

As therapists, we hope that our clients leave therapy empowered, not only by a better understanding of their story and the way they function in the world, but also with a desirable idea for their future, giving them a precious sense of direction. I often suggest to my clients who are ready to leave therapy one final narrative experiment—a coda of a kind—that allows them to depart with their own account of the work done. This written therapy conclusion created and re-discussed together in the final sessions parallels my own notes taken and reflected upon all throughout the work. In this way both the therapist and her client depart with a tangible object—a witness to the journey taken. This document can be helpful, especially if and when clients decide at a later stage to resume therapy.

As Thompson insists,

> When writing is part of the therapeutic contract, issues such as how much time will be spent on reading clients' writing outside of sessions or what sort of response to e-mails is expected are all part of the contract which needs to be negotiated.
>
> (Bolton et al., 2006: 28)

The (fluid) blueprint that I have developed though years of integrative practice is broadly about welcoming written exchanges (mainly by email), but also suggesting that anything substantial should be shared in the "here-and-now" of the session. Allowing some flexibility is essential as, especially in the initial stages of therapy, clients' shame is omnipresent and easily gets in the way of their disclosure. When this happens, having a written channel (which should be agreed in advance) makes the sharing of sensitive material less daunting. An early small-scale and practice-based research into clients' experience of written therapeutic exchanges confirms that this "'sense of being hidden" within email counselling helped overcome pre-existing barriers for some" (Dunn, 2012: 321). I had clients coming out as gay or acknowledging the real extent of their suicidal thoughts by email or WhatsApp. They simply could not yet say those scary truths out loud. Of course, following up on these disclosures made outside of the therapy room, no matter whether physical or virtual, is essential.

Emigrant writers

In his seminal book, Akhtar echoes Freud who advised his fellow analysts to inquire from their "own experience of life, or turn to the poets" (Akhtar, 2004). Akhtar followed this advice by looking at the poetry of exile and travel. Actively engaging with emigrant literature can enrich our work with displaced clients. Even without practising bibliotherapy, it is fruitful to develop a certain familiarity with such a literature in order to share these titles with emigrant clients. Sharing some reading and engage in discussions of those books that have touched our clients is always a way of deepening the therapeutic alliance. Especially for those therapists who have not experienced displacement first-hand, engaging with such literary accounts of dislocation shows the client that we care and are ready to walk the extra mile to understand their experience.

World literature is abundant with displacement stories from exiled and emigrant writers such as Vladimir Nabokov, Joseph Brodsky, Edward Said, André Aciman, and Eva Hoffman. Emigrant literature—or the fiction of self-begetting, as Kellman describes it—conveys the experience of an author or character torn by migration, which captures and crystallises the shared human condition of transience (Bevan, 1990). It deals with objects that are mainly absent. The Russian poet Anna Akhmatova observed that "absence is the best remedy against oblivion … the best way to forget forever is to see every day" (Volkov, 1998: 17). The heightened sensitivity of emigrant writers for the absent objects, and their concern for the lost place and memory, are shared by therapy clients with similar backgrounds.

Brodsky himself makes a convincing case for looking into the exiled writer's experience in his address to the Wheatland Foundation conference in Vienna in 1988:

> Yet talk we must; and not only because literature, like poverty, is known for taking care of its own kind, but more because of the ancient and perhaps as yet unfounded belief that should the masters of this world be better read, the mismanagement and grief that make millions take to the road could be somewhat reduced.
>
> (Brodsky, 1991)

In emigrant writers' fiction the "aspiration towards self-creation or self-recreation emerges as a potent response to the dislocation and tenuousness of the émigré condition" (Bevan, 1990). Displaced therapists and their clients, all around the world and online, unite in a similar activity, which has a similar scope.

Displaced clients wrestle with the very psychological struggle that has been extensively explored by emigrant writers. These texts provide us with a deeper understanding of the multiple facets of displacement, offering insight into the condition of emigrant or peripatetic clients. Engaging with these accounts and sharing them with our clients is a powerful fertiliser for growing one's displacement rabbit ears.

Amongst the topics dear to emigrant writers, such as loss, memory, home, and nostalgia, there is also multilingualism. The typical split of a bicultural individual caught "between languages" or "lost in translation" is described in a variety of ways by numerous emigrant writers (Hoffman, 1998; Said, 1999; Aciman, 2007). Multilingual quandary is often central to the inquiry of those writers who grew up in a multicultural environment or were displaced early enough to acquire a second language in their childhood. Their wrestling with their multilingual identity through the pages of their books is of a particular interest to therapists and their clients who grew up in multilingual families— bicultural or those who identify as Third Culture Kids.

> I have never known what language I spoke first, Arabic or English, or which one was really mine beyond doubt. What I do know, however, is that the two have always been together in my life, one resonating in the other, sometimes ironically, sometimes nostalgically, most often correcting, and commenting on, the other. Each can seem like my absolutely first language, but neither is. I trace this primal instability back to my mother, whom I remember speaking to me in both English and Arabic, although she always wrote to me in English—once a week, all her life, as did I, all of hers.
>
> (Said, 1999)

For therapists who are not bilingual or did not grow up in a multilingual environment, engaging with such first-hand accounts can lead to a better understanding of their multilingual clients' experience.

Mythology of displacement

Displacement is as old as human history. Humans always moved from one place to another, in search of better life conditions. This has resulted in a particular displacement mythology, deeply rooted in the collective consciousness.

Grinberg and Grinberg (1984) traces this mythology back to the biblical myths. Both the myth of Eden, in which Adam and Eve were exiled from Eden and lost their ideal world, and that of Babel are metaphors for human displacement and the existential condition. These powerful myths are deeply rooted in the Judeo-Christian traditions, but there are other myths and legends, developed collectively, which affect the way people relate to their own experience of displacement. The stories that our clients tell about their own migrations often have unconscious reminiscences of these older collective narratives. Uncovering them can help deepen the therapeutic work.

One of these powerful stories is the myth of return to the original place. Fantasies of return animate many emigrant daydreams, nightmares, and come up in sessions with stubborn frequency. In therapy, allowing a space for elaborating on these fantasies helps clients make sense of their present emigrant experience (Bolognani, 2016). These collective narratives and archetypal stories include a hero returning home, be it from war or from another dangerous mission. From children's fairy tales to all kind of popular culture narratives,—movies and books—these stories are always about the treasure or knowledge that he the hero brings back home from his adventures. "I cannot go back home without a husband, or children, or a brilliant job", some of my emigrant clients complain as we discuss their fantasies about returning to their original place. To return empty-handed is humiliating, and the perspective of their relatives or friends looking at them in disappointment is scary. "All this suffering and separation led to nothing?" they are afraid to be told. This myth is often associated with the anxiety that keeps these emigrants frozen, preventing them from travelling back home, sometimes for years.

Another story which feeds the collective imagination of the Christian world is the Parable of the Prodigal Son (Luke 15: 11–32). After spending his father's inheritance in foreign lands, the youngest son returns to his family home. He is met with forgiveness. "For this my son was dead, and is alive again; he was lost, and is found", the father exclaims, to his oldest son's bewilderment. Many themes in this story illustrate the various facets of conflict that come with migration. Beyond the hope of forgiveness that the parable offers to the displaced, there is also the tension between those who left and those who stayed behind. The envy and the understandable scorn of the oldest son, who never left and "dutifully served" his father, illustrates rather literally the tension that many expatriates experience in relationships with those they have left behind—their parents, siblings, and friends.

The prodigal son's return also offers a lesson of courage. In the myth of the hero returning home, there is an intrinsic expectation for a migrant to come back with a treasure acquired through his travels. No matter what our cultural tradition is, the belief internalised from this paradigm causes much anxiety for emigrants whose travels have not been obviously fruitful. The prodigal son's story shows us the courage it takes to return empty-handed.

Boym notes about the writings of Brodsky and Shklovsky that "the myth of the prodigal son returning to his fatherland, forgiven but never forgotten, is rewritten throughout these texts, without its happy traditional denouement" (Boym, 1996: 514). This can be said about any emigrant, even if these variations are less dramatised and publicly acknowledged. The myth of the prodigal son is inherently present in the subconscious of anybody who has left their original home behind. I grew up in Saint Petersburg, where, as a child, I spent countless hours in the Hermitage Museum, as my mother was lecturing to her History of Arts students. Rembrandt's painting, "The Return of the Prodigal Son" always fascinated me, long before I knew I would have to leave my beloved city. Rembrandt was a Dutch Jew, familiar with exile. The emotional charge that he was able to create in this painting speaks to any human psyche, universally imprinted with the existential experience of loss and mourning involved in growing up and leaving our original objects.

Of course, these examples originate in the Christian tradition, but in most other cultures, such mythical paradigms will exist in some form or another. To be curious and inquire about the collective narratives that animate our client's psyche should be a fruitful lead.

Considering return

Return to one's original place is probably one of the most powerful themes that animate the narratives of the displaced. Return-related material will invariably come up in therapy with emigrants, be it a fantasy, a dream, or a nightmare. The therapist's readiness to recognise its importance will impact on whether the clients give it full attention or not. This material is emotionally charged and often associated with pain, guilt, and shame—the emotions that are uncomfortable enough for both client and therapist, if they are displaced themselves, to eventually collude in just skimming the surface or avoiding it completely.

Grinberg and Grinberg (1984) emphasise that the possibility of return always impacts the emigrant experience, but when migration has a clear end date, such as for expats or foreign students, it is easier for the individual to enjoy his experience. Now, are these "temporary" displacements really experienced as temporary? Deep down inside, no displaced individual can be sure that he will ever return home. No one knows when and where death will find us. Some expatriates have more choice than others in making this decision. Those who are lucky to have freedom of choice face the additional weight that this uneasy decision carries—the bitter-sweetness of the resulting responsibility. At the deeper existential level, no matter whether return is an option or not, every displaced person still has to work through it. Therapy can facilitate this process in various ways.

Homecoming dreams and fantasies are widely reported in therapy with emigrants (Tummala-Narra, 2009a; Sinatti, 2011; Bolognani, 2016), which confirms the crucial importance of this theme for the displaced psyche. This is an area of their emotional life that displaced clients cannot share easily with their significant other. If their partner is also an emigrant, they may fear triggering their own painful feelings about their condition; if on the contrary they are partnered with a non-displaced person, then they may not want to burden them or make them feel guilty for tying them down to the new place. Often these dreams and fantasies are overlooked or stored for private use, for example in daydreaming or binge-watching television from back home. Faced with this storing-away, the emigrant reinforces the already present inner split, often resulting in feelings of alienation from either his old or his new reality.

Any good enough therapy with the displaced offers clients plenty of time and space for exploring the home-related dreams and fantasies.

A non-emigrant therapist will do this with kind curiosity. Letting her client guide her through his memories and the places left behind, will confirm for the therapist that these places are still part of her client's inner landscape. If there is a space for them in the therapy room, there may also be one in his new reality. As Nabokov puts it in the foreword to his autobiographical volume, the story told becomes a "conclusive evidence of my having existed" (Nabokov, 2000). Integrating these lost worlds from the pre-emigration past into the narrative co-created through the therapeutic conversations leads clients to identity integration.

For displaced therapists, the challenge is different. A client's wrestling with his own lost realms will certainly trigger similar struggles for the therapist. Playing out the possible and impossible returns with my own clients sometimes brings up material that I would rather avoid. This happens to be precious for supervision, especially when teaming up with a displaced supervisor or peers familiar with that experience. Many emigrant therapists who have written about this subject (Grinberg and Grinberg, 1984; Akhtar, 2004) report on the benefits of such a displacement-savvy supervision or a writing group with a "displaced" angle.

What are the psychological functions of homecoming fantasies? Some of them are defensive to cope with on-going frustrations experienced in the new place (Tummala-Narra, 2009a); others are there as a vehicle for the mourning process. Many of these fantasies serve as a practising field, where clients can rehearse some of the most difficult unresolved conflicts that await them back home. These fantasies verbalised in therapy allow clients to confront their back-home demons together with their therapist, their ally in this journey. Through this work, we empower clients, getting them ready to encounter old demons if and when they return to their original place.

Relational psychoanalysis shifts the focus on the intrapsychic and inter-subjective quality of fantasy (Gerson, 2008). Homecoming dreams are intrinsic to the therapeutic process and are created by the client's psyche, also in relation to his therapist. This relational value opens a possibility for working through difficult emotional material, especially the one related to shame. Clients who constantly feel not-good-enough are disempowered in face of the risk of a home-visit. Emigrants often feel that the new merged identity (Akhtar, 1995) that they have created in the new place is not welcomed nor acceptable in their original place. They may indefinitely postpone their plan to travel back home and avoid bringing up this topic in therapy altogether. Reading in the literature examples of dreamwork with emigrants' fantasies of return may make us feel that, somehow, other therapists are more gifted to help their clients bring up the neat dreams full of relevant material about homecoming. In my experience, many displaced clients actively try to avoid these confrontations, and step back, even in front of their fantasies or dreams.

So, there is no need to be impressed by the literature, and we should open our displacement-related rabbit ears to identify clients' disguised hints about return-related fantasies. This may be even more challenging for those therapists who are displaced themselves. They may be still in the process of battling with their own demons left back home. A tacit unconscious alliance between the therapist and her client to avoid the painful home-related material is a more common situation than often acknowledged, and supervision is where this can be unlocked.

In the case of one of my clients, let us call him Pablo, this avoidance scenario was epitomised. He was going by a more French-sounding first name, Paul. He was extremely articulate and had a poignant, self-deprecating sense of humour in all the three languages that he used with ease. Paul's French was perfect; he had spent most of his adult life in Paris. His relationship with Spain, his country of origin, was as cold and uneventful on the outside as it was dramatic and complex on the inside. He spoke reluctantly about his childhood spent in a small coastal town of southern Spain. From the very few clues that he had given me, I figured out a poor, ugly and hot place from which he had felt mostly alienated. He was a bright child, and throughout his early years was deprived and under-stimulated, until finally, in the third grade, a new French teacher arrived at their school and made Paul discover that new language, offering him access to unexpected novels and poetry that changed his world. Reading became a secure bubble for Pablo/Paul—a transitional space where he took refuge from his alienating reality (Winnicott, 1971). Paul insisted on using French for his therapy. He decided to consult because he felt stuck in a terrible dilemma: for a few months already, he had been having an affair, and now his lover wanted him to leave his wife. A professor of modern literature at a Paris university, Paul was married to a beautiful French woman, as he had stressed during our first session. Their relationship seemed to be at a fading stage that produced frustration and resentment on both sides.

Every time I inquired about his native town, Paul would cut it short. He was not interested in going back there in any way—neither literally (he almost never visited), nor in our sessions. He did not feel any connection with his birthplace and preferred to focus on his current dilemma. Which woman should he choose?

Paul's relationships with women seemed as unhappy and unexamined as his relationship with his birthplace. He had never been able to maintain any long-term interest with any of his multiple lovers. He had lost interest in his wife a few months into their wedding. It seemed that as soon as the novelty dissipated, nothing was left for him to enjoy. His own inconsistency scared him, and this justified fear was the main reason why he was unable to trust his current feelings for his lover, no matter how strong the initial attraction was. Torn between the two women and unable to enjoy his everyday life, Paul was on the brink of depression.

Until I explicitly asked, Paul did not mention that his lover, Clara, was originally from Spain. How did he feel about being with somebody who shared his cultural background and spoke his mother tongue? He seemed embarrassed by my question. They spoke French as Clara was unaware of their shared cultural background. Was it at all possible? They had been dating for a year and she still did not know this one important thing about him? Embarrassed, Paul confirmed that he had never dispelled her impression of him being French.

This bewildering reality of Paul's sentimental life created an opening to finally talk about his original place. It took him a few sessions to mention that he had conducted an affair with his French teacher during his last year at high school. Her small family had landed in this unremarkable town to follow her husband's new position as manager of the local factory. She was feeling depressed and deprived of her beloved Paris. Tall and blonde, she was for a Spaniard the epitome of a French beauty. She had quickly become the object of his first sexual fantasies and romantic dreams. With her sober but beautifully cut clothes, she stood out from the colourful and noisy crowd of local female teachers who all looked at her with suspicion and envy. She had been the one who had shown him the way out of his misery and boredom. Paul knew that he was her favourite pupil; she would look straight at him while reciting a poem or reading from Maupassant or Balzac. For the first time in his life, he had felt worthy of interest.

Now, Paul recognised that she had probably been bored in this foreign place to which she had been dragged against her will. Maybe playing with the feelings of a local boy had provided her some solace and an opportunity to punish her husband. She might have distracted herself with a Pygmalion scenario. One day, Paul had found a few folded handwritten sheets in one of the books she regularly lent him—a pocket Paul Verlaine edition. It was a kind of personal journal entry, which described his native town and its people in a cruel, sarcastic way. Reading these notes of hers, Paul had felt a terrible shame bearing down on him; he could still remember how hot his face had felt, and how he had been impelled to run to the barn and hide for a few hours, not wanting to see his town ever again. It was painful to discover that this was how she felt about his place, and probably about him as well.

Paul's rejection of his origins was deeply rooted in this moment of shame experienced as a child, when he came to see his native town through the eyes of his beloved French teacher whose taste he admired. Since then, this internalised shame had been barring him from believing himself worthy and capable of a real attachment. He had sided with her in despising his own place.

As we stepped into this previously unexplored territory of shame and belonging, Paul decided to finally disclose his true origins to Clara. Their relationship hit a few bumps but flourished despite his fears. They switched to Spanish, and after a few months he left his wife, who seemed relieved, at least according to his account. The last time I saw Paul, he was considering travelling to Spain with Clara. He was anticipating this trip with trepidation, as he had not been there for almost two decades.

Paul had come to therapy with a clear relational dilemma, but his deeper agenda was about resolving his interrupted relationship with his childhood place, the shame he had been made to feel about it, and the consecutive avoidance of that integral part of his life.

Emigrant literature abounds in tales of return, possible or impossible, real or imaginary. These stories can be instrumental in nourishing our understanding of displaced clients. One of the most striking explorations of a journey back to the original place comes from Anita Brookner's novel *Latecomers*. One of the two main characters, Fibich, was brought from Germany to England as a child during the Holocaust. All through his adult life, Fibich struggles with the void left by the absence of childhood memories. He has little recollection of his parents or his family home and with time becomes possessed by the fantasy that "the past would be returned to him as an illumination, and that that illumination would render him whole" (Brookner, 2010: 199). In his older years, he finally performs the terrifying trip to his native Berlin, as he is convinced that his son needs to know his history "to be a man among men, and not simply the terrified creature he [Fibich] knew himself to be" (Brookner, 2010: 200). The anxiety that Fibich experiences in the few days preceding the trip puts him directly in touch with the emotional material that he has been avoiding for all his conscious life: "Restless and homesick, he entered upon an altered state. The homesickness, he knew, he was attempting to sort out. The restlessness—and the realization came to him only slowly—would be with him to the end" (Brookner, 2010: 198). By the end of his visit to Berlin, Fibich liberates himself from the burden that had been with him for a lifetime. In a striking effort of self-therapy, Fibich concludes that he had been feeling guilty for having survived his parents, for having been spared. Here, Brookner reminds us of the therapeutic power of the existential truth. What frees Fibich is

> the thought of his own death, which he somehow knew was not far off, and he brushed aside the past—remote now, dully coloured, almost dark—in the interest of seeing to whatever future remained to him, leaving matters in good order for those who came after him.
>
> (Brookner, 2010: 209)

As he turns towards his present and future life, Brookner's hero counts his blessings—his loving wife, his brilliant son, and his valiant fellow emigrant friend. Once in the native place that had kept eluding him, Fibich reconnects with the terrified displaced child in himself. He comes to a vivid realisation that it may be necessary to "abandon the stock of time that one carries within oneself, to discard it in favour of the present, so that one's embrace may be turned outwards to the world in which one has made one's home" (Brookner,

2010: 210). But to stop looking back, chasing the ghosts of his traumatic childhood, Fibich had to summon the courage and return to his original place. Towards the end of his Berlin trip, the hero undergoes a metamorphosis and recognises himself as being "just a traveller" and accepts the fact that he will never see his lost parents again, and somehow now he can live with that. In an ironic turn, on Fibich's return as his plane lands in London, his childhood nightmare with his last image of his parents (his mother fainting in his father's arms as their son (him), is carried away to safety by the train), returns to haunt him, prompted by the view of a woman fainting, unable to cope with the airport crowd. This is the cautious reminder about the limits of what can be achieved in therapy—some ghosts will never depart, nevertheless clients can learn how to lead fulfilling lives alongside them. Upon his return from Berlin, Brookner's hero sinks into a deep depression, and not even his loving wife nor his dear childhood friend can re-engage him with the present. At the end of the novel, we discover that upon his return from Berlin, Fibich has started writing a memoir, in which he reclaims his lost past. We will never know the childhood facts that he was eventually able to retrieve, but with the notebook containing his memoir he passes the names of his lost ancestors to his son. The trip back to Berlin, where his family home was now unidentifiable, was somehow instrumental in retrieving the lost parts of his identity, but this identity integration would have not been possible without processing that return through writing his memoir and sharing it with his son.

This fictional tale demonstrates the dramatic power and therapeutic potential of return, real or imaginary, for displacement therapy. This theme may be replayed in any displaced mind, and for those emigrants who cannot wrestle with their ambivalent feelings about possible return through writing, therapy stands as the only safe space available for such wrestling.

Re-evaluating the decision to leave home

Reasons for departure vary; some are pragmatic (fleeing an unsafe environment or seeking better economic opportunities); some are of a deeper unconscious nature. The reasons given are not necessarily the true causes of leaving (Madison, 2011). At the time of departure, many do not have an opportunity or the capacity to scrutinise their decision. The anxiety naturally triggered by migration is often too much to bear, and defence mechanisms, such as denial and deflection, guard would-be-emigrants from too much untimely introspection.

Later, when the emigrant deals with the consequences of his departure and the incurred loss, the emotional discomfort can become overwhelming. This is a good time for inquiring into doubts about the initial decision to leave, as well as haunting thoughts about return. This confusing period can happen at any stage of displacement. It can be triggered by a scene from a film, a book, an encounter with or a visit from someone from back home. Therapy then offers an opportunity to look back and reflect on the earlier life-changing decision to leave home. Re-evaluating this sometimes "untaken" or unprocessed decision turns into an important therapeutic task, which can instantly deepen the work at hand. As we step into the delicate waters of discussing the initial decision to expatriate, the therapist is let into the most intimate and sometimes concealed areas of her client's world. Many hidden truths reside in that secret space. At the initial stages of therapy, many clients will not trust their therapist and allow her access to these inner places. Sometimes they are still too dark and too scary for the client's psyche, and his equilibrium can be threatened by revisiting them. We must be patient and prepared, our displacement rabbit ears out, to spiral back to these topics of home and belonging.

For displaced therapists (like myself), these topics will always trigger some very personal home-related material. When a client is finally ready to address this area, we may have to deal with some strong emotional responses, which we must be able to keep at bay, at least until we write our notes or until our next supervision session. There are cases, of course, when some level of self-disclosure can be considered. In some situations, offering to the client a hint of our own displacement-related experience can be helpful in strengthening the kinship and the alliance, but generally, these topics are so intimate that I would think carefully and often leave them out.

For those who left as children, hastily and out of necessity, or against their will, re-evaluating the early departure helps to regain some power in the process. As Grinberg and Grinberg stress (1984), children can hardly be considered as emigrants; their situation is better described as exile. Eva Hoffman, who left her native Poland as a teenager, describes her experience of emigration as "a notion of such crushing, definitive finality that to me it might as well mean the end of the world" (Hoffman, 1998). Children, especially young, are rarely involved in the decision-making process: "I was shipped as a parcel", they often comment bitterly. Even when their parents' decision to emigrate was the only viable path to survival, adults who were displaced as children rarely have the full picture, since their seniors generally avoided sharing much. Young children have not yet developed the emotional tools to process the trauma of dislocation. With their family moving to a new place, not only do they have to face the loss of the familiar objects, but also, they must adapt to the sudden reshuffling of the family system, with re-adjustments of its dynamics to the new situation. Children are rarely given a space for dealing with their confusion. Freshly emigrated adults are too busy with resettling and putting some roots in the new place. These exiled children turn to therapy later, as adults, in search for answers outside of their family system.

Many of those who left at a young age end up developing an idealised version of the pre-emigration world. They can feel as they were "pushed out of the happy, safe enclosures of Eden" (Hoffman, 1998). Such idealisation is only natural when the child cannot cope with the overwhelming reality of the displacement trauma. In some cases, this idealised version of home is challenged through stories shared by older members of the family, visits back home or fellow emigrants' accounts of their life in the original place, but often, especially when return is impossible, and other members of the family collude in maintaining this mythical version, the idealisation may persist. It impedes emigrants building a new life in the new place. Some come to therapy armed with their new personas—they have mastered the language and seem well settled—but the internalised version of the lost paradise may be well entrenched, impacting their experience of the present reality, as no tangible place can compete with an idealised home. Being trapped in the Golden Age can push these emigrants to hold onto their accent, avoid intimate bonds outside of their local community of fellow expatriates, or never fully engage with their present existence.

Some of the ways emigrants use to deal with loss can be disguised in unexpected ways. For Lena, whose family emigrated to the US from Colombia when she was a child, the idealisation of her lost world happened in the form of a projection on another culture. Through the colourful accounts of her parents, she knew that the world they had escaped was dysfunctional. She therefore could not create her own portable version of a lost paradise. Instead, she fell in love with another distant culture, Russia. She travelled there extensively, learnt some rudiments of the language, read translated novels and watched Russian films. In therapy we started exploring this peculiar passion, and eventually she was able to reflect on the relationship with Colombia, the country that she had to leave behind as a child. Reflecting on her passion for Russia helped Lena better understand her earlier rupture with her original country and decide how she wanted to relate to it as an adult; this time, it was her own decision.

As I am finishing this book, the Russian war in Ukraine is ravaging cities, individual lives, and tearing apart entire families. As a Russian myself, this has brought up many personal considerations, and one of them is about my decision to leave my country, nearly three decades ago. The few Russian clients on my current case load fall into two neat categories—those who left and those who stayed. Never before has the chasm between them been as striking as now. For any Russian who does not support Putin's regime has had to consider whether to stay or to leave. Considering the psychological cost of both options has become central to our work. Those who have already left have once more had to process their decision, and the guilt about leaving some people behind in the process has now grown exponentially, to point of suffocation.

Any therapist who works with emigrants should keep in mind the question of the circumstances of her client's initial departure, and their implication in the decision-making process. Did this decision belong to them? How much power did they have at the time? Revisiting this decision is always a fruitful path towards deeper therapeutic work.

The notion of choice that is part of any voluntary migration is at the core of any decision to leave. As Masha Gessen, an American writer who emigrated from Russia as a teenager, argues:

> Immigrants make a choice. The is not in remaining at risk for catching a bullet but in making the choice to avoid it. In the Soviet Union, most dissidents believed that if one were faced with the impossible choice between leaving the country and going to prison, one ought to choose exile. Less dramatically, the valor is in being able to experience your move less as an escape and more as an adventure. It is in serving as living reminders of the choicefulness of life—something that immigrants and most trans people do, whether their personal narratives are ones of choice or not.
>
> (Gessen, 2018)

No matter how much of a choice our emigrant clients had at the time of their leaving, no matter how conscious that choice was, they can be empowered by revisiting that decision. As they do, with their therapist as witness, they gain an opportunity to make this choice consciously, as adults, and based on their actual experience of life in displacement.

Visits back home: how to use them?

Holidays usually bring turmoil to any therapist's practice, but this is particularly true for those working with displaced clients who around that time are planning to visit (or not) their original country. Their return to home is a meaningful and complex event that requires close examination in therapy (Tummala-Narra, 2009a). Whatever the reason why they left, and however long ago, these visits back home are always a time for confrontation and reflection (Grinberg & Grinberg, 1984). Going back to familiar surroundings and revisiting people from the past naturally triggers unresolved inner conflicts, which go back to their original departure. In therapy, this time turns into a precious opportunity for revisiting the initial decision to leave, to confirm or question it.

> In fact, everything here repels her. Suddenly she's utterly baffled by this phenomenon of people actually choosing, of their own free will, to go back and visit the different places of their youths. What is it they think they're going to find? What is it they have to have validation of—just the fact that they had been there? Or that they'd done the right thing in leaving? Or perhaps they were urged by some hope that recollecting more precisely these lost places would work with the lightening speed of a zipper to unite the past and the future, creating a single stable surface, tooth to tooth, a metal suture.
>
> (Olga Tokarczuk, 2018: 307)

These poignant lines were written by Olga Tokarczuk, but they could have been written in an email by one of my displaced clients from their holiday trip to their original place.

Akhtar uses the term coined by Furer of "an access to refuelling" in order to picture a migrant's need to visit home (Akhtar, 2004). This refuelling in the motherland can only work when there is no attachment struggle, which is rather rare for displaced individuals. More often, what is supposed to be "refuelling" turns into a re-traumatising experience. Instead of getting the emotional support and closeness they crave, emigrants can be rejected and shamed again by their original family and the place itself. The myth of the Prodigal Son rarely materialises. The repeated experience of not fitting in, not belonging, or even worse, being unwanted and rejected, only reminds them of the deeper reasons for leaving home in the first place.

The recent Covid pandemic has hit many of those who were used to travelling, forcing them to skip those traditional visits back home for major holidays, be it Christmas, Thanksgiving, Diwali, or Ramadan. Many of my clients acknowledged their relief at this and felt liberated by this unexpected turn of events. Even if this escape from duty was happening against their will, they nevertheless still felt guilty—unruly sons and daughters, not honouring their family duties. "To go or not to go?" is the question that many displaced clients were bringing up in our post-lockdown sessions. After a break imposed by the global crisis, this familiar dilemma grew out of proportion. The imposed impossibility of travelling broke the rhythm of the habitual visits, offering an unexpected escape from what was previously an unquestionable duty imposed by loyalty to the family or motherland.

Most clients who live abroad feel anxious before travelling back home or being visited by their family members. When they do return to their old family homes, they may sleep in their old bedroom filled with well-known items, and bump into old acquaintances or family friends. Sometimes being back at their parents' place makes them feel exactly as it "should"—warm, protected, loved. But often it does not, and instead the old scenery makes them feel sad, angry, or depressed. In any case, the original place offers an array of powerful triggers.

These trips back home can be turned into a powerful opportunity for re-examining clients' childhood experience. They can often trigger a dissonance between the story that they were told and the emotional responses that these visits back home trigger. These thoughts easily cause confusion and guilt. Usually, clients regress when they return home, so they are unable to deal with anxiety-producing situations. This regression does not help them deal with the powerful family dynamics, which have often remained unchanged since their departure and eventually return them to the darkest places of their childhood.

They may seek some form of validation of the not-that-ideal version of reality that they have experienced. They need somebody who will acknowledge that they are entitled to have some not-really-positive feelings about it.

They are not going crazy or making things up. If they have siblings, and have a good enough relationship with them, they can compare their earlier experiences. This often helps, and together they can ascertain how it had been and how it had made them feel. Acknowledging the influence of the places, landscapes, and people of their common past on their current lives already feels painful enough.

Often, for those who left home early, the obvious reason for that decision is identifiable. For example, they think they were primarily interested in exploring the world, seeing new places. Itchy feet do exist, but often there are deeper reasons, carefully hidden from themselves and others. This emotional truth resurfaces when they come back home, even for a short stay. They have to face it all again.

One of my clients, Sarah, a young Scottish woman resettled in Italy, told me about the discomfort she had experienced during her recent visit back home: "There was a strange smell around my parents' house ..." She could not identify it, but was haunted by it all through her short stay at her childhood home. She was deeply disturbed by the uncanny experience—the smell was familiar but yet disconcerting in its new foreignness. "What did it smell of exactly?" I asked, with an increased curiosity. "Something slowly rotting ... my father's cigarettes maybe", she responded, visibly confused. As we explored her discomfort about the smell in her childhood home, Sarah told me of something that had remained hidden throughout the several months of our previous conversations: the neglect she had experienced in her childhood. Her mother had been through various bouts of depression, and each time her father had escaped into his work. From those times Sarah remembered the goldfish rotting in the murky fish bowl; the dishes piling up in the sink, unwashed for weeks; the absence of food in the fridge ... Her mother's depression would usually get worse during the autumn months, and the house would slowly sink into desolation. From outside it still looked the same, nobody knew what was really going on behind the expensive heavy curtains. Every time her mother recovered from another depressive episode, she would throw herself into organising a big garden party. She would invite all the neighbours and her husband's colleagues, to display a perfectly kept house and a well-run family. Sarah always had a role to play in this show—performing at the piano, dressing up, helping with the decoration of the garden.

It took Sarah an expatriation to be able to look back and recognise how much desolation there had been in her childhood home. She had not brought it up until after that holiday at her parents'. All these years later, Sarah kept feeling terribly ashamed about what her home looked like during her mother's episodes of depression. Talking about the haunting smell was the only way she had found to start talking about her childhood in more truthful way.

It is helpful for clients to recognise that every family, including theirs, is a well-established system with its specific dynamic. Once distanced, they remain a part of its functioning or malfunctioning. The missing piece (as in a jigsaw) tends to become the most representative one. Coming back, even for a short time, they tend to quickly fit in again at the very place and role they initially had in the system. During stays at their parental home, clients face the emotionally challenging reality that they had been avoiding by leaving. Examples include the drinking habits of a family member, a shameful secret that all collude to avoid mentioning, an unacknowledged chronic illness. Plunged for a few days into the old family dynamics, clients bring to therapy some fruitful grist for the therapy mill.

"Too much food!" is a complaint I often hear from my displaced clients back from a visit to their family home. Mum's food is difficult to avoid (think of Bridget Jones' turkey curry!). While it is a natural sort of communion, it can also be a way of avoiding some deep emotional truth they were not ready to meet. The prodigal son fed to his teeth, to lure him back, is an unsuccessful replay that creates disappointment for the parent as well as for the child. These unresolvable dynamics bring up shame on both sides—the mother who has not been able to keep the child close, and the child who has left without finding a true emotional intimacy.

It can be a painful experience to look back, especially when one has learnt so well to burn their bridges and keep running away. Revisiting the childhood home and the earlier chapters of one's life story can be a challenging but enriching experience. Even if it takes effort and courage to make sense of this kind of experience, it is an important step for growth.

This is precisely why the weekly periodicity of sessions should be maintained as much as possible during a client's trips back home, which the online setting makes possible. These sessions also provide the therapist with precious access to their clients' original home. In the case of Anna, the session we had during her visit to her native town became a turning point in her therapy.

"I was born in a small Russian town, a very cold and dirty place", was one of the first elements Anna shared about herself in a long introductory email as she reached out for online therapy. In this description of her native town, I could sense her sad childhood: a lack of emotional warmth and possibly some neglect.

The way people describe their early physical surroundings usually tells something significant about their emotional life story. We develop early bonds with our carers, but also with a place. We end up internalising the qualities of the landscape or family home where we grew up. Can we ever detach ourselves from our original place? Does it not persist inside us, long after the physical building may have been knocked down?

Anna had left her native town early, to study and work in Moscow, and then she had moved abroad. Her departure had been more of an escape: eager to leave, she had barely said her goodbyes. Since then she had changed countries several times, and had finally landed in London. But the original coldness and dirtiness had followed her, as a malevolent shadow from her past. It was only our second session, and I was experiencing Anna as frozen and difficult to connect with. She complained that no town ever felt good enough to her: "too cold" or "too dirty". Her camera gave me a glimpse inside her current London flat, which looked impersonal and rather messy. By contrast, she was always impeccably dressed.

Anna's restlessness was partly due to her conscious desire to find a more nourishing environment, but this desire was conflicting with a deeper sense of hopelessness and despair: she believed that such a place did not exist for her. Even in a warmer and more welcoming country, she would always feel alienated by a feeling of guilt—as if she had betrayed her motherland. But at the same time, she never felt that she truly belonged to this new and "better" place; she felt painfully different. Deep inside she remained a girl from a "dirty and cold place", her life forever stained by her early unhappiness.

As often happens with expatriates, something shifted when Anna went back home for a holiday. She took part in her weekly online session from there. As her face appeared on my screen, I was struck by how different she now looked—instead of her usual white shirt or impeccable jacket, she was wearing a loose t-shirt; and without make-up she looked younger. She was staying at her parents' flat—the one in which she had grown up—and was getting in touch with some early emotional experiences from her childhood.

"Internet connection is always bad here, so maybe we will need to switch off the video at some point", she warned me, preparing for a retreat in case the session triggered too much shame. She was also reminding me how imperfect her childhood place was. Shame was indeed present for the full hour, but Anna was brave enough to stay with it, and we managed to navigate this experience together. Carrying her laptop with its built-in webcam, Anna showed me around. This was a real risk-taking, and I could appreciate how exposed and vulnerable she felt. The place was indeed muddled and testified to an un-nourishing childhood environment.

Anna's mother, born just after the war, was a hoarder and had been stockpiling all sorts of things that were piling up and covered by dust in every corner of their flat. Understanding her mother's struggle helped Anna make sense of the level of messiness she had grown up with, and the shame she was feeling about it. That "back home" session was a turning point in our work. She realised how much she was painfully attached to her birthplace, unable to leave it completely behind.

Making better sense of her mother's mental condition, Anna was now able to re-evaluate her own relationship with her family home and her native town. This place was not her; it did not define her. Her experiences may have started in that town, but they did not have to end there. Choosing to move on from there had been her choice, which turned out to be quite an empowering realisation.

Once back, Anna made quick progress in her therapy, as we capitalised on our unique session from her original place. In a way she was now more able to complete her move away from home and from her mother. Soon after that trip, she decided at last to buy her own place in London: after all this is where her life was now happening. She recognised that she needed an anchor, a safe and familiar place to come back to from her frequent work trips. Neither her hometown nor her parents' flat were that anchor for her.

When clients come back from visiting home, they often need a transitional period, and it is their therapist's responsibility to offer them that kind of time and space, to make clear links between the insights they gained during their time back home and the issues experienced in their current situation. This work contributes to building bridges between these two worlds separated by space and time, addressing the archetypical emigrant concern voiced by Eva Hoffman: "I can't throw a bridge between present and past, and therefore I can't make time move" (Hoffman, 1998).

Some clients bring back local food from their trip back home, even when it is available in their new country. This food has a highly symbolic meaning—it is a transitional object by which a client tries to unite his two realities, especially when they feel estranged and incompatible. One of my clients, a South-Asian woman, would bring me a small plastic bag of dried mangos from each of her trips back home. I accepted them gratefully. For her it was probably a way of bringing her two separate words together. She was also letting me know of her respect and how much she valued our work.

Foreign backgrounds

Susie Orbach describes her practice as "a room with a view" (Orbach, 2000); for an online therapist, it is rather "a room with an angle". We meet in a couch-less space unattached to any physical location, or rather suspended in between the two places—the therapist's office, and the often-fluid and ever-changing locations of her fidgety clients.

"Where do you come from?" is a haunting question for many displaced individuals. After years of meeting such clients in the online space, this question has naturally evolved into a more grounding one: "Where are you right now?" Starting with locating them levels the ground (they know that I am based in Paris) but also helps us to settle into the "here-and-now" of the session.

In adapting to the ever evolving and changing environment, and, more recently, to the rollercoaster of the Covid-19 pandemic, the psychotherapy profession has had to extend online. In that transition we lost the comfort of the traditional couch but gained access to new sources of additional information. In the traditional set-up the client comes into his therapist's universe, or at least the image of it that she decides to project in her therapy room. Connecting for an online video session, we open a window into our client's physical realm. It is somewhat equivalent to the home call that rarely happened in the past but that was precisely useful in order to better understand the client's context.

It is always good practice to pay attention to where our client chooses to bring us, which part of his life he chooses to show. Most online communication platforms now offer of choice of virtual backgrounds. These technologies will most probably keep expanding and will get increasingly sophisticated. Clients may opt for such a prefabricated world—a tropical beach or an impersonal office—hiding from you their real surroundings. I even saw recently some creative uses of the pre-set background technology. For example, one of my clients used a picture of a house on fire as a virtual background. This was an efficient and immediate way of communicating his state of mind. Of course, these choices are generally less dramatic, but it is always worth considering the more or less subtle clues provided by their choice of pre-set background. Reflecting with him in the "here-and-now" of the session on a client's choice of background does help to access their emotional state or fantasy.

Clients can connect to their sessions from hotel rooms, cars, or even from various Starbucks around the world. When a new background behind my patient sparks my curiosity, I naturally inquire about that place, and we spend some time locating ourselves. The client may tell me about the country or town he is currently in, about this particular area or hotel. This curiosity overtly expressed by the therapist helps the client realise the connection between his mobile lifestyle and the way he feels, and its relevance for the therapy work.

Seeing peripatetic clients connecting from their hotel rooms brings up what the itinerant writer Anna Badkhen described, in another context, as "a sense of discomfort that resembles lostness—a feeling of displacement, of not-quite-being there" (Badkhen, 2018).

The hotel universe, in which evolve some highly mobile clients, was depicted by the emigrant journalist Joseph Roth in the aftermath of World War I. An Austrian Jew, Roth lived out of his suitcase in various hotels across Europe, reporting on a continent ravaged by change. His collection of essays *Hotel Years* describes his peripatetic life throughout Europe between the wars. Roth's own homeless condition makes his observations particularly poignant. Simultaneously with Roth's hotel life observations, the sociologist Norman Hayner was undertaking his research into the condition of those working and living in hotels. The son of American missionaries born in China, Hayner had personal experience of displacement. His dissertation, *The Hotel: The Sociology of Hotel Life*, was later (1936) published by the University of North Carolina Press and reprinted recently (Hayner, 2013). The picture of detachment, freedom, and loneliness that emanates from Hayner's interviews with bellboys, maids, and waiters helps us better understand the experience of homelessness of highly mobile clients.

Also, around the same time, in the bubbly Paris of the 1920s, the Jewish emigrant Chaïm Soutine was painting a large series of hotel and restaurants' staff, often young emigrants themselves. Those who paused for Soutine might have been the very people depicted by Joseph Roth:

He is an Italian. The waiter is from Upper Austria. The porter is a Frenchman from Provence. The receptionist is from Normandy. The head waiter is

Bavarian. The chambermaid is Swiss. The valet is Dutch. The manager is Levantine; and for years I've suspected the cook of being Czech.

(Roth, 2015: 157)

There are various ways to interpret what Soutine was seeing in these faces, but with my displacement rabbit ears (or eyes?), I watch these moving paintings and see displacement-induced struggles. Soutine did not leave explanations on his series of portraits, but as he sat in front of the young pastry cook, or the young butcher's apprentice, did he also see his own homelessness, insecurity, and the shame induced by his condition? Wright spots this mirroring effect:

Soutine was a misfit. Looking along the line of his portraits of hotel and restaurant stuff, it is clear that they are misfits too. [...] Soutine was drawn to these people because he saw something of himself in them, or something of his own situation—an outsider who did not quite fit the mould.

(Wright in Serres & Wright, 2017: 21)

These misfits of the 1920s were drawn to hotels where they were able to find not just means for survival but also a community of other displaced individuals, and a home, as temporary as it might be.

In the modern globetrotters' community, my client Lorraine was an international consultant always on the move, always connecting from a hotel room. She would usually spend four months in a row in a particular country, and then move to the next assignment in a different one, often on a different continent. Lorraine was in her mid-30s, bright, successful, and extremely lonely. After a few sessions, I finally asked: do you have a "base"? Lorraine marked a short silence—her beautiful pale face rarely showed any emotion. No, not really. Her few belongings were stored in her parents' basement in Canada. She travelled light, just a big suitcase and a laptop. Lorraine lived in hotels of large chains—convenient, comfortable, impersonal. And as the British author Suzanne Joinson puts it, "it was fun, for a few years, until suddenly it wasn't" (Joinson, 2015). Lorraine reached out to me when suddenly it wasn't fun anymore. However, she never complained— it was "not too bad", and, after all, every couple of months she would be allowed a break to spend a few days elsewhere. These short trips would be just enough to preserve her sanity.

In our co-created placeless bubble, we communicated in English—a second language for both of us. We also had French in common, but Lorraine had unequivocally chosen English from our first email exchange. She had acquired it as a teenager, when her family relocated to Canada. Lorraine was half-Korean, half-French, a Third Culture Kid, brought up by a bi-racial family in a country that was not the original home of either of her parents.

Why was she in therapy? Sometimes I wondered, as she seemed rather content with her transient life. Talking with her often created a strange cognitive dissonance—I sensed her distinct unhappiness, but she would never verbalise it, never express any deep dissatisfaction or nostalgia for a home or a relationship.

Lorraine had friends of course, spread around the globe. She would visit them between assignments, for an adventurous holiday with some of them, or at the homes of those freshly settled and building a family. After these trips, she would not express a particular desire to settle or find some attachment. "It was nice", she would comment with detachment. She seemed devoted to her itinerant lifestyle more than to anybody or anything else. She did not miss her parents. Their presence in her adult life seemed more of a hassle, for example with their requests to help them with their paperwork. With her constant relocating from one place to another, Lorraine had developed paperwork efficiency as a critical survival skill. Efficiency was something Lorraine valued highly. In her vocabulary "being inefficient", meant many other things too: being overwhelmed, exhausted, or emotional.

When she was a child her family had moved a few times for her father's professional assignments. I never got a real sense of how it could have been to grow up in her family. She was an incredibly docile child, and then a capable adolescent, never creating any trouble for her parents. She simply did what she was supposed to do and did it well. She worked hard at school, gained a commendable degree, and went on to take a lucrative job. In her family everything was about efficiency. Her Korean mother was a perfectionist and would get upset if something was not done exactly how it should be. Her French father was hard on people who did not live up to his expectations.

Emotions had little or no place in this family. For somebody as well educated as Lorraine, she had little awareness of her emotions and struggled to name her feelings, usually using the words "bored" or "frustrated" to cover up other emotional experiences.

In therapy, Lorraine was hard work for me. Occasionally she would travel back to Canada to spend holidays with her parents. Each time I offered to maintain our session during those holidays, she would politely but firmly decline—too busy with playing catch-up with family and friends. So, I never had an opportunity to get a glimpse of her childhood home, and my attempts to suggest that such session "from home" would be interesting, never produced results. This house in Canada that she never really described felt ghostly to me, and I wondered whether she had the same feelings about it. When her parents retired and decided to sell their family house, Lorraine seemed indifferent. They bought an apartment in the South of France, in the village they used to visit during their European holidays. Wasn't she sad about seeing her childhood home go, along with her memories, and her things in the basement? No, she was not. After all, she always knew her family would never settle there forever. Almost all her friends from that area had already left and had either settled elsewhere or were travelling around the globe.

Would I feel the same numbness if I was to lose connection with my original town? This one thought fills me with sadness. Even after living all my adult life abroad, I still feel attached to my native Saint Petersburg, where all my childhood memories reside. Lorraine's displacement was of a different nature; she grew up out of place, with no deep roots in any of the cultures she was surrounded by. The Korean world was only barely familiar to her; she identified herself as French, but even that belonging had some clear limits.

This state of things went on for a while. Lorraine moved a few times from one country to another, and I grew increasingly frustrated with the lack of depth in our work.

Occasionally, I would be travelling too, and connect for our sessions from a hotel room. The first time this happened, Lorraine looked strangely annoyed. She was even less talkative than usual, and I could sense that something was going on, but as usual she resisted my questions.

"Would your bad mood be linked to my being elsewhere than in my office?" I asked. She paused, seemingly perplexed: "Maybe". She was used to seeing on her screen my office background filled with bookshelves and artwork, which was now for her the most familiar and stable surrounding. The consistency of that space in our sessions was something that meant a lot to her. The "session from two hotels" did not actually constitute a spectacular breakthrough, but something had shifted.

Several weeks after, Lorraine stopped in Paris, and we finally arranged meeting in-person in my practice room. I generally feel a mixture of excitement and apprehension in such a case. Not having a screen between us breaks the settled frame; with some clients it feels like a welcome change, with others less so. In Lorraine's case, I was hoping that the encounter would produce some interesting material.

She sat in front of me; composed, pale as usual, and shorter than I had thought (that happens often with on-screen relationships). All the semblance of closeness we had been able to build online seemed to dissipate. Lorraine was back in her shell.

She was between assignments, but not for long, and seemed ready, almost eager, to move into a new hotel somewhere in South-East Asia. It would soon become her "home" for the next few months. She had already checked the hotel situation—it was one of her favourite chains and was equipped with a decent gym and swimming pool. She seemed a bit lost, homeless for real, without the hotel room that usually would contain, at least temporarily, her belongings and her life. She made no comments about my part of the town, or about the therapy room that she had only seen on her screen before.

"How do you feel about us being in the same room?"

"Not much, maybe a little uncomfortable".

She was not used to sharing a room with anybody; she never had. Her childhood family house was large enough for everybody to have their own bedroom, she said. They rarely spent time together downstairs; her parents both had their own office room. Coming back home from school, she would usually grab something from the fridge and retreat upstairs, directly to her bedroom.

This was the first time that Lorraine was sharing some tangible details about her childhood. As she spoke, I could finally picture this big, perfectly organised house, surrounded by snow. The white lacquered furniture that her mother loved and kept in perfect order, spotless. This was probably why Lorraine was not allowed to invite friends; none of her birthday parties had taken place at home. Her home had always felt like a hotel to her—it was comfortable, clean and temporary. Since an early age, Lorraine had known that she would leave and go elsewhere later. Her childhood had been about waiting for it to happen.

Now, as an adult, she did not know how to do differently. She still had to learn how to develop an attachment, to a place, or to a person. Our shared online space was a tentative model; a little relational bubble in which this process could hopefully start. At that point, Lorraine was not ready to fully grasp how the life she had built was as dysfunctional as her childhood. The defensive walls that she had built in the past were still in place, protecting her from the terror of her attachment-less reality. And she was not yet ready to confront this.

Therapy clients are always creative in communicating their hidden truths to us, even though they are not yet able to verbalise them openly. Online clients have more sophisticated options, making our exploratory work even more fascinating. Marco, who had been one of my recent clients, broke up with his girlfriend after a tumultuous and dramatic relationship. The next day, when we connected for an emergency session, I was surprised by the view of him lying in his bathtub. "I am destroyed", he commented, explaining his soaking in the hot bath. The bare upper part of his body was visible all through the session, in which he struggled with the feelings of shame and belittlement that he had experienced in the relationship with his verbally and physically violent partner. The striking contrast, that was literally in my face, between his displayed Latin masculinity and his experience of being abused in this relationship for years, was his way of communicating to me his being hurt and his shame, at the same time as the contrasting image of a strong man. I opted for not addressing in that session his decision to display his maleness. Marco was too upset and struggling with shame to engage in such a challenging conversation. It took us a few more months of consistent talking before discussing the bathtub setting, but it finally paid off. Marco managed to verbalise his fear of "turning into his father", who consistently lied and cheated on Marco's mother almost openly, often using his young son as a cover. This deep fear drove Marco to choose partners who mistreated him greatly, as his father had done to his mother.

There is something counter-intuitive about the importance of place in a place-less online setting, but it is this very absence of a shared physical space that makes the concept of place and physicality central to the therapeutic process. Therefore, addressing displacement starts with some attunement to the place in the background of the client, often visible on the screen.

Note

1 Making the most of such "travelling" offered by online therapy was illustrated in *Unlocked* (Piatakhina Giré, 2022)

References

Aciman, A. (2007). *Out of Egypt*. New York: Picador.

Akhtar, S. (1995). A third individuation: Immigration, identity, and the psychoanalytic process. *Journal of the American Psychoanalytic Association*, 43(4), 1051–1084. doi:10.1177/000306519504300406.

Akhtar, S. (2004). *Immigration and identity: Turmoil, treatment, and transformation*. Oxford: Rowman & Littlefield.

Badkhen, A. (2018, Nov.). An anatomy of lostness. *World Literature Today*.

Baldick, C. (2015). *The Oxford dictionary of literary terms* (4th edn). Oxford: Oxford University Press.

Bevan, D. (1990). *Literature and exile*. Amsterdam and Atlanta GA: Rodopi.

Bolognani, M. (2016). From myth of return to return fantasy: A psychosocial interpretation of migration imaginaries. *Null*, 23(2), 193–209. doi:10.1080/1070289X.2015.1031670.

Bolton, G. (2011). *Write yourself: Creative writing and personal development*. London: Jessica Kingsley.

Bolton, G., Field, V., & Thompson, K. (2006). *Writing works: A resource handbook for therapeutic writing workshops and activities (writing for therapy or personal development)*. London: Jessica Kingsley.

Boym, S. (1996). Estrangement as a lifestyle: Shklovsky and Brodsky. *Poetics Today*, 17(4), 511–530. doi:10.2307/1773211.

Boym, S. (2001). *The future of nostalgia*. New York: Basic Books.

Brodsky, J. (1991). The condition we call exile. *Renaissance and Modern Studies*, 34, 1.

Brookner, A. (2010). *Latecomers*. London: Penguin.

Burgo, J. (2018). *Shame: Free yourself, find joy, and build true self-esteem*. New York: St. Martin's Press.

de Grève, M. (2008). L'autobiographie, genre littéraire? *Revue de littérature comparée*, 325(1), 23–31. doi:10.3917/rlc.325.0023.

Dowd, A. (2019). Uprooted minds: Displacement, trauma and dissociation. *Journal of Analytical Psychology*, 64(2), 244–269. doi:10.1111/1468-5922.12481.

Dunn, K. (2012). A qualitative investigation into the online counselling relationship: To meet or not to meet, that is the question. *Counselling and Psychotherapy Research*, 12(4), 316–326. doi:10.1080/14733145.2012.669772.

Ferro, A. (2006). *Psychoanalysis as therapy and storytelling*. London and New York: Routledge.

Gerson, S. (2008). Unconscious phantasy and relational reality. *Psychoanalytic Inquiry*, 28(2), 151–168. doi:10.1080/07351690701856906.

Gessen, M. (2018). To be, or not to be. *New York Review of Books*, February 8.

Grinberg, L., & Grinberg, R. (1984). *Psychoanalytic perspectives on migration and exile*. New Haven CT & London: Yale University Press.

Hayner, N. (2013). *The Hotel: The Sociology of Hotel Life*. Chapel Hill: University of North Carolina Press.

Hoffman, E. (1998). *Lost in translation: A life in a new language* (Vintage edn). London: Vintage Books.

Joinson, S. (2015). Hotel melancholia. *Aeon*, June 8.

King, S. (2000). *On writing: A memoir of the craft*. London and New York: Hodder & Stoughton.

Lembke, A. (2021). *Dopamine nation: Finding balance in the age of indulgence*. London: Headline.

Madison, G. A. (2011). *The end of belonging: Untold stories of leaving home and the psychology of global relocation*. New York: CreateSpace. ISBN: 9781449534165.

McAdams, D. P. (1996). *The stories we live by: Personal myths and the making of the self*. New York: Guilford Press.

Nabokov, V. (2000). *Speak, memory*. London: Penguin Books.

Nathanson, D. L. (1992). *Shame and pride: Affect, sex, and the birth of the self*. New York and London: W. W. Norton.

Norman, S. H. (2013). *Hotel life* (2nd edn). Chapel Hill: University of North Carolina Press.

Orbach, S. (2000). *The impossibility of sex*. New York: Touchstone.

Piatakhina Giré, A. (2022). *Unlocked: Online therapy stories*. London: Confer Books.

Roth, J. (Ed.) (2015). *The hotel years: Wanderings in Europe between the wars*. New York: New Directions.

Roth, P. (1997). *The facts: A novelist's autobiography*. New York: Vintage.

Said, E. W. (1999). *Out of place: A memoir* (1st edn). New York: Knopf.

Serres, K., & Wright, B. (2017). *Soutine's portraits: Cooks, waiters and bellboys*. Exhibition catalogue. London: The Courtauld Gallery and Paul Hoberton Publishing.

Sinatti, G. (2011). "Mobile transmigrants" or "unsettled returnees"? Myth of return and permanent resettlement among Senegalese migrants. *Population, Space and Place*, 17(2), 153–166. doi:10.1002/psp.608.

Szekacs-Weisz, J. (2016). Emigration from within. *American Journal of Psychoanalysis*, 76(4), 389–398.

Tokarczuk, O. (2018). *Flights*. London: Fitzcarraldo Editions.

Tummala-Narra, P. (2009a). The immigrant's real and imagined return home. *Psychoanalysis, Culture & Society*, 14(3), 237–252. doi:10.1057/pcs.2009.9.

Tummala-Narra, P. (2009b). Teaching on diversity: The mutual influence of students and instructors. *Psychoanalytic Psychology*, 26(3), 322–334. doi:10.1037/a0016444.

Volkov, S. (1998). *Conversations with Joseph Brodsky*. New York: The Free Press.

Winnicott, D. W. (1971). *Playing and reality* (1st edn). London: Tavistock Publications.

Yalom, I. (2017). *Becoming myself*. New York: Basic Books.

Yalom, I. D. (2009). *The gift of therapy*. New York: Harper Perennial.

Chapter 5

Importance of working with attachment

Place and memory

No matter the efforts humans employ to modify their landscape, they are heavily dependent on their environment and are naturally sensitive to their surroundings. Our biological capacity to locate our bodies in space is a function embedded in our brains. Neuroscientific research into the complex structure of the hippocampus has identified the specialised cells for the brain's spatio-temporal representation of the environment, which are necessary for human survival in the physical world. This is where the complex interconnection between place cells, grid cells, head position cells and other cells responding to self-locating purposes is taking place (Moser et al., 2015). This brain activity is responsible for creating dynamic self-maps which include information about the specific places we are evolving in, and it is not independent of another function of the brain—emotional memory formation. These simultaneous neural activities lead to unique emotionally coloured stories about oneself in a place. As Dowd puts it,

> It is into these "place maps" that our emotional experiencing in relation to our total environment, human and non-human, becomes embedded or encoded as "organised spatial stories". It is these processes that give rise to the special, temporal and relational links [...] essential to a sense of self-cohesion, self-continuity and belonging.
>
> (Dowd, 2019: 252)

The current view in neuroscience is that the primary function of the hippocampus is to generate cognitive maps and to mediate episodic memory processes. A recent focus has been on the specific contribution of place cells to episodic memory, confirming that spatial geometry of the environment plays an important role in memory formation (Smith & Mizumori, 2006; Leutgeb et al., 2005). This phenomenon is successfully exploited by the "Method of Loci", an ancient method of memorising information by placing each item to be remembered at a specific point of an imaginary journey through a familiar

DOI: 10.4324/9781003144588-5

place (Kelly, 2017). This method has many variations, but its origins go back to Ancient Greece. Therapy with clients whose emotional history is anchored in many scattered places is a similar journey into recovering and organising their narrative, by re-visiting those places.

There is an additional value in looking at the past places through the magnifying lens of loss. Emigrants learn this art naturally. When we lose a significant place, with time and distance we re-create its image in our mind—fabricating a memory. This creative process is akin to any artistic endeavour. Proust, in *In the Shadow of Young Girls in Flower* describes a turning point when a provincial church is transformed for the narrator's mind after he contemplates the painting of that church by an artist friend. The building in the painting moves him in a way the original building had not done. This transformative power of the creative process is used in therapy, which is quite similar to literary storytelling. As our emigrant clients tell us about their lost places, they use this power of transformation; by allowing these places to move them (and us), they re-create a version in their memory that is meaningful and aligned with their narrative.

The biological link between memory formation and physical places is of crucial importance for a better understanding of displaced clients' experience of therapy. When a therapist inquires about a remote and trauma-infused event, it should be kept in mind that these events are always associated with a place in which they happened. The place itself can be a good starting point from which we can start a journey of discovery.

Importance of place

Environmental psychology, an interdisciplinary field that gained recognition in the 1970s, shifted the focus to the transactions between humans and their surroundings. Hofer is a psychiatrist and author of *Roots of Human Behaviour* who has contributed to adding biological evidence to attachment theories (Hofer, 1981; Hofer & Sullivan, 2008). He concludes that "place … is important to human being right from the beginning" (Hofer, 1981). The American philosopher Edward Casey studied the problematics of space and place. As he puts it, "place belongs to the very concept of existence … [it is] the condition of all existing things" (Casey, 2009: 15). We all evolve within the boundaries of our own physical bodies, and our bodies evolve within the boundaries of physical spaces. No matter how many technologies we invent to break this interdependence, humans are bound to places. Humans constantly challenge their physical environment—sometimes to the point of exterminating it—but places will always return to haunt us and restore their primacy, whether by a natural disaster or in our scariest nightmares. Even though there is some truth in the idea that the natural environment of our species is no longer a geographical but a relational landscape (Cozolino, 2006), there are no relationships that happen outside of some form of a place, or space for those who evolve entirely in a virtual reality. Many highly mobile individuals who chose again and again to uproot themselves are defying this dependence on a place. Jhumpa Lahiri makes sense of her own breaking away: "I am working to free my work from geographic coordinates, and to arrive at a more abstract sense of place" (Layshon, 2018). But ironically, she also shows us an inspiring example of developing a powerful emotional bond with Italy, turning a foreign land and its language into a home (Kellman, 2017; Lahiri, 2017). As Dowd summarises, "there can be no person without a place to be a person" (Dowd, 2019: 4). This statement propels the place-related matters to the core of any identity-related quandary, and as a result to the very centre of any therapeutic endeavour with displaced clients.

In the last two decades, in response to ever increasing mobility, there has been a broader interdisciplinary effort to bring together knowledge about humans' relationship to places and mobility (Dixon & Durrheim, 2000; Cresswell & Merriman, 2011). Researchers in the fields of human geography and social psychology have been routinely linking place with meaning (Dixon & Durrheim, 2000; Cresswell, 2015; Kearney & Bradley, 2009; Simandan, 2011): "We grow up in place, we experience our lives in place, we foresee our future in place" (Simandan, 2011: 6). "Questions of 'who we are' are often intimately related to questions of 'where we are'" (Dixon & Durrheim, 2000: 7).

Simandan (2011) makes an appealing call for his fellow human geographers to engage more actively with recent psychological research, and I would like to make a convergent call for my fellow psychotherapists and other mental health practitioners to engage more with research in human geography. A more focused and refined interest in human experience of place, the process of place making, and the storytelling about places becomes even more crucial at a time of broad displacement of individuals all around the world.

Geographers insist that we make places, and it is our subjective experience of the things we are doing in a particular surrounding that impacts our sense of place (Cresswell, 2015; Simandan, 2011). Since the early 1980s, environmental psychology has developed a concept of *place-identity* (Proshansky et al., 1983; Dixon & Durrheim, 2000) as a "pot-pourri of memories, conceptions, interpretations, ideas and related feelings about specific physical settings as well as types of settings" (Proshansky et al., 1983: 60).

Unfortunately, therapists rarely share geographers' fascination with the place concept. In my clinical practice I have met peripatetic clients who had moved places and cultures more than once, without it being explored in their previous therapies. If a therapist ignores the personal geography of her clients, her displaced clients miss an opportunity for a deeper self-exploration, in a strange parallel with the loss they have actually experienced with their multiple dislocation, thus leaving blind spots, and an incomplete narrative and sense of self for her clients that may unconsciously avoid addressing them. It is the therapist's responsibility to help them look back to re-integrate their experiences related to the multiple places they have left behind. This is often a significant condition for restoring a more complete sense of self. A geographically fragmented, peripatetic life may result in multiple attachments and a complex concept of place. This complexity leads to confusion about one's identity and one's place in the world.

What the Bible calls "high places", also identified as "sacred places", have been part of stories that humans tell about themselves and an intrinsic part of any kind of self-narration. No matter how we explain the supernatural phenomena that may occur in these places, the human brain, with complex, electronically sensitive structures in its limbic system, tends to assign meaning to sensory input produced by certain places. This meaning-making activity around our physical surroundings, be it a natural landscape, a building, or even a virtual scenery, is wired into the human brain.

In displacement, we become even more attuned to our surroundings; our attention naturally shifts onto the unfamiliar landscape as we try to master it for survival, and the question of location becomes central. The feelings of lostness and confusion, described by many exiled or peripatetic writers, often lead to a heightened preoccupation with places (Badkhen, 2018).

When they first reach out, displaced clients generally define themselves with some geographic characteristic: "an American living in Paris"; "a British expat to Singapore"; "a Third Culture Kid currently based in Beirut". For sedentary clients, there is no need to specify their cultural background in relation to a place or their current status in their current location; the displaced clients reaching out to a therapist naturally share this kind of detail. Starting therapy with an exploration of how the displaced person identifies himself quickly opens the door to the displacement-related material. Thus, the therapist, from an early stage, shows her client that she is ready to welcome this material into their dialogue and recognises the importance of this approach.

As some of my clients pass through Paris on their way to a vacation or professional trip, they sometimes take the opportunity to meet me in person (for more detail see Chapter 8). As they settle down and take time to scrutinise the bookshelves and artwork on the walls of my therapy room, we talk about their experience of making their way through Paris—a necessary self-locating activity. For some, it has turned into an anxiety-provoking endeavour: "This was such a nightmare!", while for others it was an exciting adventure from which they extract some pride: "I made it here so easily!"

Centrality of place and its meaning for clients who experience displacement puts the question of place attachment at the core of therapeutic work with this population. Rogers specialises in expatriate issues in therapy. He insists that "consideration of the human–place relationship is vital to effectively assisting people who have been traumatized by displacement, are considering a major move, or are in transition" (Rogers, 2013). For peripatetic clients, the place-attachment problematic moves from a theoretical ground to a real-life experience.

Therapists who turn to human geography can integrate this consideration into a displacement-sensitive practice.

Place attachment

Practitioners from different theoretical backgrounds routinely recognise the central importance of attachment in human development and include the concepts from Bowlby's attachment theory into their practice. But the developmental role of place attachment is mostly ignored (e.g. Howe et al., 1995; Aldgate et al., 2006). There has nevertheless been an awakening call recently for psychology researchers to integrate place attachment into their thinking about human development (Jack in Atkinson et al., 2012), but it seems to be slow to penetrate clinical practice with displaced individuals.

Attachment theory (Bowlby, 2012; Ainsworth, 1997) provides a solid basis for understanding early relationship experiences within social systems. It describes the impact of human bonding on the development of identity and personality. Early attachments leave important psychological imprints that later serve as operational guides and reference points for all future relationships. The emotional bond that humans develop with their meaningful environments is known as *place attachment*. It is characterised by a reciprocal relationship between an individual and "a beloved place" (Fullilove, 1996).

Place attachment has gained much scientific attention since the turn of the century (e.g. Giuliani, 2003; Scannell & Gifford, 2010; Manzo & Devine-Wright, 2014; Cresswell, 2015). Following the early 1990s when it was at concept stage, place attachment now seems to be moving to an application stage, being applied to practical issues (Scanell & Gifford in Manzo & Devine-Wright, 2014). Its implications for the place-making professions (urbanists, architects, designers, etc.) have been clearly stated (Hester, 1985), but what about the meaning-making professions, such as counsellors and psychotherapists?

The "frayed knot" hypothesis, elaborated by human geographers, is about how repeated upheaval undermines the function of place (Fullilove in Manzo & Wright, 2014: 141), impacting how people develop attachment to places. There are multiple ways in which an emigrant's relationship with his new place can be explored, and place attachment is one more area in which creativity is a differentiator for therapy.

Multiple displaced artists use various visual arts as means to reflect on a place–person relationship. One striking example is the work of Joan Archibald, a Californian artist known as Kali, who used photographs and multi-layered superpositions to create daunting surrealistic images mixing portrait and landscape. After first seeing her work, I was barely surprised to find out that Kali, in 1966, had made a life-disrupting move from Long Island to California, and from a housewife's life to that of a hippy artist. Without this drastic self-imposed displacement, she could not have broken with a life that she was finding restrictive, bound by strict social norms, to embrace a life of creativity. In her art, Kali constantly wrestled with her relationship to places. The media she used, such as collages of images from magazines, photography, and other printed materials, can supplement and enrich any talking therapy with displaced individuals.

"If this place were a person, what kind of relationship would you have with them?" is a question I often ask to my peripatetic clients who struggle with their new place. Using such a personification leads to fascinating reflections about how they feel and about their current and often temporary home. These conversations provide insight into their personal geography. Clients' relationships with their new places vary greatly, but there is always some ambivalence or complexity about them. Exploring them in any depth comes with making links with clients' earlier attachment figures.

In the case of Anna, making such a parallel helped us to revisit her relationship with her mother. Anna had left her home country, Poland, a decade earlier. When we started our work she was based on a small British island, married to another emigrant, and had a good job. Despite the superficial stability of their situation, she constantly felt unsettled and kept wondering why she could not be content. "Why can I not be just like other people who are simply happy where they are? Why am I always discontent[ed]?" she often wondered, with some self-contempt. When I asked her what kind of person the island would be, she came up with an answer that did not surprise either of us: "It is scornful and possessive ... it wouldn't let me go. If I leave, it will not let me back." The island was often cut off for days from the mainland and the rest of the world, with all flights cancelled. The anxiety and fear of abandonment that Anna expressed led us right back to her mother, who had brought her up alone, and who, over a decade later, would still use every opportunity to remind Anna how "abandoned and lonely" Anna's departure had made her feel. Anna had always felt responsible for her mother's wellbeing; she was sending her a good share of her income, gave her expensive gifts, and spent way too much money on trips back home that always left her emotionally exhausted and even physically sick. The kind of attachment she developed to her new place was only a variation on her main attachment theme, which was not allowing her to engage in a more trustful way with the island. Somewhere in the middle of our therapy work, Anna had to cancel our weekly session: "I am stuck in London, there is fog on the island again". This rather common meteorological event sent Anna into turmoil. The next time we met she was still anxious and upset. Her new home or "the damned rock" started to feel like a rejecting parent. When I mentioned this analogy to Anna, she smiled sadly "Yes, when I was a teen-ager and wanted to go out with friends, my mother used to warn me not to come back late: she would lock the door and not let me in if I came back after the time limit ..." Once she did lock her out of their flat, punishing Anna for something that she had experienced as a rejection. Her mother's unresolved attachment anxieties were now resonating as a distant but threatening thunderstorm in Anna's emigrant existence.

Emigrant women often have a particular difficulty to take up space. Many of my displaced female clients struggle with the relationship to their bodies; they feel "fat" or that their body is not right in some way. As Susie Orbach insists in her manifesto *Fat Is a Feminist Issue* (Orbach, 2016), exploring clients' relationship with their bodies, we routinely bump into an earlier attachment figure, often a narcissistic parent who would make aggressive comments on their appearance and put pressure on their child to live by their unreasonable and overwhelming expectations. Those who have this unfortunate background and then experience displacement see this kind of early developmental history resonate in their emigrant existence, impacting their embodied experience of self in the new place. For example, one of my clients, Alyson, a young American woman, would often comment on how scared she was to shop in Paris, where she lived. On the rare occasions when she ventured into one of the fancy boutiques that abound in the French capital, the salesgirls, "always thin and snobby", would make her feel "like I am too fat and completely inappropriate". Clearly, Alyson's experience of displacement was triggering the older shame that her mother had routinely made her feel as a child. As she was growing up, Alyson always knew that her mother, a very thin, cold woman, disliked her and resented her for "taking her husband's genes", and Alyson had always been told that they were bad genes. Her father had left them when she was a young child. She experienced Parisian women as an army of her mother's soldiers, all repulsed by her large frame and plump arms. Blinded by her powerful projection, Alyson was unable to notice any genuinely kind gaze, any positive comment or compliment that her French colleagues might give her. The earlier traumatic attachment to her mother was getting in the way of her engaging with her new place and with the people there. Making this simple link allowed Alyson to reflect on her relationship with her mother, to question how "wonderful" it was, and eventually to open up to her new place and to the prospect of new attachments in Paris.

Attachment tendency and the choice of online therapy

At the beginning of my career as a therapist, I was experiencing online therapy as a client myself. Reflecting on my own reasons for turning to remote therapy helped me to better understand my displaced clients' choice of this medium. Meeting my distance therapist through the screen felt easy; it probably fitted well with my own avoidant attachment tendency (Ainsworth, 1997). "'Avoidance' refers to the tendency to evade intimacy with other people, but also to defend against certain feelings, impulses, memories, and needs that arise internally" (Cundy, 2018: 72).

As a child, I had learnt to ask little from my parents, who were often unable to respond to my needs. Both were passionate about their successful teaching careers, and my father had a mentally ill brother to take care of, so I had to be strong and self-reliant. As a young adult, I felt unable to turn to others at times of emotional distress—only comfortable when relying on myself—self-sufficiency was high on my list of human qualities. In short, I qualified for a "dismissive avoidant" label (Howe, 1995). As often happens, my adult experience of emigration reinforced this attachment structure; away from home and alone I had to take care of myself if I was to survive. This childhood story and the resulting attachment tendencies closely echo the three case examples described by Cundy (Cundy, 2018), as well as many of my own online clients' narratives. By the time I started therapy online, these defence mechanisms were well in place and entrenched. The fact that my therapist lived on another continent and spoke a different language made me feel safe, giving me an opportunity to control my exposure. As Winnicott points out, it is a joy to be hidden, and a disaster not to be found (Winnicott, 1971). We all play hide-and-seek with others, and the therapeutic relationship is no exception. The online space, limited by the screen, offered many opportunities for successful hiding; but the hope of being found persisted and was eventually compensated by the acceptance and affection that my online therapist was able to demonstrate throughout our work.

In my experience, it is not unusual for a client to exploit the hiding potential of the online setting; they connect from a poorly lit room with a window behind them, or choose a place with a terrible internet connection, so that their face becomes a pixelated image.[1] The "body-less" nature of the online encounter makes it easier for both client and therapist to fail each other. From my side of the screen, I certainly did not make my therapist's job any easier, but over the following years he offered me a safe space during yet another international move. I retreated weekly to the small room under the roof of my temporary Spanish home, with an iPad on my lap showing his always-calm familiar face.

The preference of clients for the online therapy option has been under-researched (Simpson, 2009), but based on sparse accounts in the literature (Dunn, 2012) and my own observations, some clients express a clear preference for meeting their therapist online. The distance makes them feel safer. Reeves, an attachment-based psychoanalytic psychotherapist who also works online, wonders whether the attachment style of the client influences his choice of the technology mediated therapy:

> I have no doubt that there are clients who choose this medium because it enables them to keep emotional distance and, therefore, maintain some of their defences, but it is not by any means the main or the only reason for this choice.

(Reeves in Cundy, 2015: 139)

Reflecting on my own online work I have come to the same conclusion. It is reasonable to put forward a hypothesis saying that there may be some insecure attachment in the background when the individual leaves his home country; especially when this rupture happens repetitively. There is certainly more fascinating research to be done into the complex links between attachment tendencies and the choice of a particular therapy delivery method.

"Avoidant individuals are masters in the art of evasion and disguise, employing a remarkable range of defensive manoeuvres that indicate the quality of their relationships with other people" (Cundy, 2018: 78). These manoeuvres are facilitated and amplified by developing technologies. Whilst many clearly state their preference for meeting with their therapist through the screen, the recent pandemic pushed most people in therapy all around the globe to move their sessions online. From my own close observation of this process and from what has been reported so far in the literature, the variety of responses to this move are fascinating: some disliked online sessions and could not wait to return to an in-person setting; some felt relieved and had a hard time making their way back to their therapist's office (Dunn, 2012; Dunn & Wilson, 2021; Vostanis & Bell, 2020). Looking at this phenomenon from the attachment perspective helps us make sense of these preferences. Avoidant clients may be much more comfortable with the protective barrier of the screen and the physical distance between them and their therapist.

In the same way their clients do, therapists may display the avoidant-attachment style and be uncomfortable with too much intimacy. Carl Rogers admitted that the intimacy he was able to develop with his clients in the therapy room "without risking too much of his person" compensated for his inability to take such risks in his personal life (Adams, 2013). I guess Rogers might have embraced the screen-mediated connections, and eventually become a keen online therapist.

As Cundy insists, the therapeutic aim with avoidant clients is about "helping them become less defended and inhibited, more spontaneous and alive in relationships" (Cundy, 2018). The disinhibition effect of the online interaction is well described in literature (Suler, 2004). It becomes an unexpected ally for any online therapist. Easier self-disclosures or more frequent act-outs play a significant role in any remote therapy process. Many clients who opt willingly for technology-mediated therapy would find the in-person interaction with a therapist impossible to handle, as the amount of exposure and shame such intimacy would trigger would be overwhelming or emotionally unaffordable. With the physical distance it precludes, online therapy opens a precious window for avoidant clients to start their therapeutic journey in a more manageable context, retaining more control over their environment.

"I can make you disappear in one click," Sam said mockingly. His face beamed with a childish smile on my screen. This fantasy of power over a carer perceived as unpredictable is precious material for the therapeutic mill. Sam had grown up in a British family with both parents struggling with alcohol abuse and depression, neglectful, and often violent. As a young boy he was often left alone to cater for his own basic needs, and whenever one of his parents finally gave him some attention, it was mainly to scold him, aggressively discharging their own load of unacknowledged shame. With this early relational history, Sam knew that giving too much power to the unpredictable adult in an authority position could be extremely dangerous. Now a young adult, he craved my attention, but was also constantly scared of what it may result in. Despite the anxiety our sessions were triggering for him, Sam never did use his power to make me disappear at the push of a button. At times he asked me if he could switch off the camera, or would cancel his session at the last moment, under a rational pretext that we both knew was covering up his compulsion to flee. At first, we reflected together on his choice of meeting online (Sam lived just a short subway ride from my office), then further down the line we routinely observed how his anxious avoidant attachment style was playing out in our online interactions, impacting the way our therapeutic relationship was developing. This on-going attention to the online process helped Sam learn about how he behaved in relationships with others. Slowly, he started to take more relational risks, for example exploring online dating opportunities. Only after a year did he eventually mention the possibility of having a session at my office.

Interpersonal and place attachments

My mother tongue has an idiom that was extensively used by Soviet ideologists: "Rodina-mat" or "mother Homeland". One of the first rules I learnt during my Russian lessons at school was that I had to write Homeland (Rodina) with a capital letter. The awe we were made to feel towards our motherland was extended to the ruling Communist Party. In the juxtaposition of these words—mother and homeland—that have merged into one English word—motherland, I see an interesting question: what is the relation between the attachment bonds we form with our caretakers and those we develop simultaneously to the place in which these relationships develop?

Until recently, knowledge about place attachment evolved separately from knowledge of interpersonal attachment. For millions of displaced clients in therapy there is an obvious benefit to identifying the nature of an individual's attachment tendency, regardless of the object (Scannell & Gifford in Manzo & Wright, 2014). Exploring the possible interplay between the interpersonal attachment styles (Ainsworth, 1979) and their potential place-associated counterparts is a fascinating topic for those working with displacement-related issues.

To this day, there is little literature available on this topic (Lewicka, 2011; Scannell & Gifford, 2010). It seems reasonable to bring forward a hypothesis that the place-attachment we form is closely linked to the bonds we simultaneously develop with others. If so, interpersonal and place attachment would form a symbiotic system, that would lie at the basis of early human development.

I intuit some clear similarities in developing an insecure, for example avoidant, attachment to early caregivers and a rejecting stance for an emigrant who left a society he had being experiencing as neglectful or shaming. "I hate my home country!" a Russian client once told me during our first session. She had grown up in a neglectful family with an emotionally unresponsive mother and an alcoholic father.

"Home" is often associated with our attachment to people developed in our original place. Lack of connection in early relationships can leave people longing for a sense of belonging and lead to desperate searching for the experience of the archetypal home that is nowhere to be found (Rogers, 2013). As these early bonds develop in parallel, in a constant relational interplay with people and/in places, they must be addressed in one shared therapeutic effort. This effort can only succeed if the relationship we offer is safe enough, creating a space that feels stable and predictable. In his recent book, Salman Akhtar (Akhtar, 2022) argues that one of the first prerequisites of working developmentally with clients is offering them a "safe" physical place—an office—that is neutral, but warm enough, and stable. The importance of creating a safe and nurturing place, a substitute for "home", is evident and widely recognised, but when we work online this becomes more challenging. Of course, we can make sure we position our camera in such a way that clients can see a reassuring background, for example bookshelves, but the place-less nature of the interaction makes this task even more ambitious. No matter how much we try to maintain a predictable environment, if we work online, our clients will at some point disrupt the scenery on their side of the screen, connect from a new place, for example from a friend's home or from their car, and on the therapist's side, we may connect from a country house or hotel room when some sessions need to be fitted into a holiday trip. This dynamic context shifts even more weight onto the therapeutic relationship itself—away from a physical place and towards the interpersonal connection. Simply put, an online therapist can rely much less on the physical realm to create safety and predictability for her client; she has to rely entirely on her own relational skills and work hard to make sure her clients end up with a reparative experience.

This natural shift from place towards relationship facilitated by the place-less reality of the online work highlights the cooperative nature of the therapeutic endeavour. It is about co-creating the "secure relational base" in a "place-less" realm, so that the client experiences an emotional bond and a closeness not fully associated with any physical environment. In the traditional in-person therapy, the therapist is responsible for maintaining the "safety" of the surroundings. In online therapy, that responsibility is shared, and paradoxically, the client gets a renewed opportunity to acquire a new understanding of his functioning and develop better relational skills. This is one of the "unexpected" gifts of online therapy that a skilled therapist can exploit for the benefit of her client, a shift in relational dynamics that presents an exciting opportunity for developmental work.

Another fascinating group that is naturally drawn to online therapy consists of young professionals often displaced as children, who have not quite settled down as adults, and have kept moving around, often with a successful international career. They are generally extremely self-reliant and find it hard commit to one romantic partner or one place. They often believe that their peripatetic lifestyle does not allow them to settle, and there is some truth to that. But when we look deeper, we often realise that it is the fear of an exclusive emotional bond that keeps them moving. Clara clearly belonged to that category. She grew up in Canada in an emigrant family. Her Italian father was a prominent academic, and a workaholic. Her Italian mother had dedicated her life to following him, adapting to his needs that evolved around his demanding work. Not much time was left for Clara, and she quickly learnt how to survive alone. As an adult she was based in Switzerland, but she travelled extensively for work. During one of our online sessions, she announced that her parents were selling their Canadian house, where she had grown up and spent most of her childhood. Clara's white face remained blank. She did not plan to travel there to retrieve her few belongings stored in the basement. When I asked her how she felt about this, she insisted that she did not feel much. She had always known she would not settle there anyway. Her lack of emotional response, not unusual given her generally calm mood, was still surprising. I offered a hypothesis that her avoidant attachment to her absent parents might be extended to her childhood home, but she dismissed it somewhat defensively "So what?" Despite her insistent reassurances about all the friends she had, I constantly felt that these relationships lacked depth, and in our own therapeutic relationship I also felt that I was being held at a distance. Meeting through our respective screens was efficiently reinforcing her strategy there. She did often travel to see her always distant friends and stay with them for a few days. These were short non-committal trips to visit people who, just like her, were busy young professionals with demanding jobs. They too lived across borders and had fragile attachments to the place in which they were "currently based"—an expression favoured by these peripatetic clients, as opposed to the more settled and dangerously definite "live". As I drew her attention to such matters, Clara would shrug, bored with my interventions. With my frustration growing—our sessions seemed increasingly flat and lacking in depth—I was starting to wonder whether I could ever help her. She might end our work at any time, probably out of sheer boredom, so I challenged her, asking for her reasons to stay in therapy. "Life–work" balance and other rather mundane matters came up. "What about romantic relationships?" I asked. "I am not particularly interested right now", she answered, impassive as usual. And yet, she stayed. With many interruptions, sometimes disappearing for weeks, she would always return. And stubbornly we both kept going despite the shared frustration. Despite her financial possibilities, Clara was living in a smallish furnished flat that she constantly complained about. She resisted making herself comfortable, such as by acquiring furniture, or getting to know local friends. After a few years though, she slowly started engaging more with her surroundings, spending more weekends in the Swiss town, rather than travelling across Europe to see distant friends. Eventually she rented her own flat, small and still temporary, but for the very first time unfurnished. This process of starting to trust a place, relying on its resources for survival and meeting her various needs was extremely slow and anxiety-producing for Clara. But she pushed forward. It took her even more time to extend this trust to people. The day she invited a couple of new local friends into her newly decorated flat, I knew something major was shifting in her life.

Exploring the relationship with the motherland

"Perhaps it is simply this: having lived in Russia, I know in my bones how complicated a place it is", states the Russian-born American journalist and academic Keith Gessen (Gessen, 2018). The essence and the complexity of the place where one was born is encrypted into one's body, into its cells, turning any definite separation into a tricky matter.

The relationship that displaced individuals develop with their original place is rarely an easy one. The departure can be a rupture. Many emigrant clients, when asked at the initial stages of therapy, how they feel about their original home, respond with some noncommittal abbreviated version, hardly explaining the reason why they left. One of them, Pierre, a young Frenchman, first left Paris at the age of 15 to study abroad for one year, and has not returned since, having multiple brilliant academic and professional achievements. At the initial stages of our work, he insisted he adored his father, and his mother was the most caring and supportive parent one could have. This narrative, stubbornly constructed through years of early but nevertheless voluntary displacement, was his way of shielding himself from a reality that was emotionally unbearable and did not fit with the family narrative, in which five children, all raised with high Catholic and bourgeois standards, were expected to perform excellently and be grateful for what they were given. It took us a few years to elaborate a different version, more aligned with Pierre's loneliness, his deeply rooted shame, and his chronic and unexplained depression. Pierre's buried and unrecognised emotional reality followed him in his new place, as far away from home as it could be, in this instance the antipodes: Australia. He was lonely, had no close friends, and no romantic partner had ever survived the first date. His parents seemed untouchable, as Pierre resisted any deeper exploration of their relationship; but after a while we were finally able to talk about his experience of growing up in the chic Parisian suburbia, where he had felt "not at his ease" and "different". His passion for sports was not aligned with what were collectively implied as noble interests. Pierre had grown up feeling restricted and misunderstood, disempowered by the parental authority of his intimidating father, a successful businessman. The only way Pierre had found to escape this environment was to physically remove himself from it. We mostly worked online, but the pivotal session happened in person, during one of his holidays at his parents' home. Enquiring into his experience of physically being in the house in which he had grown up gave us hints on his childhood. What he was describing sounded so similar to his current life in Australia, as if the loneliness and misalignment had become the emotional feature for "home". This paradox of a home that never felt homely was at the core of Pierre's peripatetic journey through places and cultures. For years, he tried hard to put his motherland and his parents behind but remained loyal to his old home and its rules, endlessly repeating with some superficial variations the old themes of his past. Moving beyond his initial narratives and re-evaluating his relationship with his childhood home helped Pierre reclaim some ground, to build a new kind of home on a different basis.

As Boym points out in her essay on nostalgia:

> The home that one leaves and "a home away from home", which one creates, sometimes have more in common than one would like to admit. A portable home away from home, which an émigré ferociously guards, preserves an imprint of his or her cultural motherland.
>
> (Boym, 1996: 514)

What seems relevant to therapy here is to explore what these bits of homeland are that displaced individuals keep or re-create within their inner landscape or in their new place. Unfortunately, these parts are neither the most comfortable ones nor separated from what made people leave in the first place. This presents an obvious potential for inner conflict and widens the therapeutic field.

The ambivalence of experience with the original home is even more unavoidable when the motherland has a history of provoking war or genocide, or mistreats its own people. Many individuals I see in therapy come from such places. In particular, the Russian war in Ukraine has wreaked havoc for my Russian clients, wherever they may be. It becomes unsustainable to relate to one's motherland when its rhetoric and acts go deeply against one's moral values and beliefs. For those over there who had been living in a state of internal emigration, managing to tolerate the ambivalence without using the drastic solution of emigration, a breaking point was reached, and that strategy suddenly stopped working, leaving lost individuals in a system gone mad.

The situation may not often be as paroxysmic as that, but the displaced clients' ambivalence towards their motherland is here to stay, bringing the more or less hidden agenda that must be addressed. The American journalist Margaret Renkl pointedly recognised in reflecting on her original place, the American South, that

> People can hardly help loving the hands that rocked their cradles or the landscapes that shaped their souls, but I doubt there's a single writer in the South for whom life here isn't a source of deep ambivalence. And yet all the writers I've mentioned had opportunities to leave—many actually did leave for a time before returning to stay.
>
> (Renkl, 2018)

Nevertheless, some places just do not welcome back their migrants, or the return feels unaffordable for other, usually internal reasons. Whereas returning emigrants get an opportunity to address their ambivalence within their original place itself, those who stay away face a different challenge. All therapists know how difficult it can be to work with the problematic parental figures when they are unavailable for any dialogue, be they absent or unresponsive because of death or a mental illness. The offspring then has to take full responsibility for disentangling the ambivalence. A therapist then stepping into this process and facilitating a dialogue with the absent parental figure (or motherland) will make this process a bit less lonely and alienating.

Here again, emigrant writers can be a source of inspiration, for their creative wrestling with such an ambivalence. The American siblings Masha and Keith Gessen, who emigrated with their parents from Soviet Russia as children, both turned to writing to cope with the unavoidable ambivalence that they had inherited alongside their culture and their displaced condition. For both, their careers turned into a battlefield, and their writings mostly deal with topics as unavoidable as autocracy, totalitarianism, and emigration. With his novel, *A Terrible Country*, Keith Gessen attempts to make sense and eventually peace with the problematic motherland that his parents "had fled, too many times" (Gessen, 2018). The main character of the novel, Andrey, returns to Moscow for a book-long reflection on his and his family's relationship with Russia. There is no simple resolution, but the process turns into an existential path towards self-realisation.

Therapy with displaced individuals who feel ambivalent about their motherland is always a wrestling space where we can turn to creativity, ours or that of our client. Just like Pierre, many expatriate clients will repress their negative feelings about their original home and will hardly report on what had not felt quite right in their life before emigration. One of the ways therapists can gain access to this repressed emotional material is by keeping an open eye (and the displacement rabbit ears on) for any complaint about their current place. Exactly in the same way as we would use the relational clues from a client's present or our own relational observations of the therapeutic process to better understand clients' relational past, we can use their experience of their new place as a departure point for exploration of their deeper feelings about their motherland.

Exploring the relationship with the new place

Exactly as attachment theory suggests, the ambivalence experienced in the early bonds, be it with the parental figures or the motherland, will always resonate in the later intimate relationships that we develop with people or places.

Whereas expatriate clients often avoid looking into their early relational wounds, they are more ready to explore their current relationships and point out the discrepancies they experience in their attunement or mis-attunement to their new place. Complaints about the new places come in endless forms, and always represent a rich source of material for exploration. Emigrants may feel unwanted, rejected, constantly misunderstood, and sometimes mistreated in their new location. This alienation from their current reality causes a lot of torment to those who had already felt alienated from their motherland or their people. It leads them to question not only their initial decision to leave their original home but also their own worth. Exploring these feelings and placing them in the context of their relationship with their original place always moves therapy forward.

One of the creative experiments that can be used with clients who have mixed feelings about their new place is to have them associate the current place that they express ambivalence about with a person. In the case of Helen, a half-French, half-American journalist, such an experiment was a turning point in her therapy. When we first met, Helen had been living in Algiers for a few years, covering northern Africa for a French news channel. She lived alone with two cats that did not require much commitment or care. As they appeared on my screen passing by, Helen commented that she loved them for this exact reason—they were exactly like her—self-reliant and minding their own business. In one of our initial sessions, Helen complained about feeling constantly uncomfortable outdoors, in the streets of Algiers. Back in Paris she used to jog along the riverbanks, and running was a source of joy for her, as well as an emotional and physical conduit. In Algiers, even though she lived by the sea, she felt too uncomfortable to venture outside in sports gear. A woman walking alone became an object of intense scrutiny for male bystanders. Young men sitting outside cafés drinking tea would watch her, sometimes in silence, but often commenting in Arabic. They presumed this tall blond, white woman would not understand, but Helen spoke Arabic and it would be a strain to try to ignore their comments and abstain from responding with an insult in Arabic. Helen spent most of her time writing from her apartment, she rarely left it except for a quick trip to buy groceries. I was surprised to learn that Helen did not really have to stay in Algiers for her work, she could perfectly well have moved to freer and foreigner-friendlier Morocco. Sometimes she would mention this possibility, but then never take action to relocate. In some strange ways, her restricted life in Algiers felt comfortable. Questioning this paradoxical attachment to a place that she did not enjoy naturally led us to her father. Helen's "American father"—as she referred to him—was a colourful character, a brilliant rock musician, recognised as an authority in the New York musical circles. Helen was born after the year he had spent in Paris, working on an album with a French band. When she was two, he returned to New York, leaving her mother and her, with debts plus an expensive guitar as a gift to his daughter. All through her childhood, Helen would wait for his impromptu visits, which were rare, and feel torn between her desire to see him again and the anger and resentment she felt because of his absence. The "American father" was also constantly torn between bouts of depression and maniacal élan. Drinking, drugs, and one woman after another kept making his life a hell. The promiscuous life he lived was a source of much of her adolescent confusion about sex and romantic love. Growing up, Helen went through all possible emotional states vis-à-vis her father—her relationship with him was a constant and mostly exciting rollercoaster. It was rarely about her though, and always about him. Her father, too preoccupied with his own creative life and his never-ending emotional crises, was generally absent, and then would suddenly re-appear with a major upheaval. These comebacks would always disrupt her plans, but then he would retreat again into the vortex of his life under the spell of his music, and Helen would feel troubled and terribly lonely for months in a row, until his next reappearance. When she talked about her father in therapy, she usually struggled to find a storyline, to stick to a version that would make sense—he was the most terrible but also the most terrific father one could imagine. Her friends, especially those who were into the rock scene, called her by her last name to pay tribute to him. Helen's father had died from an overdose a decade earlier, but her story about him and their relationship remained unsorted. With all this in mind, I asked her to describe Algiers as if it were a person: "What kind of person would it be?" Helen stayed silent for a moment, then responded "Rejecting, absent … but also captivating and inspiring in some strange ways." When I commented that this fitted well with her description of her father's character, she nodded. By sticking to this place, was she still trying to change or repair something in this relationship with her evasive father? Both her father and Algiers made her feel unwanted, alienated but at the same time they were a source of a strong identification—with her father she was the daughter of a dark but brilliant American rock musician, and being based in Algiers led to a strong professional identity as a journalist specialising in this complex region. By stubbornly investing in her relationship with Algiers, Helen was trying to resolve her relationship with her father. As we pursued this parallel, we managed to better understand the ambivalence that was part of her earliest attachment. She used to idealise her dysfunctional father in the same way as she now did with Algiers, looking for any crumbs of beauty in its culture, its language, its people. This was a beautiful relational effort, but by staying there Helen was depriving herself of a more fulfilling life.

The online setting: a "no-place" space

In traditional face-to-face therapy, clients return over and over to the same therapy room, and thus gradually develop an attachment to that physical place while their attachment to the therapist grows. But in the online setting, the therapeutic relationship develops outside of a single physical space. Clients may connect from a variety of places, and therapists who have become more confident with their online media may work from multiple locations, for example while travelling or from a holiday home. At the very beginning of psychoanalysis, therapists put much thinking into the decoration of their offices. It was supposed to be neutral, without objects that could give away too many clues about the therapist's private life, but also warm enough for the client to feel welcome. Today, it is not unusual for therapists to opt for a bare white wall as a background. When meeting through video, clients have limited access to their therapist's surroundings, and with the rapid qualitative development of online communication tools, therapists may soon be able to choose a background with virtual bookshelves and art or whatever else they want to project as an image. Clients already do these experiments, as they are not bound by any ethical code nor concern about the impact it may have.

Humans tend to create meaningful spaces, as in the case of religious or spiritual place attachments. If traditional therapy offers a "sacred" place for individual growth, online therapy offers something different—through the two on-screen representations, therapists and clients connect with each other in a space, rather than a place. This is an ironic turn for those clients (and their therapists) who wrestle with displacement, which at the core is a rupture of attachment to the original place. This irony is not lost on many displaced clients who consciously make the choice of easing this attachment expectation and opting for the online medium; in this way they avoid having to attach to yet another physical space—the one that belongs to their therapist.

With the invention of the internet, humans expanded their meaningful place-making activity to its vast and intangible territory. Since the creation of the first virtual chat rooms in the 1980s, people have used their potential as a gathering place, sharing a virtual space that differs from any of the individuals' "real" environments (Biocca & Lanier, 1992). The natural ability of the human brain to interpret flat images moving on a screen or fixed words printed on a page makes it possible to create worlds that feel "real". They can be a perfect escape from boredom and from challenges from the physical world, or a thrilling source of development for various addictions, or sometimes a promise of connection (not always kept).

Now, what is the online space? Philosophers from the phenomenology school of thought explore human consciousness and perception, thus helping us in this rather philosophical questioning. Merleau-Ponty put forward the definition of space as

> not the setting (real or logical) in which things are arranged, but the means whereby the positing of things become possible. This means that instead of imagining it as a sort of ether in which all things float or conceiving it abstractly as a characteristic that they have in common, we must think of it as the universal power enabling them to be connected.
>
> (Merleau-Ponty, 1962: 243)

This definition comes from Merleau-Ponty's seminal book, first published in 1945, establishing him as the philosopher of the body, and the *vedette* of French existentialism. The space created by the internet was of course not something Merleau-Ponthy could ever have figured out, but since that time the connecting potential of the online space has actually been exploited to develop and maintain all kinds of relationships: from dating, playing and work to therapy. Therapy is one field that takes up the challenge of its potential for the benefit of others—making use of its connecting potential and reducing the underlying risks of the opposite kind.

Sherry Turkle (2011) warns us about the risk of using the easily and constantly accessible others as objects and using them only for the characteristics we find useful or gratifying (Turkle, 2011: 154). This is also the risk that online therapists run—to be used by clients in this limited way. Online therapists are only one click away, and, in my experience, there is always a risk of short-changing them by offering only a superficial support with short-lived results. Turkle also points out the potential that the internet provides in exploring one's identity. Younger and older adults create avatars for themselves, explore their fantasies, engage in intense virtual worlds, play games. This potential is successfully exploited by online therapy, where clients get creative with changing their settings, playing with variety of backgrounds, and may even introduce us to their significant others and pets. Again, it is possible that the problem contains a solution—if we consistently aim at working at relational depth, maintain the existential stance, and engage with the medium creatively, then we should be able to offer to our online displaced clients what they often crave the most—a meaningful and genuine relationship that can survive their mobility and embrace the fragmented parts of their complex identity.

Cozolino suggests that the natural environment for our species is no longer a geographical landscape but a relational one. For highly mobile individuals, the concept of home is dynamic rather than fixed (Cozolino, 2006). They develop complex attachments to multiple places. In constant movement, their relationships with others become as much home as the environment in which they are temporarily evolving. In every successful emigration, there is a point where the attention shifts from place to people. The place-less reality of online work facilitates this natural shift from place to relationship. Effective psychotherapy delivered online then becomes about co-creating a meaningful relationship in a place-less space, so that clients can experience closeness without any physical environment, especially at those early stages of their migration when they feel alienated in their new place, grieving the social links that their move upended, and when new social links have not yet been built, which naturally takes time.

Bridging the worlds

Reeves claims that digital natives use communication technologies as a way of "bridging" rather than "being separated" by distance (Reeves in Cundy 2015:

137). For displaced individuals, maintaining meaningful connections from a distance, such a "bridging" is a question of psychological survival. As therapists engage with their displaced online clients, they constantly re-enact this paradox, creatively turning an obstacle to connection into a connection.

A bridge is an important symbolic object for those who had to cross borders through their journey. Anybody familiar with displacement is sensitive to its metaphorical power, which is associated with separation, loss, and time passing by.

Humans developed the art of building bridges early in their history in order to increase their ability to cross chasms, and therefore to expand their world. In their stubborn desire to move, humans seek expansion; there is no emigration without crossing a metaphorical bridge. For certain displaced people these bridges even had to be burnt, avoiding any possibility of a return. For some, this is a condition of getting a sense of security.

A bridge is also an archetypal image. Jung defines the archetypal image as a universal, primal idea, "a first model", a sub-stratum of the psyche that cannot be grasped in its entirety, so we perceive that phenomenon through representations or symbols (Papadopoulos, 2006). Any individual perception of these symbolic representations is shaped by history, culture, and personal context, thereby giving them a specific perspective. If displacement had its own symbolic vocabulary, then the bridge would be one of its central elements. Other strong images would be organised around moving a body through the space—roads, crossroads, airports, train stations, and other scenery familiar to migrants. The archetypal bridge suggests a transition, a progression from one state to another. In many dreams reported by my clients, bridges seem to mark an important change, a transition. Many emigrants will be familiar with nightmares involving packing belongings, rushing to the train station or airport, not finding a taxi, missing the boat, or crossing a bridge. These dreams, through which the displacement-related anxiety makes its way to the surface, offer a precious path for exploration of their displacement journey.

If the bridge stands for a change, there are usually obstacles to this transition—either external or internal. As it often does, mythology offers us a hint of the older universal narratives that animate cultures. A Norwegian folktale, "The Three Billy Goats Gruff", tells the story of three goats wishing to travel across a river bridge to the bank where there is plenty of grass. That foreign grass is of course greener than theirs. As the three goats make their way across, they are confronted and stopped by the evil troll, whom they must defeat to continue to the other side. This challenge represents the final test on their path to the green heaven. They overcome the trickery and make their way to the green hills where they happily feed on lush green grass. The troll retreats to the dark under-bridge world.

Beyond fairy tales, scary trolls are often within us. With their ugly mocking faces they scare us in our dreams, reminding us the imperfectness and finality of our worlds. The mythical beasts—griffons and sphinxes—guarding bridges in my native Saint Petersburg figure as reminders of these inner monsters. Our displaced clients, whether stuck on one side of the ocean or in the middle of their crossing, often come with a need to solve the bridging. "I can't throw a bridge between present and past, and therefore I can't make time move", writes Eva Hoffman, the Polish American writer and academic, relating her experience of displacement and nostalgia (Hoffman, 1998). She captures the frozenness many emigrants feel, unable to resolve the conflictual tension between their loyalty to the original home and the newly found attachment to the new one. I often witness how a displaced client may feel stuck on one side of the world—standing on the "foreign" side of the river (or sometimes ocean), unable to cross back. On the other side, the old world still exists, even if its familiar shape has been lost forever. This adds even more tension to the conflict.

One of my clients, Michael, an American just returned to his native California after a decade in Europe, developed a phobia of bridges. This happened suddenly, as he was crossing the Golden Gate bridge on his way home from work. This bridge had been a consistent element of his childhood imagery. His family had always lived in the Bay Area. He had driven across it countless times, never feeling anything special apart from annoyance at the fog or frustration with the traffic. But this time, stuck in the traffic on the bridge, he was suddenly struck by a wave of anxiety. Terrifying thoughts and images flashed in his mind—the crumbling bridge, his lifeless body in the car… Reflecting on this disorienting incident, and on his fear that was now extending to all bridges, we stumbled on a feeling about his return home, something he had not shared yet. His repatriation had been accelerated by the redundancy of his position in Europe, with a different position back in the US. For a decade he had been travelling around Europe, living in three different countries, never for more than two or three years in a row, and this mobility and the high demands of his lucrative job had never enabled him to build strong relational bonds. He had been drifting, carried by the changing winds of his employment without ever questioning the next move nor putting much willpower into the resettling process. From afar, his expatriate life looked appealing to friends and family who had stayed back home. Michael often heard envy in their comments about his lifestyle. His own sister, who lived a few miles away from their parents, had started calling him "stranger". When accepting the only option offered to him of a forced return, Michael had broken the news to me somewhat passively: "Time to go, I guess". When the bridge incident happened, he had been back in California for a few months. Until then, no matter how much I inquired into his feelings about being back home, Michael had been dismissing the topic with a joke or by switching subjects. Now, with bewilderment, he was telling of his feelings of "being trapped" on the bridge, unable to cross and reach the bay. Now, his feelings were overwhelming and taking over him: "Am I going crazy?" he asked with terror. Somehow, in the middle of that mundane crossing, the emotions that he had been repressing all along had broken free. He felt adrift, without solid ground beneath his feet, trapped in his car (or was it a symbol for his job?). His fear that the bridge would collapse, unable to carry him to the other side, was standing for his unrecognised fear of not being able to resettle in California, where he was starting to feel foreign, confirming the nickname his sister had mockingly assigned to him. Once we openly addressed his fears, and his regrets about not quite having engaged with life in Europe, Michael took the decision to give expatriation another chance. He soon resigned from his company and returned to Europe, on the lookout for new business opportunities. In the process, his phobia of bridges dissolved; and on the day of his departure for France, as he was crossing the bridge on his way to the airport, Michael felt a wave of nostalgia and longing. This was confusing. It related to both places—Paris, to which he was about to return, but also this very special place he was leaving behind again. Paying attention to the symbolic value of the bridge helped us go beyond the usual surface level at which Michael felt most comfortable, and access the underlying anxieties that displacement was activating in his psyche.

A bridge is a stable, solid element thrown across water—a changeable element underneath it—which accentuates its stability. By nature, displacement is a dynamic and unsettling condition, filled with novel experiences and uncertainties, which always lead to anxiety. In addition to its connecting function, therapy in displacement offers highly mobile clients a stable ground, which remains consistent, no matter how much they move around. It is fascinating to witness this group of clients in their transitions from one place to another all through our shared therapeutic journey, which has its own pace and its own destination. For them it is crucial to find me where they had previously left me, on their screen and with the usual reassuring background of my therapy room, with its furniture, bookshelves, and artwork. This way, therapy becomes the kind of solid bridge needed to cross the rivers of our personal despair. Metaphorically, any therapeutic journey is a crossing, coming with its own obstacles, the trolls of our past, that we must face and defeat in order to come out on the other side, alive. Facilitating the crossing, I find myself sitting on top of the bridge, like the sphinx and griffons guarding the bridges of Saint Petersburg, in a way that is actually benevolent.

Note

1 Fictionalized case examples of how the avoidant-dismissive tendencies play out in online therapy are described elsewhere: Piatakhina Giré, 2022.

References

Adams, M. (2013). *The myth of the untroubled therapist: Private life, professional practice.* Abingdon: Routledge.

Ainsworth, M. S. (1979). Infant–mother attachment. *American Psychologist*, 34(10), 932.

Ainsworth, M. S. (1997). The personal origins of attachment theory: An interview with Mary Salter Ainsworth. Interview by Peter L. Rudnytsky. *The Psychoanalytic Study of the Child*, 52, 386.

Akhtar, S. (2022). *In leaps and bounds: Psychic development and its facilitation in treatment*. Manila, Philippines: Phoenix Publishing House.

Akhtar, S. (2022). In leaps and bounds: Psychic development and its facilitation in treatment. In Akhtar, S., *In leaps and bounds: Psychic development and its facilitation in treatment* (pp. 1–188). Manila, Philippines: Phoenix Publishing House.

Aldgate, J. (2006). *The developing world of the child*. London: Jessica Kingsley.

Atkinson, S., Fuller, S., & Painter, J. (2012). *Wellbeing and place*. Farnham UK: Ashgate.

Badkhen, A. (2018, Nov.). An anatomy of lostness. *World Literature Today*.

Biocca, F., & Lanier, J. (1992). An insider's view of the future of virtual reality. *Journal of Communication*, 42(4), 150–172.

Bowlby, J. (2012). *A secure base*. Hoboken NJ: Taylor and Francis.

Boym, S. (1996). Estrangement as a lifestyle: Shklovsky and Brodsky. *Poetics Today*, 17(4), 511–530. doi:10.2307/1773211.

Casey, E. (2009). *Getting back into place: Toward a renewed understanding of the place-world*. Notre Dame: Indiana University Press.

Cozolino, L. (2006). *The neuroscience of human relationships: Attachment and the developing of social brain*. New York and London: W. W. Norton.

Cresswell, T. (2015). *Place: An introduction* (2nd edn). Chichester: Wiley-Blackwell.

Cresswell, T., & Merriman, P. (2011). *Geographies of mobilities: Practices, spaces, subjects*. Farnham, UK: Ashgate.

Cundy, L. (2015). *Love in the age of the internet: Attachment in the digital era*. London: Karnac Books.

Cundy, L. (2018). *Attachment and the defence against intimacy: Understanding and working with avoidant attachment, self-hatred, and shame*. Abingdon: Routledge.

Dixon, J., & Durrheim, R. (2000). Displacing place-identity: A discursive approach to locating self and other. *British Journal of Social Psychology*, 39, 27–44.

Dowd, A. (2019). Uprooted minds: Displacement, trauma and dissociation. *Journal of Analytical Psychology*, 64(2), 244–269. doi:10.1111/1468-5922.12481.

Dunn, K. (2012). A qualitative investigation into the online counselling relationship: To meet or not to meet, that is the question. *Counselling and Psychotherapy Research*, 12(4), 316–326. doi:10.1080/14733145.2012.669772.

Dunn, K., & Wilson, J. (2021). When online and face to face counseling work together: Assessing the impact of blended or hybrid approaches, where clients move between face-to-face and online meetings. *Null*, 20(4), 312–326. doi:10.1080/14779757.2021.1993970.

Fullilove, M. T. (1996). Psychiatric implications of displacement: Contributions from the psychology of place. *American Journal of Psychiatry*, 153, 12.

Gessen, K. (2018). *A terrible country*. London: Fitzcarraldo Editions.

Gessen, M. (2018). To be, or not to be. *The New York Review*, February 8.

Giuliani, M. V. (2003). Theory of attachment and place attachment. In Bonnes, M., Lee, T., & Bonaiuto, M. (Eds.), *Psychological theories for environmental issues* (pp. 137–170). Aldershot: Ashgate.

Hester, R. (1985). Subconscious landsapes of the heart. *Places*, 2(3).

Hofer, M. A. (1981). *The roots of human behavior: An introduction to the psychobiology of early development*. New York: W. H. Freeman.

Hofer, M. A., & Sullivan, R. M. (2008). Toward a neurobiology of attachment. In Nelson, C. A., & Luciana, M. (Eds.), *Handbook of developmental cognitive neuroscience* (pp. 787–805). Cambridge MA: MIT Press.

Hoffman, E. (1998). *Lost in translation: A life in a new language*. London: Vintage Books.

Howe, D., & Campling, J. (1995). *Attachment theory for social work practice*. Basingstoke: Macmillan.

Iyer, P. (2019). *Autumn light: Japan's season of fire and farewells*. London: Bloomsbury Publishing.

Jack, G. (2012). The role of place attachments in wellbeing. In Atkinson, S., Fuller, S., & Painter, J., *Wellbeing and place* (pp. 89–103). Farnham UK: Ashgate.

Kearney, A., & Bradley, J. J. (2009). "Too strong to ever not be there": Place names and emotional geographies. *Social & Cultural Geography*, 10(1), 77–94.

Kellman, S. (2017). Jhumpa Lahiri goes Italian. *New England Review*, 38(2), 121–204.

Kelly, L. (2017). *The memory code: Unlocking the secrets of the lIves of the ancient and the power of human mind*. London: Atlantic Books.

Lahiri, J. (2017). *In other words*. London: Bloomsbury.

Lau, D. (1974). *The Tao Te Ching*. London: Penguin.

Layshon, C. (2018). Jhumpa Lahiri on writing in Italian. *The New Yorker*, January 22.

Leutgeb, S., Leutgeb, J. K., Moser, M., & Moser, E. I. (2005). Place cells, spatial maps and the population code for memory. *Current Opinion in Neurobiology*, 15(6), 738–746. doi:10.1016/j.conb.2005.10.002.

Lewicka, M. (2011). On the varieties of people's relationships with places: Hummon's typology revisited. *Environment and Behavior*, 43(5), 676–709. doi:10.1177/0013916510364917.

Manzo, L. C., & Devine-Wright, P. (2014). *Place attachment*. London and New York: Routledge.

Marciano, F. (2015). *The other language*. London: Vintage.

Merleau-Ponty, M. (1962). *Phenomenology of perception*. London and Henley: Routledge & Kegan Paul.

Moser, M., Rowland, D. C., & Moser, E. I. (2015). Place cells, grid cells, and memory. *Cold Spring Harbor Perspectives in Biology*, 7(2), a021808. doi:10.1101/cshperspect.a021808.

Orbach, S. (2016). *Fat is a feminist issue*. New York and London: Random House.

Papadopoulos, R. K. (2006). *The handbook of Jungian psychology: Theory, practice and applications*. London: Psychology Press.

Piatakhina Giré, A. (2022). *Unlocked: Online therapy stories*. London: Confer Books.

Proshansky, H. M., Fabian, A. K., & Kaminoff, R. (1983). Place-identity: Physical world socialization of the self. *Journal of Environmental Psychology*, 3(1), 57–83. doi:10.1016/S0272-4944(83)80021-8.

Renkl, M. (2018). What is a Southern writer, anyway? *Te New York Times*, July 9.

Rogers, D. E. (2013). Place, purpose, and potential: Examining narratives of self-initiated expatriates. Available from Dissertations & Theses Europe Full Text: Social Sciences. Retrieved from http://search.proquest.com/docview/1412656382

Scannell, L., & Gifford, R. (2010). Defining place attachment: A tripartite organizing framework. *Journal of Environmental Psychology*, 30(1), 1–10.

Simandan, D. (2011). On time, place and happiness. *New Zealand Geographer*, 67(1), 6–15. doi:10.1111/j.1745-7939.2011.01192.x.

Scannell, L., & Gifford, R. (2010). Defining place attachment: A tripartite organizing framework. *Journal of Environmental Psychology*, 30(1), 1–10.

Simpson, S. (2009). Psychotherapy via videoconferencing: A review. *British Journal of Guidance & Counselling*, 37(3), 271–286. doi:10.1080/03069880902957007.

Smith, D. M., & Mizumori, S. J. Y. (2006). Hippocampal place cells, context, and episodic memory. *Hippocampus*, 16(9), 716–729. doi:10.1002/hipo.20208.

Suler, J. (2004). The online disinhibition effect. *CyberPsychology & Behavior*, 7(3), 321–326. doi:10.1089/1094931041291295.

Turkle, S. (2011). *Alone together: Why we expect more from technology and less from each other*. New York: Basic Books.

Umebinyuo, I. (2016). *Questions for Ada*. London: Amazon.

Vostanis, P., & Bell, C. A. (2020). Counselling and psychotherapy post-COVID-19. *Counselling and Psychotherapy Research*, 20 (3), 389–393. doi:10.1002/capr.12325.

Winnicott, D. W. (1971). *Playing and reality* (1st edn). London: Tavistock Publications.

Chapter 6

Language

The centrality of language to any talking cure is indisputable; it is the main tool used by clients to elaborate their stories, and by therapists to engage with them. We listen, we talk; language is the medium.

Displacement fosters multilingualism and propels language even further to the centre of the therapeutic encounter. If a monolingual dyad can ignore the question of language, a multilingual one cannot; as soon as the displaced client enters our therapy room, it naturally comes to the foreground. Gaining in linguistic awareness can help therapists, no matter their mono- or multi-lingual condition, to better address their needs.

The recent development of various technology-mediated psychotherapy services, accelerated by the Covid-19 pandemic, has dramatically expanded cross-cultural and cross-lingual therapy. Therapists' awareness on the topic of multilingualism, an additional layer to simple language awareness, is therefore as urgently needed as ever.

Theories of language have been elaborated by the disciplines directly interested in language such as sociolinguistics, psycholinguistics, or cognitive psychology. These fields are removed from the realm of psychotherapy rooms, where therapists and clients use language to elaborate together on clients' stories and facilitate the necessary personal growth and change. The way we approach language varies from one psychotherapy school to another, and from one modality to another. For a practitioner who does not have any background in linguistics, the question of language can be particularly confusing. Being confused about the tool we use daily for our work leads to a paradoxical situation: imagine a baker confused about his oven, or a shoemaker perplexed by his shoe hammer. Such confusion may naturally result in a feeling of discomfort and shame that stops us from engaging with the questions of language. Especially for multilingual clients, this blind spot covers an area that they constantly wrestle with, in direct relation to their identity.

Current psychotherapy training and counselling programmes rarely include extensive modules on multilingualism. My own professional training, which was run by a couple of British psychotherapists relocated to France, did not contain any material on cross-cultural counselling or multilingualism. At no

DOI: 10.4324/9781003144588-6

point was the fact that some members of the group (myself included) were using a different language than their mother tongue mentioned, during a 4-year otherwise extremely well-tailored programme. I left the training feeling lonely in my own displacement and multilingualism, with no tools for the cross-cultural and cross-lingual practice that lay ahead. Since then, I have been exploring this topic relentlessly, mainly in my consulting room, alongside my displaced multilingual clients.

Over a decade later, I am actively practising in four languages (Russian, English, French, and Italian). The relationship I have developed so far with English is nevertheless the most meaningful one. It has become for me the language of personal growth, the language of therapy. With many of my displaced multilingual clients we use English as a lingua franca, a neutral vehicle to create a shared understanding of their life story.

Theories of language are a separate topic of inquiry, well addressed in the psycholinguistics literature (Pinker, 2015). The common ground with this book is mostly the topic of multilingualism and cross-lingual communication, I will thus only briefly elaborate on the particular points about language that may be helpful to address.

Lately, the dream of Babel has been animating the interdisciplinary field of contemporary theoretical linguistics and the cognitive neurosciences (Pinker, 2015). Looking for a unifying language of therapeutic treatments is also an old quandary for the psychotherapy field, which has been growing only more fragmented with the constant emergence of new approaches and modalities (Miller et al., 1997). This theoretical quest for a unifying language takes on a more immediate turn and intensity in clinical work with multilinguals.

The location of our early attachments, the original "home", is always associated with a language or several languages. It is the most ancient element of our culture, closely linked with belonging to a place and to a community. Throughout a child's development, language is a way to make meaning of his experience of the world, of others, or even of himself. This meaning-making role of language brings it to the core of one's identity. In order to create any sort of self-narrative, we must use a language, or in a case of more complex multilingual identities, several languages.

Since its early days, the psychoanalytic tradition has been paying close attention to the use of language (Lacan, 1968; Ogden, 2016). Psychoanalytic writers are particularly interested in the relation between language and the mother. Developmentally, language is a means of preserving a relationship with the mother but also a means of separating from her (Greenson, 1950). As we learn a new tongue, we further separate ourselves from our first language and our original objects. Ironically, the foreign language becomes a vehicle for separation but also a way of coping with the pain produced by such separation.

Some issues relevant to psychotherapy with multilingual clients have been widely discussed in the literature (Gulina & Dobroliubova, 2018). Among themes that researchers have been exploring is the use of the mother tongue in therapy with bilingual emigrants (Buxbaum, 1949; Greenson, 1950; Mirsky, 1991; Kogan, 2010). Amati-Mehler insists that there may be advantages to using a second language in therapy, which may allow access to more mature levels and to object relations of a more adult nature (Amati-Mehler et al., 1993). Pérez-Foster proposes that bilingual speakers may possess different representations of self that are organised around their respective languages (Pérez-Foster & Moskowitz, 1996). Those who learnt their second language(s) after puberty experience a different emotional impact when speaking their first or second language(s) (Dewaele & Pavlenko, 2002).

The duality of two opposing categories—native language or mother tongue vs second language—is now shifting towards a more polyphonic reality, in which several languages can be welcomed into the therapeutic space, and the multilingualism of the client (and therapist) is taken into account. Another landmark of this multilingual reality is the wider use of a shared second language (often English) as a more neutral third language, a lingua franca. Online therapy seems to offer a perfect floating container for such a polyphonic dialogue.

Burck uses the word hybridisation to refer to this kind of multilingual experience of self and the world. His notion of "identity as an on-going project" is relevant to bilingual people's endeavour in therapy (Burck, 2011).

Schauf's impressive work on bilingual autobiographical memory indicates that the therapeutic space for bilinguals has to include a heightened awareness of linguistic and therefore cultural "selves" (Schauf, 2000). He argues further that the self-representations activated in such memory retrieval activities as therapy are uniquely tied to the bilingual's consciousness of being bilingual and bicultural. Echoing Schauf, Costa & Dewaele (2012) make a call for exploring the creative therapeutic potential of the language gap in therapeutic work with multilingual patients. They insist that individuals who are multilingual may have access to a greater emotional range and have a more developed facility for managing plural cultural identities than their monolingual peers (Costa & Dewaele, 2012). This particularity should be acknowledged and worked with in online therapy with displaced individuals.

More recently, two Russian-British researchers, Marina Gulina and Vera Dobroliubova, inquired into the bilingual therapist's experience of working in a second language and the potential impact of language on the therapeutic encounter (Gulina & Dobroliubova, 2018). Their small-scale research's topic is now becoming central in the mental health world transformed by technological advances.

Freud, like many other early psychoanalysts, was displaced and multilingual (he spoke eight languages). Goldschmidt argues that the Freudian approach consists in seeing what language has to say and paying attention to it (Goldschmidt & de Rubercy 2006). Freud's curiosity for his patients' narratives, their words, was probably deeply linked to his multilingualism. Gay mentions

Freud's anxiety about working in his second language (Gay, 2006). Today this anxiety is certainly shared by many therapists who are expanding their services into the online space. Curiosity, as well modelled by Freud, can be the answer and a driving principle for any therapy with multilingual clients.

Language lends itself to a variety of psychodynamic uses (Ainslie et al., 2013). For a dislocated individual, mastering a new language represents one of the foremost challenges, and that process transforms his identity. Which language is used in therapy with displaced clients is therefore critical, as this is how we achieve individual growth and change.

My aim here is to explore ways in which displaced clients' multilingualism impacts the psychotherapy process, and to start a dialogue about how mental health practitioners—mono- or multilingual—can better engage with their clients' multilingualism.

I Language and displacement

As I am writing this book in English, my other languages are constantly popping up, uninvited, interfering with the thoughts I am trying to express. This usually happens when I have indulged in reading a French book the evening before, or after a particularly emotional morning session with one of my Russian clients. Sometimes simply overhearing a conversation of two Italian tourists sitting next to my table during lunch in a restaurant transports me to a different linguistic realm. This is part of the process, which closely parallels what is going on with many of my bilingual clients.

Aneta Pavlenko, a Ukrainian-American applied linguistics scholar, describes her academic writing as "a story of ways in which I gained membership in a scholarly community and constructed an authoritative voice, with a trace of an accent (which I prefer to see as bilingualism and double vision)" (Pavlenko in Casanave & Vandrick, 2003: 177). This "double vision" effect is exactly what, as an emigrant multilingual therapist, I have been actively fostering in my clinical work with displaced and bilingual clients. Practice for over a decade has been nurturing the ground for my reflections on multilingual therapy.

Language is ubiquitously central to displacement and to the process of change that any emigrant undergoes (Grinberg & Grinberg, 1984). It is closely related to identity formation in children, but it is also central for identity maintenance in adults (Ainslie et al., 2013; Pavlenko, 2014). When an emigrant is learning a new language there is a natural identity re-adjustment. Adult language learning is a slow process; the integration does not happen instantly, leading to a stage in which the older monolingual identity is shaken and under threat. During that stage, many recently expatriated individuals experience a deep psychological discomfort, which they often cannot verbalise yet, in either of their tongues. They may feel confused, lost, incompetent, and in some cases, utterly disoriented. This is generally when they come to therapy, and we must use this opportunity window to assist them in making the transition; to mourn the lost parts of their identities, to readjust, and finally integrate the newly acquired parts.

Reflecting on bilingual clients' use of their languages creates a fascinating situation, in which language is simultaneously the tool and the object of our shared explorative effort. As we engage in this process together with a client, we elaborate together on their life story, but also their (and our) language evolves through this dialogue. Our individual vocabularies, reflecting our personal life journeys and carrying our cultural beliefs, norms, and stereotypes, bump into each other, leading to the creation of a common meaning, a co-constructed narrative of their life. This continued process, renewed from one encounter to another, is constantly re-shaping the shared version of the language used by the therapeutic dyad.

Some of this identity readjustment struggle can only be properly addressed—and eventually resolved—in a dialogical encounter, which what any good therapy is.

2 Multilingualism and identity

The current situation in academia is such that multilingual researchers mostly write about this topic in English, which is a second language for many of them. This is also my case. As a result, it creates a kind of emotional distance from the topic. As I am writing these lines, I am trying to observe what is happening in my mind, and I can almost physically sense how some of my other parts, put aside, are watching me writing in English, in sheer bewilderment.

"I am a tricolor Russian, an American brought up in England, a St. Petersburger with a Parisian burr in Russian but who, in French, rolls my 'R's in the Russian manner" (Nabokov, 2019: 365). In this reflexive passage Nabokov gives a telling picture of his multilingual self-narrative. He also provides a rare example of self-translation, or as I would rather put it, of stereo-writing. In addition to Russian, his first language, he learnt English and French as a child. He describes his work on the English and Russian versions of his memoir as a diabolical task. "Such multiple metamorphosis, familiar to butterflies, had not been tried by any human before" (Nabokov, 2000: xii). Six decades later, when reflecting on her own peculiar linguistic shift from English to Italian, Jhumpa Lahiri echoes this metaphor, referring to Ovid's *Metamorphosis*:

> Metamorphosis is a process that is both violent and regenerative, a death and a birth. It's not clear where the nymph ends and the tree begins; the beauty of this scene is that it portrays the fusion of two elements of both beings.
>
> (Lahiri, 2017: 163)

Many multilingual therapeutic dyads reproduce this metamorphosis: displaced clients share their memories, engraved in their mother tongue, with their therapist in the language they share. It is not always a first language for the therapist, the dyad can also use a lingua franca. The therapist will then have to process this material in her own native language, which can differ from her client's, and switch back to the lingua franca to respond.

This constant linguistic metamorphosis is a dynamic and creative process, with the scope of re-defining a client's identity. Engaging in this multilingual narrative, therapist and client collaboratively re-define and re-adjust the client's identity, disrupted as it was by his experience of displacement.

If displacement is a challenge to the original identity, language takes on multiple and various roles, from a resistance tool to a catalyst of change. In my work with clients wrestling with their displacement and newly acquired multilingualism, I often observe extreme attitudes to their language, mother tongue or second language. These emotional responses probably have something to do with splitting, a psychological defence mechanism well known by therapists: "When we feel unable to tolerate the tension and confusion aroused by complexity, we 'resolve' that complexity by splitting it into two simplified and opposing parts, usually aligning ourselves with one of them and rejecting the other" (Burgo, 2012: 83). Paradoxically, multilingualism is simultaneously the complexity that one tries to resolve and the tool for maintaining that split:

> For people who are multilingual, the way in which experiences and emotional reactions are encoded becomes more complex when more than one language is spoken. One of the ways in which multilinguals cope is by splitting and creating new selves for each of the languages spoken.
> (Costa & Dewaele, 2012: 20)

This juggling with several selves, creative in its very nature, is an important part of any multilingual identity. Addressing it in therapy is an opportunity of integration for the client.

3 Linguistic repertoire

In the current deterritorialised context, linguists are increasingly interested in how multilingual individuals negotiate their crossings of the language boundaries (Rampton, 1995; Li Wei, 2011; Busch, 2012). In moving away from conceiving languages as separate clear-cut entities, a greater focus is placed on bilingual speakers and their creativity in language use. Li Wei develops the concept of "translanguaging space"—a social space for the multilingual individual that brings together "different dimensions of their personal history, experience and environment, their attitude, belief and ideology, their cognitive and physical capacity" (Li Wei, 2011: 1223). A therapeutic dialogue with a multilingual client naturally turns into such a space, in which the act of translanguaging, if allowed to happen, facilitates the emergence of various and often parallel dimensions of the client's identity.

Brigitta Busch (Busch, 2012; 2017), a professor of applied linguistics at the University of Vienna, makes an inspiring call for revisiting the earlier concert of linguistic repertoire brought forward by Gumperz in the 1960s (Gumperz, 1964; Gumperz, 1970). In expanding the original concept to the lived experience of language, Busch defines a linguistic repertoire as an "heteroglossic and contingent space of potentialities which includes imagination and desire, and to which speakers revert in specific situations" (Busch, 2012: 19). For studying linguistic repertoires of multilinguals Busch proposes a multimodal biographic method—"language portraits"—previously used to research language awareness in primary school education. Participants are presented with simplified body silhouettes and multi-coloured pencils and they are invited to think about languages, codes, and means of expression that play a role in their life. Using the silhouette, they then represent or map their linguistic repertoire. This method goes beyond the strictly linguistic research, away from the scope of eliciting explanations about language practices and towards a meaning-making practice. That makes it organically adaptable for the scope of therapy. For clients who lack awareness and vocabulary to talk about their complex or ambivalent relationship with their languages, this research method turned therapeutic experiment facilitates the emergence of the client's self-narrative. This kind of practice should directly benefit displaced children or descendants of emigrant parents, whose stories were not properly told. As clients guide their therapist through their linguistic portrait, they gain a better understanding of their displacement history.

In her conceptualisation of the linguistic repertoire Busch insists on the first-person perspective based on biographical narrative (Busch, 2015), which propels any individual linguistic repertoire into the interpersonal dialogical space. When the linguistic portrait method is used as a therapeutic experiment, this dialogical dimension comes to the foreground. Practising this method is a concrete means for co-creating a self-narrative through the linguistic lens, organically available to multilinguals.

Busch points out that "a linguistic repertoire may not only include what one has but also what one does not have, what one refused but is still present as desire" (Busch, 2012: 7). For clients whose ancestors' original languages are out of reach, integrating them into the language portrait may be the first step of their journey. When such a misplaced, lost, or dreamed language appears on paper, it becomes visible to the therapist, and re-integrated into the fabric of their linguistic repertoire and eventually into their complex identity.

One of my young clients, Becca, had recently moved to Paris with her mother. She grew up in San Francisco, living with her mother and maternal grandmother. Although she seemed settled in her new Parisian life, she complained about anxiety and insomnia. When we first met, I was struck by the overall confusion that surfaced in her uncertain speech and vague looks. Clearly a bright young person, she was perplexed about her imminent graduation and fearful of the not-so-far-ahead adult future. In the first session, as

I inquired into her experience of Paris, she briefly mentioned her mother's emigrant background. It turned out that her Jewish grandmother had emigrated from Russia to the US with her 10-year-old daughter, who then struggled to adapt to the new place and learn English. Now a successful businesswoman, her mother never spoke Russian outside of their old Brooklyn flat, it was a kind of secret language she had with her mother—Becca's grandmother, and she never taught it to Becca.

When asked about her father, Becca seemed even more confused. She had never met him, and only knew that he was "a Latino". Did she speak Spanish? She shook her head, clearly taken aback by my question.

With her under-recognised displaced background and her shyness, Becca seemed an ideal candidate for the linguistic portrait experiment. When I gave her a sheet of paper and a few crayons, she seemed doubtful. She thought and timidly started drawing. At first, her silhouette looked rather empty. Then she coloured the torso green—"This is English", she commented. French was a little red lump located somewhere in her throat. "I struggle to learn French, but I really want to", she explained with a sudden ardour. Russian then found a place outside of the body shape, in the upper right corner of the sheet. "It looks a little lonely there", I noticed. "When mum and grandma speak in their language, I feel lonely", Becca volunteered. Placing Spanish was another difficult task. She eventually wrote Spanish in childish letters in a corner of the picture. "How do you feel about Spanish?" I asked. "Not much", she said. Then, after some thinking, she admitted feeling jealous of her friends who all spoke Spanish effortlessly.

Talking with me while drawing seemed to help her stick to the emotionally challenging task. She kept elaborating more on what her languages meant to her. What quickly emerged was a sense of exclusion and abandonment. Her father never showed up, and her mother never talked about him. Spanish belonged to him, this absent and hidden figure. She fantasised him as a sort of dangerous drug dealer. Therefore she felt that his language was forbidden to her. Learning it would be to step onto dangerous ground, somehow betraying her mother.

When her mother and grandmother spoke in their cryptic and yet familiar tongue, she felt excluded, infantilised. As a little girl, she knew they used it as way of hiding things from her. But then it stayed. Her mother seemed unwilling to make any effort for her daughter to learn Russian. Until she drew her language portrait, Becca never thought about why. "Maybe she did not want me to return there one day?" she wondered. Indeed, her mother seemed scared about returning to Russia, and with the war in Ukraine, she kept repeating that "they so much better off away from that shithole". Becca had never visited Russia and had a vague idea about what kind of place it really was. Her lack of curiosity seemed astonishing. "Any other languages that you are aware of?" I asked. After some reflecting she answered in an inquisitive tone "Hebrew?" This was another missing language. Becca was aware of its existence because her grandmother had started learning it a few years ago. She attended some classes and would often lock herself in the kitchen of their small apartment to do her homework. Every time she did that, she seemed upset and angry. Becca felt that there again, she was not welcome. Even worse, she had absolutely no right to that language. This was her grandmother's territory, not even her mother could venture there. Her grandmother was constantly angry, often with Russians but even more often with Americans. She seemed stuck between her two places; neither of them seemed friendly to her. Becca was used to her angry attitude. As a child, she would stay on her own in her room to avoid any topic that might trigger another burst of anger from her.

Exploring her linguistic repertoire, her lonely past came back to life. It also helped her make links between her learning French and her mourning the other languages of her family, long unavailable to her. At the end of the session, Becca elaborated on her desire to learn French: "this will be my own language, just mine". This "other" language, unrelated to her family's displacement struggles, promised a way out. It would be an existence outside of that tiny apartment full of secrets where she constantly felt superfluous. With Becca we had a long way to go but working on her language portrait in that first session set the tone, opening a path for further exploration of the family's displacement trauma. As Becca departed, the folded portrait in her hand, in contrast with her initial presentation she seemed excited about the future of her therapy.

As Busch suggests, "the linguistic repertoire points both backwards and forwards" (Busch, 2012: 18). Any individual repertoire is a dynamic, fluid phenomenon that happens only in relation to others. As the client engages in this mapping activity, the therapist gains an opportunity to make links between client's past and their present and explore their attachments to meaningful places and people, and their impact on the client's present and eventually future self.

4 Accent and identity

An accent is a person's distinctive pronunciation, and as the British linguists develop further:

> They're among the most personal parts of ourselves that we show to the world, revealing our life history and experiences to date simply by the way we sound our speech [...] Accents lie at the heart of what makes us human. We can use make-up or get plastic surgery to look different and our choice of clothes sends an incredibly strong signal about how we would like everyone else to perceive us [...] But an accent is the person-ality flag that we all fly with brighter colours than any garment, and most of us can do little to hide it.
>
> (Crystal and Crystal, 2015: 11)

Every accent is individual and unique; it expresses our identity, whether subtly or loudly, it communicates some important information about our belonging to a certain group, culture, social class, or place. It also gives away our education history and can convey our professional occupation. An eclectic accent is the auditory mark of our mobility history.

Therapists' and clients' accents interplay in any therapeutic encounter, but in a cross-cultural setting they have a particularly significant role.

No matter how much fluency we may develop in our second language, if we learned it later in life, after the biological window has closed, our ability to master this language will always remain limited by the evolutionary logic. In Pinker's clarifying words, "learning a language—as opposed to *using* a language—is perfectly useful as a one-shot skill" (Pinker, 2015: 291–293). Many multilinguals will of course challenge and sometimes transcend this biological realm, but even for the most successful adult learners, the accent often remains. When learning a new language as an adult, we can master its grammar and syntax, but our biological tools have already been shaped by our first language(s), those to which we were exposed in our early childhood.

For many emigrants, accent is a constant piece of luggage pointing to their difference; a reminder of their displacement displayed to whoever they are speaking to. A few words are often enough to break the spell of mimicry. Even after a quarter of a century in France, I am often asked after a few sentences whether I come from Belgium. "No, I am Russian", I usually clarify, feeling the well familiar ping of embarrassment. Accent makes us feel exposed and vulnerable. Even without any hostile response to it, a feeling of shame is naturally triggered by such an exposure of our foreign self, well hidden behind our second language.

The way we feel about our accent reflects our relationship with our original place. This is the audible mark of our displacement history. The way we speak tells others about where we came from; how we experience our accent may reflect the level of our integration. With some of my displaced clients, we share two languages, but they consciously avoid using one of them. Why do they privilege one language over the other? They often mention their accent. This is the case for bilingual individuals who grew up in a family where one dominant language was mainly used, pushing the language of the other parent (often an emigrant) to the margins. I observed a similar attitude with my teenage daughter as she became self-conscious about her missteps and mispronunciations in Russian.

Consciously or not, we all make assumptions broadly based on stereotypes, based on the accent of another person's speech (Nesdale & Rooney, 1996). Depending on the cultural stereotypes and our own earlier experience linked to a similar accent (or the lack of one), we may develop a particular attitude to the individual involved, no matter how little we know about that person.

To my surprise, I sound "British" to my American clients, or "American" to the British ones. The way they experience my speech and make sense of my accent, based on their life experience, probably impacts the early stages of our work. When a therapist, like myself, works in their second, accentuated language, inquiring into her client's emotional response to this linguistic set-up can bring some additional grist to the therapy mill.

"How is it for you to have a therapist who speaks with an accent?" I asked Don, one of my American clients, a sedentary man from Florida.

"I love it, actually", he responded. Developing further, he mentioned that despite the fact he had never lived abroad, he always dreamed about other places. Digging into this topic brought us to his regret about missed opportunities, and shame about not taking greater risks. These regrets have a direct link with the existential crisis that brought him to therapy in the first place. His choice of an emigrant Russian therapist based in Europe was his way of getting more adventurous in his choices. My accent-related query in the very first session actually put us in touch with Don's existential issues.

Any therapist will at some point have a client whose speech is more or less heavily accentuated. Paying attention to our own emotional reaction, and the stereotypes his accent triggers for us can help us get a better sense of what this person is often dealing with when interacting with other people. Checking in with oneself, using this awareness to better understand the client's unique experience of being in the world, or even self-disclosing these responses in the here-and-now of the session, can propel the therapy forward. This kind of work with countertransference can also be successfully modelled in a cross-cultural, cross-lingual supervision.

5 Multilingualism and online therapy

In the places where displaced individuals live, they do not necessarily have access to therapy in their mother tongue, or even in their second language. Reaching out to an online therapist makes this possible. Many therapists use technology-mediated work to expand their outreach and experiment with more international, cross-cultural work.

Findings of the online survey, which was a used as a preparation stage for this book, indicate that the population choosing online therapy is multilingual (4 in 5), hence the paramount importance of this topic. A variety of mother tongues was mentioned (17 including English for 105 participants).

- 42% reported English not being their mother tongue
- 20% were multilingual. The rate of multilingual clients seems high, but we do not have solid statistics on that category in the in-person setting to conclude a preference of multilingual people for online therapy
- 27% of participants did not use their mother tongue to communicate with their therapists, of which 64% were not able to switch to their mother tongue if needed
- 24% of participants indicated that they did not have access to therapy in their language in the place they lived

Only about 20% of participants who chose online therapy in English were monolingual native English speakers. Due to the small-scale quality of the research, the knowledge gained here about the use of languages in online therapy with displaced individuals can only be considered partial and would benefit larger-scale studies.

"Having the ability to meet with a therapist online was essential to my work schedule and enabled me to have productive sessions with someone fluent in my language so that we were not caught up in a loss of meaning between languages", one of the survey respondents commented.

Situations in which a therapist or client (or both) are not using their mother tongue are common in the online setting: "Funnily enough English was not my therapist's mother tongue", noted one of the participants.

As Bernstein suggests, the multilingual therapy world is a world in which "knowing different languages no longer constitutes merely a mastery of different vocabularies but affords the ability to play within one language and between languages" (Bernstein in Beltsiou, 2015: 132). The survey participants showed appreciation for the possibility of "switching" between languages: "I am extremely lucky to have a therapist who speaks multiple languages, so we can do back and forth".

For some participants the mother tongue assumed the quality of a "private language" or a "language of convenience": "The languages we used made a difference in the topics we discussed. My native language was a 'private' language that I used to express thoughts that I would not share with anyone else".

My questionnaire was only in English, and for 42% of the respondents (all fluent in English) it was not their mother tongue. How did this influence their responses? Byford suggests that the second language, learned later in life, may be the language of an observing ego (Byford, 2015).

6 Therapy with bilingual clients

The term "bilingual" refers to an individual who uses two or more languages in his or her everyday life, regardless of the context of use (Grosjean, 2008). The cross-disciplinary dialogue at the boundary between linguistics and social sciences can help us better grasp what happens in a multilingual therapy practice. Since the early 2000s, multilingualism has been actively explored by Aneta Pavlenko, for her psycholinguistic work focussing on multilingualism as cognition, emotions, and narrative. Back in the early 1990s, a freshly arrived graduate student at Conwell University, she realised that the mainstream linguistics simply did not reflect the outer reality in which "more than a half of the world population was multilingual which made monolingualism and monolingual-like competence an exception rather than a rule" (Pavlenko in Casanave & Vandrick, 2003: 184). Since than Pavlenko herself and other researchers have explored the different facets of multilingualism across the disciplines of social science and applied linguistics (Costa & Dewaele, 2014;

2012; Rolland et al., 2017). The "bilingual turn" that eventually took place in the study of language and cognition in the 1980s and 1990s is a "natural consequence of globalization, transnational migration, and increased ethnolinguistic diversity in the Western world" (Pavlenko, 2014).

A few decades later, the situation in the mainstream psychotherapy field is not dissimilar, and with most of the published discourse dealing with monolingual clients and monolingual therapists, authors like Beltsiou, (2015) or Costa (2020) are exceptions, focusing as they do on bilingual clients and therapists' experience. In the field of psychotherapy, the multilingual turn is unavoidable and probably overdue.

In the last decades, the world has evolved even further towards multilingualism. For lack of world statistics, there is no way of accurate estimates of the number of multilinguals in the world, but the general consensus puts the multilingual population close to being a majority of the world's population (Ansaldo et al., 2008). Given the large number of languages spoken in the world, and considering that world migration is growing each year, it is highly probable that bilingualism will continue to increase over the years. So it is high time we recognised that soon a majority of individuals seeking therapy will be bilingual, and therefore we should adapt the therapy process to their needs, without ignoring their multilingualism and the identity quandaries that come with it.

These developments are challenging the earlier mainstream view, widely popular in the late 19th and 20th centuries, influenced by the social context of global colonisations, that presuppose that one language (the more powerful) has to replace the preceding ones that have somehow become obsolete. This paradigm of linguistic imperialism has resulted in the now broadly deplored situation of a declining number of languages, with English and a few other Western languages predominant in academia (Phillipson, 1997). Calls for challenging the monolingual fallacy, which is part of linguistic imperialism (Phillipson, 2012; Phillipson, R., & Skutnabb-Kangas, 2012) should probably extend to the mental health field as well. This process of decolonising multilingualism (Phipps, 2019) should also happen in the way we practise psychotherapy, starting with individual therapists shifting their linguistic stance towards a more inclusive one in the intimacy of their therapy rooms.

Beverly Costa has put forward *the multilingual therapeutic frame* (Costa, 2020), which is timely and "introduces a linguistic perspective so that anxieties around language can be explored and contained actively, relationally and constructively in the clinical encounter—by clients and by practitioners in training and supervision" (Costa, 2020: 9). This framework encompasses such concepts as linguistic privilege, linguistic empathy, and linguistic attachment and loss. My aim here is to throw a bridge between this multilingual frame and the displacement-focused stance, as it seems artificial and counter-productive to separate the problematic of language use by multicultural individuals from their existential experience of displacement. Integrating these topics broadens the dialogue further into areas like attachment and loss, introducing new elements (such as linguistic shame) that should be helpful for a more efficient and deeper work with multilingual clients.

7 In which language?

Steven Pinker insists on the complexity of human communication which "is not just a transfer of information like two fax machines connected with a wire; it is a series of alternating displays of behaviour by sensitive, scheming, second-guessing, social animals" (Pinker, 2015: 227–228). When this behavioural interplay is complicated by the use of several languages for at least one of the participants, things get more complex and at the same time fascinating. When a therapist meets a monolingual client, the question of the choice of language simply does not come up. But when a multilingual therapist and a multilingual client meet, they are presented with a dilemma. Epstein's fantasy about the polyphonic writing (Epstein, 2012) turns then into reality in such a therapeutic dialogue.

Bilingual clients are presented with a variety of choices: they may opt for therapy in their mother tongue or in their second language acquired in childhood or later in life. Choosing a monolingual or a bilingual therapist able to operate in the same set of languages is a powerful enabling dimension for them in their language choices (Byford, 2015). Some bilingual clients make these choices consciously; others are simply driven to a certain option that only later in therapy can reveal its deeper unconscious reasons and consequences. In any of these situations, it is crucial for the therapist, whether monolingual or multilingual, to address this choice, or in Lahiri's words "To provide a key, to clarify the issue" (Lahiri, 2022).

The most obvious reason, which may stop a monolingual therapist from openly inquiring into his multilingual client's linguistic preferences, is the lack of awareness and understanding of multilingualism. This could easily be addressed by including more material about the multilingual brain into the counselling courses and programmes. This shift towards a more inclusive linguistic stance in our therapy practice is finally happening (Costa, 2020).

Therapist's shame is another obstacle which gets in the way of multilingual clients getting heard more fully in the therapy room. Monolingual therapists can naturally feel shame about being less linguistically competent than their multilingual clients. When working in our second language, shame is always present—be it about our accent or a poorer vocabulary than the one of our clients using their mother tongue. Being able to tolerate this shame and the anxiety that goes with it is an important resilience to foster for any therapist working cross-culturally and cross-linguistically. As shame often leads to silence, few therapists recognise this particular facet of their experience. The feeling of shame, or its higher nuance—humiliation—is mentioned by Lijtmaer (1999) in a rare acknowledgement of the emotional impact of shame on therapist's process.

Of course, one does not have to master multiple languages in order to work well with this ever-growing population, just as one does not have to be a cancer survivor to sensitively support cancer patients. It can be a plus, but it does not have to be the case. It is rather a question of developing a sensibility and an understanding of patients' experiences, even if they greatly differ from ours. Welcoming our client's "other languages" into the therapy room instantly deepens the work and, as findings of one recent small-scale study indicate, such meta-linguistic conversations are welcomed by multilingual clients (Rolland et al., 2017). And we can invite our clients to explore their linguistic choices without being fluent in their "other" language. Another set of rabbit ears—the multilingual ones—ought to be integrated into the skill set of a therapist who aspires to work with the displaced population.

In some cases, reaching out for support is only possible in a second language. In the case of Alex (earlier described in Piatakhina Giré, 2015), he did not have to be fluent in English to use it as a message in a bottle thrown into the ocean in a desperate cry for help. His first email looked like spam, and I nearly deleted it. He wrote in an abrupt English, with neither a greeting nor a sign-off. When I read more closely, I saw that he was seeking therapy, though he didn't say much else. In his brevity I sensed hesitation, a shade of doubt. Some hide-and-seek is not unusual in the early phase of the therapy process. Asking for help involves a degree of exposure, which can trigger feelings of shame. For Alex, using the shield of the screen avoided the physical, face-to-face confrontation of a traditional consulting room and offered the option, or at least the illusion, of anonymity.

I wrote back to Alex, asking if he might say a little more. His second email was a bit longer, perhaps because he now trusted that behind my web page there was in fact a real person available to listen. He alluded to his "continuous work on overcoming my homosexuality". At this stage, I would usually invite a client to meet me via Skype to talk at greater length. I still did not know where Alex was coming from. Something about his brisk, straightforward, and slightly aggressive mode of address felt familiar to me, and I suspected he was Russian. But why didn't he use our common native language? I wrote another email to Alex, listing the various languages in which I practised therapy, and noting that Russian was my first language. It turned out that he was indeed Russian and lived in a remote city on the periphery of the country. At that point, we switched to writing in Russian, and we set up a time to talk via Skype.

At the beginning of our first online session, I could hear Alex's voice, but no image of him appeared on my screen. He greeted me with an English "hello" heavily marked by his unmistakably Russian accent. I had anticipated that it wouldn't be easy for him to unmask. Then an awkward apology about his "bad English" followed. "Do you find it still easier to talk English with me?" I asked. "Da", he promptly agreed, this time in Russian. After a few minutes of conversation, I encouraged him to switch on his camera, and his face finally showed up on my screen.

Alex looked like any well-educated, middle-aged Russian man. He recounted his story, full of heart-breaking details: the stigmatisation of a "different" boy, using his mother's makeup to look "pretty"; the bullying in the schoolyard. He remembered being terrorised. "They called me names", he said, but he would not tell me which ones. I had to guess, again. In today's Russia, prejudice against homosexuals is widespread, and Putin's regime takes a violent punitive stance on homosexuality. There are few support groups. Alex had not been able to find a community in which to address his concerns and conflicts, so he had been reaching out to counsellors based abroad—in English.

He agreed that talking about himself felt less shameful when he spoke with "foreigners". They would not understand the nuances of the hurtful "names" he had been called. The harm would not be repeated. A foreign language kept him safe, but at the same time, Alex indicated that he had not really been touched by any of these therapeutic encounters. Now—consciously or not— he had made the move to therapy in his native language, but he still had to use his uncertain English to gather his forces.

"Could you tell me what you understood from my email?" Alex asked me. "What is my issue?" This was a strange test. From his anxious look I sensed that it was important for Alex to hear, in Russian, a description of his suffering. So, I laid out what I imagined to be his lifelong identity struggle.

The little nasty voices within ourselves usually speak our mother tongue. Alex's were no exception: They called him "bad" and "sinful". They used the same insults heard so many times in his childhood. They sounded very much like his drunk uncle, his judgmental sister, his schoolyard tormenters. Alex had internalised these voices, making them part of his own self-image, an unattractive and fragmented one. By choosing English as his initial language of self-reflection, Alex had been able to put some distance between himself and the voices in his head. He was poor, had no particular professional skills, and was no longer young. All this prevented him from leaving the place where he had been alienated since childhood.

Over time, as Alex's work with me progressed, he would discuss his mixed feelings about conducting therapy in Russian. It was somewhat like coming home, he said, to find your house ransacked by intruders. Russian felt unsafe, at times terrifying. At this stage in our work together, I focused on being there for him, supporting him during this inspection of his "home", as he cleaned up the mess, restored some order to it, opened the windows to let in some fresh air.

Alex was a courageous person. I was touched by his willingness to keep coming back, to return again and again to the thoughts and feelings stirred up by his homecoming. Alex had neither the education nor the self-awareness necessary to elaborate on his choice, and yet he intuited that his rudimentary second tongue had the potential to keep him afloat. Many displaced individuals all over the world, myself included, use English in just this way: as a language of survival, of escape, of independent thinking and unrestricted speech. There are many examples of Russian-speaking writers, most famously Vladimir Nabokov, who have used English to tell their stories. When the exile Joseph Brodsky wrote an essay about his parents after their death, he did so in English, because to "write about them in Russian would be only to further their captivity", and because, for him, writing in English was "therapeutic" (Brodsky, 2011).

But there is also something alien, and alienating, about a borrowed tongue, even if borrowed for the bulk of a lifetime. In the case of Alex, he and I, working together, made it through the arduous journey of re-living and re-describing his life's experiences, in the original language of his hurt. In the process, he grew a lot, and his narrative slowly changed. He came to accept that he was a complex person, emotionally and physically attracted to members of the same sex, and that he had feminine aspects to himself that he enjoyed, a little girl within who was alive and playful. As shame stepped back, Alex could see himself more clearly. I became a sort of mirror in which Alex could examine his newly acknowledged traits. He discovered with surprise not the disgust he had expected, but curiosity and acceptance. Sitting in front of our computer screens and studying this reflection together, in our mother tongue, we slowly learned to like him better.

8 Mother tongue

The strength of our attachment to our mother tongue is undisputable. In an online cross-cultural practice, clients employ various strategies to communicate to their therapist, often unconsciously, their intricate relationship to their original culture. It is crucial for therapists to get attuned to the potential offered by those situations that always open a path for reflecting on early bonds with others and the original place.

The place of our early attachment, the original "home", is always associated with a language, which we traditionally call our "mother tongue". This first language—or languages for those raised in multilingual families—is also the container of the childhood emotional experiences that will be shaping many of our adult behaviours. For monolingual individuals, the mother tongue is the only language of the inner and outer reality perception; for multilinguals the situation is far more complex. This complexity offers a particular linguistic self-awareness, and a different perspective on the mother tongue. Mastering several languages offers a distance from the first language, fostering an acute attunement to the meaning of each language, which is characteristic of multilingual writers and multilingual clients. It will always open up fertile fields for further inquiry into a client's inner world to try and understand the ways in which he relates to his mother tongue (or tongues).

The displacement context impacts any individual relationship with the mother tongue. Many fascinating examples of these intricate bonds come from emigrant writers; some of these accounts argue with each other, creating a fertile polyphonic dialogue on the topic. Jhumpa Lahiri, born to an emigrant Bengali family, continuously reflects on her complex and passionate relationships with her languages—her first language, English, her mother tongue, Bengali, and the Italian that she learnt later in life and adopted for her writing:

> In a sense I'm used to a kind of linguistic exile. My mother tongue, Bengali, is foreign in America. When you live in a country where your own language is considered foreign, you can feel a continuous sense of estrangement. You speak a secret, unknown language, lacking any correspondence to the environment. An absence that creates a distance within you.
>
> (Lahiri, 2015)

This accumulation of voluntary and chosen linguistic exiles, the playfulness and creativity with which Lahiri constantly explores these intricacies is emblematic of a multilingual mind. She constantly experiments with her first language, putting some distance between herself and her mother tongue, playing on the margins of it as she translates her own books from Italian back into English:

> Hearing a mother tongue is like stepping into a warm bath. But one of the disquieting discoveries that studying foreign languages brings is the awareness that your own can be a trap. By providing a steady drip of prefabricated words and ideas, your only tool for thinking and feeling can just as easily become a tool for not thinking, for not feeling; and when forced to do without those words and ideas, you realize how many of your so-called thoughts are nothing more than clichés grafted onto you by the language with which you grew up.
>
> (Moser, 2022)

Lahiri's stepping out of the comfort zone of her first language is a way of questioning not only her words, but her way of relating to herself and the world around her. The relationship she has with her mother tongue evolves, expanding the comforting limits of her first language: "I have come to think of any 'definitive text' largely the same way that I think of a mother tongue, at least in my case: an inherently debatable, perpetually relative concept" (Lahiri, 2021). This critical stance towards one's own use of the mother tongue cannot be easily achieved. It takes a lot of pondering on words, but therapists can use that method to deepen their understanding of our original bonds, and of our early attachments to those who passed on their language to us.

"Being Italian, for me, begins and ends with the fact that I speak and write in the Italian language", argues the Italian novelist Elena Ferrante, who despite her attachment to anonymity is known to be a translator and having lived outside of Italy. "I prefer linguistic nationality as a point of departure for dialogue, an effort to cross over the limit, to look beyond the border—beyond all borders, especially those of gender" (Ferrante, 2018). Ferrante's language-centred worldview is probably her own way of resolving the tensions that multilingualism brings up. She chooses to stick to her mother tongue. Her attachment to it is stronger than anything and serves as a lifebuoy when the inner waters are overwhelmingly stormy. For some multilingual clients, turning to a therapist who speaks their mother tongue can be a life-saving act. For others, in striking contrast, moving away from the lukewarm bath and out to the colder, stormier, and not always welcoming waters of a foreign language, is a powerful act. Many displaced clients do it to gain knowledge and achieve change.

When a multilingual client performs this act in front of their therapist, they invite them to dance with them. It is crucial to step out of our own comfort zone and join their dance. No matter our own linguistic capacities or our own relationship with our mother tongue, we must maintain a curious stance that allows the best therapy to happen.

In some dramatic cases, the mother tongue gets lost, and this loss can be barely dissociated from trauma. One of my clients, Marco, was adopted by a distant aunt after his parents died in a violent attack. Then, as a young child, he was taken to a foreign place where he grew up speaking a different language. His mother tongue, Spanish, was naturally dropped in the process, associated as it was with such a traumatic loss. The decision of Marco's family to displace him and remove him from the original context and language had a strong symbolic value—leaving the traumatic past behind. Years later I met with Marco, who had grown into a teenager. His sense of self was weak, as was his ability to reflect on his experience. He experienced social anxiety. His early trauma of losing his parents had actually been reinforced by the loss of his mother tongue. It seemed like with the first language, some of his understanding of the world and of himself had gone too. Speaking Spanish together created an opportunity to recover his lost past. Adults had never told him what exactly had happened to his parents. This truth seemed to have been buried with his mother tongue. His aunt was unsure about how much Marco really knew, and he showed no curiosity for the topic. At home they only spoke English, to "protect him" and make sure the horror from his past stayed away. As if she could leave the trauma behind by keeping Spanish at bay. The first time I asked Marco about his Spanish, he shrugged his shoulders "I don't speak Spanish anymore", he stated blankly. He was clearly dismissing the topic, indicating that he was not ready nor willing to go there. As long as we stuck to English, he was safe. It took us a long time before he trusted me enough to allow some Spanish words into the room. They felt like heavy stones that he struggled to move around, to make his way out of the speechless maze he was locked in. We moved through the maze together, reconstructing his lost childhood, little by little, word by word. My Spanish was limited, but good enough to follow his slow progress. I was guessing that doing this work with a therapist for whom Spanish was the mother tongue would have been too threatening at that stage. The first time I saw Marco animating and demonstrating some emotion was when he described his grandmother's house, in which he had spent his first couple of years. His recollection of the house was strangely vivid, and Spanish words came out almost naturally. As we were slowly recovering the sparse words of his forgotten mother tongue, Marco was showing more interest in his past. Soon he started talking about what he did not know but could guess about his parents' disappearance. The recovery of language eventually made him feel ready to hear the truth. This was just the beginning of Marco's journey of self-discovery (or rather self-recovery) and I hoped that one day he would be able to work with a Spanish speaking therapist, as his broader goals of integration could not be achieved without looking for his lost mother tongue.

9 The gift of a second language

Writing this book in English is not accidental for me, nor is my choice to practise therapy in the language that I learnt later in life. I come from an unescapably mono-linguistic environment; in my original home and all around me everybody spoke the unique collective mother tongue—Russian. This was a state-enforced part of the Soviet identity. My world was firmly bound by this language. Until my first grade, when at school we started learning French, I was not even aware of the mere existence of other languages. The Iron Curtain kept us away from travelling, and other places seemed surreal, almost fictional, making any exposure to another language highly unlikely. Nevertheless, as early as 12 I started reading avidly in French and became obsessed with learning as many languages as I could. My parents—both university professors—displayed two contrasting attitudes to my linguistic passions. My mother was openly supportive, my father guarded. When the time came for me to apply to university, I naturally choose the foreign languages department. To this day, I remember distinctly my father's reaction when I informed him of my decision. Usually a quiet man, he was suddenly anxious and annoyed; his dismissive words are still ringing in my ears: "Languages are not a craft. You must learn something useful instead!" However, I was stubborn; and all through my adult life my professional activities have been revolving around words, mostly foreign. Am I still trying to prove my father wrong? Do words in a foreign language have as much power and meaning as in my mother tongue?

From my early attempts to write in a second language, I discovered that using my stumbling French provided me with a distance from my then context, and this distance felt liberating. Freedom was a rare and therefore precious commodity back then. Much later, when I engaged as a now multilingual adult into a personal English-speaking therapist, it allowed me to explore my story in ways that would not have been possible in Russian. At that time also, the distance provided me with an emotional security that felt unaffordable in Russian. The neutrality of English offered a hiding place; one in which I was finally able to recognise the impact of the earlier facts of my life on the development of my adult personality. Nevertheless, it could be that my father's wariness was reasonable. After all, learning foreign tongues drove me further away from him and from my beloved Saint Petersburg. Was it what he intuited and feared? As I am writing this book, I keep in mind that my father will never read it. This simple trick keeps me safe, but also keeps my father safe—my words will not hurt him, and our relationship will be preserved. What used to be an act of defiance has now become an act of preservation. The same kind of considerations are probably valid for those who choose to engage in therapy, either as therapists or clients, in a foreign language.

When clients commit to therapy in their second language, they make a powerful choice. Even at first, when they are not fully aware of the reasons behind this choice and its meaning, reflecting on this choice should be made part of the therapeutic inquiry, as it can hardly be innocent. The conscious and unconscious elements behind this peculiar linguistic choice vary from one individual to another, but each time I explore it with my client, we stumble on the theme of freedom. Steven Kellman, the professor of comparative literature who dedicated his research to translingual writers and to emigrant narratives, notes that "When ambilinguals—writers fluent and accomplished in more than one language—commit themselves to one, it seems an affirmation of individual sovereignty" (Kellman, 2003: xiii). A similar act is performed by multilingual clients who commit to therapy in their second tongue, and this exercise of freedom becomes a starting point for their therapeutic journey. In the vast field of literary studies, such a linguistic choice is well documented and researched (first of all by the translingual writers themselves), but in the field of mental health, the topic is under-researched. With a few exceptions (Amati-Mehler et al., 1993; Szekacs-Weisz, 2004; Dewaele & Pavlenko, 2002; Pavlenko, 2007; Ivaz, et al., 2019), the impact of the use of a second language on the therapeutic process is still a grey area.

In the scarce literature on this subject, the liberating potential of therapy in a second language is nevertheless put forward "Patients can feel that therapy in their native language binds them in a position they want to move away from" (Szekacs-Weisz & Ward, 2022: 27). Moving away from their mother tongue, emigrants may claim the freedom that would otherwise be impossible to even consider. Rolland quotes one of the multilingual participants of his research:

> "Preferring to do therapy in my second language is an emotionally and therapeutically encumbered choice. My second language is linked to the future, rather my native language brings me back to the past. The native language ties me to a system. The second language means autonomy and self-power".

> (Rolland et al., 2017)

When I ask clients about the context of their learning their second language, it opens a way for them to reflect on their narrative from the linguistic perspective—how did they move from the monolingual to the multilingual identity? Or did they grow up in a multilingual family? Or were they enrolled in an international school, or sent to abroad by parents eager to make their children more worldly? The relationship they have developed with their second language impacted their choice of using it in their therapy and will also impact their therapeutic journey. When travellers chose a particular means of transportation to get to their destination—by foot, by car, by train, or plane—it does shape their journey and impacts how quickly or whether at all they will reach their destination. The language that we use in therapy is more than a mere vehicle, it is an intrinsic part of the process.

As we develop an intimate relationship with a language, we change in the process; the multilingual self that emerges is intrinsically different from the older monolingual self. Jhumpa Lahiri argues that

> a language, even a foreign language, is something so intimate that it enters inside of us despite the fissure. It becomes a part of our body, our soul. It takes root in the brain; it emerges from our mouths. In time, it nestles in the heart. The graft that I've made puts a new language into circulation, instils new thoughts within me.
>
> (Lahiri, 2022: 21)

Research suggests that most bilinguals experience less discomfort when they discuss emotionally charged or distressing topics in their second language, as well as when uttering taboo words (Dewaele & Pavlenko, 2002; Pavlenko, 2007; Ivaz et al., 2019). Foreign language effect—the phenomenon of this attenuated emotional charge—was recently studied in applied linguistics and second language acquisition studies (Ivaz et al., 2019), and a consensus was reached on the variety of ways in which it impacts our communication. Whilst this concept is still slow to integrate the cross-cultural psychotherapy field, multilingual clients naturally exploit this fascinating potential in their therapy. We just have to be ready to listen, to let the clients guide us through their linguistic universe. Here again, multilingual writers beautifully model such an inquisitorial stance—Jhumpa Lahiri with her usual curiosity towards her second tongue, shifts the focus towards its creative potential for self-exploration: "Italian remains the mask, the filter, the outlet, the means. The detachment without which I cannot create anything. And it's this new detachment that helps me to show my face" (Lahiri, 2017: 221).

The psychoanalytic authors who started as early as the 1940s to address the topic of multilingualism viewed it as a curiosity (Buxbaum, 1949; Greenson, 1950), and the underfocus culminated more recently, with for example Lijtmaer concluding that the mother tongue was the language of the unconscious and the second language was mainly used as a defensive manoeuvre

(Lijtmaer, 1999). This somewhat limited view had been greatly influencing the field of mental health for decades, until displacement became more common, and online therapy expanded accordingly. These changes in the global context are now accelerating the move away from the binary scale of disadvantages versus advantages of the bilingual therapeutic context. They shift our thinking into a more fertile field of therapeutic possibilities that can emerge from such linguistic complexity.

"Multilingual exposure enhances the possibilities of expression, not only allowing us to hide or to lie, but also allowing for different truths to emerge", argues the multilingual analyst Amati-Mehler (Amati-Mehler et al., 1993). Even for those therapists who do not master more than one tongue, an approach with sincere interest and curiosity for the subject may be sufficient to facilitate the emergence of these diverse truths. In my work with multilingual clients, the complexity that comes with this therapeutic context can be challenging to manage. In the case of Inna, a highly mobile young professional, this complexity could not hold. We only met once for an introductory session, which she crammed into her short stay in Paris. It ended with the bubbly feeling for me of a "perfect fit" that I get when I intuit that good work can be done with a prospective client. Inna was Russian as well, and we had four languages in common. It was the first time I saw such a fit in my therapy room, in fact. Maybe too perfect a fit, as I was to find out later.

Inna shared her experience of displacement, her feeling of not being in the right place anywhere, and her confusion about her multilingual self. She reached out to me in French, a second language for both of us: "I am looking for a multilingual therapist". Her name revealed her origins, as mine does, but I respected her choice of language, as I usually do, and replied in French. At this point my linguistic "rabbit ears" were already turned on and excited about the rich potential of such a multilingual fit. Inna's story was echoing those of many second-generation emigrants. She had been brought to Italy at the age of eight, when her mother remarried. She quickly learned Italian. With her blond hair and typically Slavic cheekbones, she looked different from other kids at school, but her perfectly fluent Italian allowed her to fit into this new environment. The price she paid for that fluency in a foreign language was a split of her personality. Her multilingual mind would efficiently maintain that split all through her consecutive moves. After Italy, she studied in France, and then accepted a teaching position in a British university. Now she was back to Paris for a short holiday, hoping to recover some of the bits of her self that she had left behind. In that unique session, we talked about her languages. She saw English as a tool for professional communication, one for thinking and research. She complained that it seemed difficult to bond with her new colleagues and develop friendships. In fact, the real language of the other more spontaneous part of her, the language of intimacy, was still Italian. Inna had tried therapy in French before but had found it of "limited efficiency". Her then-therapist did not speak any other language. Inna was articulate and as a result of her earlier therapies, rather self-aware, so I opted for taking the risk of using our common mother tongue: "Would you like to use Russian then?" I asked.

Switching back to the first, native language was a strong, emotionally charged act. I imagined that Inna had come to a Russian therapist (me), with the desire to express some of her troubles in her original language, even though that desire remained unconscious, since she used her "other" language to reach out. She accepted the offer to switch to Russian, but her speech was slightly uncertain, as she had stopped actively using her mother tongue after childhood. Inna told me the story of her multiple moves and her professional interests. Even if her new position offered her a good salary and a bright academic future, she felt stuck and distant. Her teaching lacked passion and her relationships with students were limited, she felt. She was unhappy and feared depression. As her story unfolded in Russian, I was becoming aware of my own strong feeling of frustration. I was suddenly tempted to say something in Italian, to connect with her using the words of a language that happens to be, for me as for her, synonymous with choice, freedom, and intimacy. Sticking to Russian, we were probably overlooking her Italian self, that little girl who had finally found some warmth and security in her new Italian-speaking home.

After all, something similar had been happening to her in England, with these "other" non-English-speaking parts of her not being acknowledged, as she had said. I was hoping that with patience and time we could eventually integrate these scattered parts of her personality, and bring together the sadness of her Russian child, her Italian emotional teenager, and her articulate adult who used English for thinking and verbalising her experiences. This integration is always the aim of therapy, but, with multicultural individuals, this road happens to be paved with the mosaics of their linguistic abilities. When Inna left my office, I was still excited about such a "perfect match" and turned away from an uncomfortable feeling that was whispering that this could not be that simple. In the following days, my excitement subdued, and the discomfort remained. Inna had not come back after that initial session, neither had she returned my follow-up email.

That unique session with Inna felt like my own failure; I kept wondering what I could have done differently. What would have happened if we had met online instead of in my therapy room? Should we have used English or French, neutral languages for us both? Inna might have felt less exposed. The neutrality of a second language might have enabled us to go further and develop a strong enough therapeutic bond in order to then allow her Russian self into the process. French, after all, was exempt from any early traumatic experience for her; it could have offered the safe and holding space that is so necessary in therapy. By introducing Russian far too early into the process, I had broken a boundary that was containing the separate parts of her identity, keeping her safe. Inna was not ready for that, and blinded by my excitement, I had moved too quickly. Unfortunately, we did not have a second chance, and I could never ask Inna these questions. We do learn from our patients (Casement, 1985), and Inna taught me a lesson about the power of language, and more specifically, the power and meaning of the second language when chosen by the client for therapy.

Is it ever possible to access each part of multilingual clients' personalities that express themselves in a particular language? Or do they remain partially locked within a specific linguistic frame, beyond the language in which therapy develops? Pondering on these questions as we move forward on our journey to discover our clients' multilingual self serves as a steady guide.

10 Using a lingua franca in therapy

With the rise of online counselling, clients can reach out to a therapist who lives thousands of miles away. This new globalised context makes it possible for many English-speaking practitioners to offer therapy in English to clients from different cultural horizons, even if it is not a first language for them or for their clients. Of course, this also happens with other languages, spoken by wide populations, like French, Mandarin, Spanish, or Russian. For the sake of simplicity, I will keep using English as an example of a lingua franca used in the field of mental health interventions.

A recent ambitious cross-cultural study has confirmed that the most common human language that is truly universal is "parentese", or the language that parents use all around the world to communicate with their babies (Courtney et al., 2021). As part of this research, 51,065 people from 187 countries, representing 199 languages, were asked via an English language website to determine whether a song or a passage of speech was being addressed to a baby or an adult. Their intuitions were more accurate than chance, predictable in part by common sets of acoustic features. Not only do these findings inform hypotheses on the psychological functions and evolution of human communication, but they also show how a particular language can facilitate communication and early-stage human development. For any therapist who believes in the importance of developmental work, this has fascinating consequences, especially for cross-cultural interventions, where a peculiar shared language is developed by the therapeutic dyad. With my Indian, Chinese, or Arab clients, we speak a very special English. With time spent in front of our screens in a shared effort to better understand their functioning in the world, it evolves into a unique "language", rich in its own peculiar words, references, and allusions. It is nourished by their and my original backgrounds, cross-referencing of each other, and shared understanding of their narrative.

A similar creative linguistic activity happens in families, where "familects" develop naturally and effortlessly, with their specific set of invented words or phrases (Gordon, 2009). Any functional family unit fosters this language-creating activity, through which the members create their own history. "Familects" usually have some specific names for their family homes, their pets, and themselves in the family context. They contain the family story with its meaningful places and people, the anecdotes about other family members or neighbours. In therapy, clients fill us in, sharing this secret language, its landmarks, and timelines, including us into their story. This process is organic to any talking therapy and takes a particularly interesting spin in a cross-cultural and multilingual context. Clients may naturally avoid naming things or people with their real names, as they may sound unfamiliar or strange for our "foreign" ear. Openly inquiring into the real names of things from their original world can have an important therapeutic value. Showing curiosity and willingness to learn these names becomes an act of caring. These minor acts of reaching beyond the boundary of language are also a way of modelling bridging, helping multilingual clients with their integration task.

Similarly, each therapeutic dyad invents its own vocabulary. When this happens in a "third" language that is "neutral" for both therapist and client, the process requires openness and collaboration from both parties. In a shared effort, they have to go to great lengths to avoid assuming too much about what words may mean for the other. In this context, nothing can be taken for granted, and both therapist and client must make an extra effort to move the process forward, enhancing its dialogical quality. This process parallels what the displaced clients experience "out there", struggling with making themselves understood in a "foreign" place. As they re-enact this challenge in a cross-cultural therapeutic encounter, they get a chance to be listened to and understood by a "foreigner", although in their second language. If this re-enactment leads to a more positive outcome than in the past, clients have a chance to better connect with others, exercised as they become with a new and working relational model.

When we exit a dichotomy of "my" versus "your" language, as prevails in more traditional cross-cultural settings where therapist's or client's first tongue is used by both parties, we shift to a more equal and more complex situation. The introduction of a third—more neutral—language leads to multiple implications. One of them is the drastic shift in the power dynamic. The therapeutic dyad that uses the lingua franca stands on a more even ground. The feeling of shame is never far away when anybody takes the risk to speak a second language (this will be discussed further in Chapter 7). When both parties take that risk, no one is shielded from shame. The therapist speaking her second language with her client exposes a vulnerability, offering a precious opportunity to model humility and resilience to linguistic shame. This is beautifully modelled by Stavans in his 1989 essay "Letter to a German Friend" (2001):

> Twice you apologize for your rotten and precarious English. You say you learned it by yourself and it's ungrammatical. Don't worry! Words serve you well in the task of describing your curiosity, puzzlement, and

existential dilemma. Besides, there's nothing to fear, English is not my mother tongue either. We're communicating in an alien yet neutral ground, neither yours nor mine. This, I believe, is a good beginning.

(Stavans, 2001: 3)

That is the kind of reparative message that each emigrant, therapist, or client ultimately longs for. Healing this displacement-related shame is one of the most precious potentials of cross-cultural therapy conducted in a lingua franca.

The online setting with its sometimes-imperfect internet connection, disruptive noises and eventual interruptions mixed with the "imperfect" accent that both the therapist and her client may have when using a lingua franca offers another opportunity for some powerful relational work. We can suddenly turn such a challenging therapeutic context into a chance to respond to one of our clients' basic human needs—be heard, seen, and understood. These relational needs are often unmet during their early relationships, whether absent or emotionally mis-attuned. The example of Claire, one of my online clients, demonstrates how this can be done. Claire grew up in a family in which her mother's physical handicap was central. Her mother was constantly pre-occupied and self-centred. Claire was never listened to nor heard. She had tried to scream, to cry, to act out, but all her attempts had failed so far. She felt angry and frustrated; this early disappointment was now impacting her current adult relationships and threatening her otherwise loving marriage.

In our first session, she asked me boldly if I really understood her well. She was a native English speaker, and I felt the familiar wave of shame. For a second I felt attacked, not trusted, and humiliated. But this simple exchange became rich material for our therapy mill. We used this opportunity to explore what it meant to her to be heard and understood. Working with this initial hint, together we managed to realise how Claire constantly put herself into the position of the "one who is unwell" in order to obtain due attention—the exact position that had made mother unavailable for her. This was somehow a comfortable role for Claire, but when she got stuck in it, her relationship with her husband suffered. He would feel unimportant and constantly strained by her overwhelming neediness (exactly in the same way as Claire-child used to feel in front of her mother). This realisation helped Claire make some important changes in her behaviour, and she was finally able to let go of this needy position, to take on a more caring stance in her relationships.

There are many fascinating consequences of using a lingua franca in cross-cultural therapy, and an acute curiosity for this topic will help counsellors to make the most of this often-unexpected aspect of their practice. Often the relationship we have developed with our shared second tongue is stronger than the differences in our cultural background. In my work with Chang, a Chinese student in Paris, it brought us together. When Chang first came to see me, he had already had an experience of therapy with a Chinese therapist. This time he opted for an English-speaking Russian therapist living in Paris because he felt that it could set him free from cultural taboos and familiar impasses. Chang's dream was to become an actor, but acting in English or French, which he spoke fluently but with an accent, was a daunting perspective. Our first session was dedicated to the exploration of what learning English and French had meant to him. Mastering these languages had expanded his world dramatically. He had grown up in small town in Northern China. His computer screen had opened for him a window on the wider world, where being gay, well-read, and creative was possible. He had spent his teenage years glued to this screen, exploring these possibilities, inventing himself. He also avidly read French and American authors, expanding his vocabulary, his worldview, and his own identity in the process. When we first met, Chang was making his first emigrant steps into the reality of a world that had mainly existed on his screen. He had made it and was now studying for a business degree, hoping to soon be able to secure a job and become independent of his parents. The reality of the Paris that been animating his fantasies for so long was cruder, rougher than the one his mind had fabricated. He constantly felt inadequate, mistreated, misunderstood and marginalised by both the local Chinese community and the white French people. I sensed how guarded Chang was; he watched me closely, almost expecting the moment when I would fail his expectations. And after all I was a white woman looking exactly like an average French person. That first session, talking openly about the anxiety and shame he was experiencing when speaking English with me, opened a precious relational channel. The meaning he found in learning foreign languages, and the role this endeavour played in his identity formation was instantly relatable to me. For many emigrants, like him or me, dreaming of leaving is a way of escaping the realities that constrain their development. As we spoke about his accent and how it could prevent him from acting in Europe, he commented that he could not tell whether I had an accent. I reassured him that I had one. This acknowledgment of my own imperfect English served the same purpose as the message that Stavans conveyed in his letter to his German friend. Chang relaxed, and his shame stepped back, opening the door for vulnerability and a better connection. Despite our obvious differences in gender, sexual orientation, and nationality, we were similar after all. The universality of our displacement-related shame and the relatedness of our linguistic endeavours brought us closer. Once this connection was established, we were able to successfully use English to build a relationship that became a safe base for Chang to use as a starting point in reinventing himself as a Chinese person implanted in Europe. Every time he or I would have to use a French word, or more rarely a Chinese one (for him!), we would remind each other about our own displacement shame and the possible alienation that is never far away, no matter how well we master the language at hand. Each time that Chang risked introducing a Chinese term, often to tell me about his dreams or his childhood, he would look wary, as if he was testing the strength of our English and our connection. These excursions back to the mother tongue were rare. Each time I attempted to ask Chang to tell me in Chinese about his emotions, he would get confused, visibly struggling to find his words. What was going on? Chang was articulate when he spoke about his feelings in English. I could sense that this was not safe territory. During his childhood, in his family, the expression of emotions was limited, his parents were too busy with work and he had to succeed in his studies. As a result, all his emotional vocabulary was in English or French. Only in his second languages was it possible for Chang to freely explore his inner experience.

11 Creativity in working with multilinguals

In her autobiographical text "L'analphabète—The Illiterate", Agota Kristof dedicates a chapter to the intricate relationship between her mother tongue, Hungarian, and her second language, French. She entitles it "Langue maternelle et langues enemies—Mother tongue and enemy languages" (Agota Kristof, 2004: 21). During her childhood, Russia invaded Hungary and the Russian language was imposed on all the population. Kristof describes how in an "act of collective passive resistance", Hungarians avoided engaging with the "language of the enemy". When Kristof arrived in Switzerland, the way she engaged with French was an echo of this earlier experience. This is an eloquent example of how our earlier linguistic history can impact our relationship with a language that we encounter later in displacement. Even after decades of thinking and writing in French, Kristof experienced French as another "enemy language". Her ambivalent feelings were fed by the fact that French was threatening to her mother tongue exactly as Russian had done during her childhood. Decades later, the combined defensive and protective stance was resonating in the adult relationship Kristof developed in displacement with the language of her new place.

Just as for Kristof, for many multilinguals taking on a second language means more than just learning its grammar and vocabulary. It is about redefining their relationship with their mother tongue and this new language. Carol, a young Dutch woman who settled with her Tyrolian partner in Switzerland, stumbled on learning German, one of her partner's mother tongues. Why was this so hard for her? Carol already spoke four languages, and had never encountered this difficulty with English, Italian, or French. "And if German were a human, what kind of person would that be?"—"A strict man in a grey suit", she promptly answered and made a grimace which showed how unappealing and threatening this man felt to her. As we elaborated on this metaphor, another image came up—that man making himself comfortable in her compartment on the train to Austria. He was there to share a part of her journey, and she had to get to know him and eventually establish a relationship with him. "He does not care for me. He is not interested".

"And are you interested in him?"

"No, not really. He looks boring".

"But maybe there is something under his strict suit? A heart? Or humorous colourful underwear?" I joked.

She smiled, unconvinced. I continued:

"What does he read?"

"A newspaper ... or maybe a book".

"A book. What kind of book might this be?"

We must find something to start a conversation with this man. Reading a book could be a way forward—Carol is an avid reader. That experiment shifted her attitude to the German language and helped her make a better connection with her partner and her new place.

Therapy with multilinguals is full of opportunities for creative work when a therapist can start co-modelling with her client a creative attitude to the crisis of multilingualism and displacement. Cairo refers to this process as "shifting from defensive to creative uses of language, from lies to truth" (Cairo in Beltsiou, 2015). This creativity can be further fostered by engaging with the work of translingual writers.

12 Translingual writers

Therapy is a private matter; what is said in the intimacy of the therapy room is rarely heard by more than the two people involved—the client and his therapist. The sparse accounts described in the literature by some multilingual therapists (Bernstein in Beltsiou, 2015; Cairo in Beltsiou, 2015) give us a hint of what happens in the therapy room when a multilingual client walks into our office, but those vignettes are often fictionalised to preserve clients' confidentiality.

Translingual writers, similarly to many multilingual clients, turn to their second language to explore the narrative of their lives. Their accounts can help us better understand their peculiar choice. Their endeavours are laid bare on their pages, enabling a better documentation and research than the use of a second language by clients in therapy can be (Kellman, 2003). World literature abounds in examples of emigrant translingual writers: Beckett, Nabokov, Brodsky, and so on. Writing in their second language, they find their creative voice: "Their words [...] are the priceless buoys with which they try to stay afloat both as professional thinkers and human beings" (Aciman, 2000: 14). Ilan Stavans, a Mexican-American writer and the child of Jewish emigrants from Russia, called his fellow translingual writers "tongues snatchers"(Stavans, 2001).

The self-directed irony of this description is illustrative of the playfulness that comes with the distance that a second language allows.

Translingual writers often place their multilingualism at the core of their creative inquiry. Contemporary fiction offers some fascinating examples of writers choosing to turn to a foreign language for their prose (Kellman, 2017).

The deliberate choice of some multilingual clients to engage in therapy in their second tongue can be understood better thanks to the accounts of the contemporary Italian novelist Francesca Marciano, who has published her four books in English, as well as from Jhumpa Lahiri, an American writer of Bengali origin writing in Italian. Their work offers not only a remarkable example of such translingual endeavour but also a deep reflection of this self-imposed transformation (Kellman, 2016).

Lahiri's book *In Other Words* is entirely dedicated to her relationship with the Italian language. As I first opened its American bilingual edition, I had to choose in which language to read it, exactly as for many bilingual clients in therapy. After some hesitation, I eventually opted for the left side of the page—the "original" Italian version. My English has taken over my Italian after years of studying, writing, and reflecting in English, so reading the English version would probably have been easier. But I was drawn to Lahiri's choice of writing this book in her second language; my reading it in Italian was putting us on an equal ground. I did not regret this choice. This book is a rare testimony of narrative self-therapy in action, with the obvious difference between the lonely process of writing and the dialogical talk therapy. Lahiri's autobiographical endeavour is exactly what displaced clients do in a therapy room, especially those who choose to use their second language to make sense of their experience of displacement and consequent multilingualism. "I am, in Italian, a tougher, freer writer", she declares (Lahiri, 2017), highlighting the most important facet of her linguistic choice. Her "falling in love" with Italian echoes Brodsky's "love affair" with English. But this love is condemned to be an unrequited one, as the language learnt after puberty never allows a satisfying mastery. As I am writing these words, I am painfully aware of my own limitations in English. Any unrequited love leads to feeling ashamed (Burgo, 2018), but despite the risk of this shame, many emigrants, writers, academics, and actors adopt a foreign tongue for their creative endeavours. This risk makes them vulnerable, and they accept the shame that comes with it. Does their choice conceal a secret hope to be finally included and loved, despite their difference and the fragility of their language?

For Marciano, the second language offers relief from the burden of the past. When she describes the experience of one of her characters—a young Italian girl who has recently lost her mother—the reasons behind this choice come to light: "Emma understood that one of the many ways to survive the pain buried inside her was to become an entirely different person" (Marciano, 2015: 14). Transitioning to a different place or a different language offers an escape from the older version of oneself and the trauma associated with that self. Another of Marciano's bilingual characters reflects on using her second language to communicate with her romantic partner:

What was incredibly refreshing [...] was that Adam and I did not speak the same language, in any sense. By speaking in English to him I inevitably needed to force something out. Not only was I obliged to be simpler, less Machiavellian, but by speaking my second language I was leaving behind a whole chunk of my history which had to do with Ferdinando. I felt lighter, as if I had been allowed to unload a weight off my back.

(Marciano, 2015: 51–52)

Many bilingual displaced clients make a similar choice to communicate with their romantic partners and friends. I am also living the realities of such a choice in my own marriage, and I know first-hand that such a choice never comes without consequences—as Marciano's character argues, it gives us an opportunity to re-invent oneself, but it also comes with a cost. What happens to those parts of us that remain behind, outside of the frame of the chosen second tongue? In doing this, do we deprive our partner of those parts that we perceive as undesirable? Or is it another unconscious trick to play Winnicott's version of hide-and-seek, torn by the contradicting desires to hide and to be found?

In my work with displaced multilingual couples, partners whose mother tongue is left out often express disappointment with their partners' lack of effort to learn their language. Exploring their feelings about this situation often leads to uncovering their grief and their guilt about letting this happen. Supporting the reflection about how a linguistic choice affects the interaction and ultimately the relationship will always help a client better understand his translingual relationships outside of the therapy room.

13 When language is a transference gift

Psychoanalytic authors have naturally explored the implications of bilingualism in how the unconscious processes of transference and countertransference take place (Pérez-Foster & Moskowitz, 1996; Lijtmaer, 1999). In the classical model, transference is defined as a repetition of an old object relation (Greenson, 1967). With the further development of relational psychoanalysis, the focus has naturally shifted towards the interactional and interpersonal context in which transference and countertransference emerges (Sugarman & Wilson, 1995). The first language is the container of and the tool for our early interactions with the caregivers, and it organically evolves within relationships that we establish later in life. For bilinguals, the early and developmentally defining relationships are stored and encoded in their mother tongue (Lijtmaer, 1999). From the attachment perspective, our early bonds develop in a close association with a language, or languages for those growing in multicultural and multilingual contexts. The complex attachment fabric of such individuals is made of various interwoven elements—language, place, and people. The kind of relationships they simultaneously develop with these objects of different nature will impact their further attachments of every kind, and most probably resurface within the therapeutic relationship. The way the dyad uses different languages in the relationship can turn into a powerful therapeutic means.

Language can be a powerful trigger for the transference phenomenon. More than anything else, personal manners, the way a person speaks, or their clothes, instantly indicate their origins. This places them firmly on the simple but deeply embedded grid on opposite sides—"same as me" / "different". Any therapist, monolingual or bilingual, will recall situations in which a client's accent has brought up some unexpected emotions, memories, associations. When a bilingual client steps into our therapy room for the first time, he brings with him the various languages that carry traces of his relational history. Some of our own relational history will also be triggered in the process, creating plenty of opportunities for transference and countertransference to happen. Recently, I met for the first time with Irina, a young emigrant woman who spoke Russian with intonations that instantly located her in a well-educated Jewish family from Moscow's intelligentsia. Up to the moment her yet unfamiliar face appeared on my screen, we had exchanged emails in English. Now, the way she spoke Russian instantly gave me access to her background, and I had to be aware of the presuppositions I was rushing towards, and make a conscious effort to put all stereotypes aside and wait for her story to unfold.

When clients from a multicultural family turn to a therapist whose first language is the same as that of one of their parents, transference emerges naturally. It provides an opportunity to address the developmental and relational history. I often see clients who choose to communicate with me in a more neutral English or French, although they know I speak Russian or Italian, like one of their parents. Their rationale usually sounds like "I am half-Russian, but I find speaking English easier". This can be a signal that they aim to sort out things with the Russian speaking parent. In this case, I put my Russian aside temporarily and listen to their perfectly aligned English words as they talk about their childhood caught in displacement. Nevertheless, our shared mother tongue is always around, as their "problematic" mother or father who demands attention.

A perfect illustration of such bicultural and bilingual clients, Clara moved to France from England. Her French father was emotionally unresponsive and bad tempered. Clara could easily recall how often her English mother used to dismiss some of his abusive behaviours with a simple "This is just so French!" In Paris, Clara was struggling with unsatisfying relationships, mostly with French men. She was often voicing bitter remarks about how "French people are", but persisted with choosing them on the dating app, despite the terrible frustration the process was causing her. My surname made her guess that I was married to a representative of this group of French men that she was angry with. "Is your husband French?" she inquired angrily in our first session. I nodded, fighting the desire to start defending the male half of the French population. We mainly spoke English, but from time to time, especially when irritated, Clara would spice her speech up with some French. In those moments I could barely avoid noticing that she probably sounded just like her father.

Her remark about my French surname quickly led us to explore the anger she felt at French men. She recognised her anger with her father. Not only was she angry with him for being verbally abusive and emotionally removed, but she also admired him and carried the burden of his anger on his behalf, as if to alleviate his load. After all, she admitted, he had good reasons to be angry. His academic career had never taken off once they had moved to England. Her mother was needy, dependant, and never happy with what they had. As we explored her deeper ambivalent feelings about her father, Clara recognised that she "hated her French half", which was at the receiving end of the contempt she expressed for the French men she was attempting to date. As we moved forward, French started making its way into our sessions, and finally replaced the English that she had originally chosen. This shift ironically coincided with her meeting a Canadian man who spoke no French and was eager to pair up with somebody who could make his expatriate life less lonely. Their partnership quickly took off, and when we talked about this sudden change in her romantic status, she laughed and commented that she "had little to say to the French at this point" and had no desire to spend her life with somebody who constantly reminded her of her angry father's tirades.

14 Dreamwork with multilingual individuals

Many clients who opt for online therapy may struggle with shame and display an avoidant attachment style. Welcoming their dreams helps with deepening the work. Irvin Yalom's call about dreams in general, "Use them, use them, use them" (Yalom, 2002: 225) is even more urgent when dealing with displaced multilingual clients. What they cannot say in words, they can communicate with the imagery of their dreams. Paying attention to this unconscious territory gives an opportunity to invite this invisible language to join the dialogue.

Beyond the never-ending debates on what dreams are and whether the therapist should interpret them or not, I am guided by Yalom's pragmatic principle: "Dreams can be an invaluable aid in effective therapy. They represent an incisive restating of the patient's deeper problems, only in a different language—a language of visual imagery" (Yalom, 2002: 226). For multilinguals, using this non-verbal language of imagery shortcuts their multilingual hurdles, and helps them get in touch with what lies beneath. Another guiding principle from Yalom is to "pillage and loot" the dream for anything that can bring therapy forward. Let us see how this can be done practically in a session:

Francesca was Italian, living in London. She had reached out to me because we shared a common emigrant background, and three languages: Italian, French, and English. She was going through a double transition: at the age of 40 and only recently married, she had been laid off by her employer. As a result, Francesca felt anxious, stuck at a crossroads between countries, lost in her professional life, and unfit for her new married life.

From the start, she had chosen to communicate with me in English, as Italian felt "boring and obsolete" to her. Having left her country in her early twenties to pursue artistic studies in Paris, she was now working in London as a designer for a large fashion house. Her adopted English was her language for "creativity and self-growth", as she put it.

One day, for the first time in the two months of her therapy, Francesca arrived early, clearly eager to share a recent nightmare, in which she was late for her own wedding. She clearly remembered standing naked in the middle of her bedroom, whilst her groom Alain was waiting for her impatiently at the church. She had to dress quickly but was unable to find her white-laced wedding gown. The clock on the wall was ticking, adding to her growing panic. She pulled the door of a huge cabinet. Inside it, a dirty pig was smiling at her, insolently. Terrified, she pulled a rope hanging alongside the pig, hoping to make the beast disappear. But as a result, a shower of vomit dropped from the ceiling, full of disgusting noodles. A strong smell of vomit then woke her up. As she reported her dream, her face on my screen looked sick with anxiety. Going through the dream again, with me as a witness, Francesca was starting to make sense of it: she realised that the tickling clock could be her biological clock (time for children), time passing on the job hunt, possibly time to return to France, where her future husband had a promising career … Nevertheless, listening to her, I felt that something was missing: usually in touch with her emotions, this time Francesca was slipping into a cognitive, fruitless field. Her storytelling made sense, but I wanted us to go further into exploring it. Two objects echoed in Italian in my mind: the tickling clock (orologio) and the noodles (spaghetti). This "stereo effect" triggered my curiosity, and I asked Francesca to tell her dream again, this time in Italian.

This was the first time I openly asked her to switch to her first language. Reluctantly, she did it. She started describing her anxiety about not being ready for her wedding. Clearly, the flow of emotions was now penetrating our shared space, giving me goose bumps. Francesca's voice had changed. She acknowledged that she had "felt much more emotional" this time in Italian. In her version in English, her mother's absence (she had died when Francesca was a child) had not seemed to trigger any particular feelings; but in the Italian account of the dream, a painful void was obvious. The sense of loss and solitude had become almost tangible, and I could see how much Francesca was missing her, at this stage of her adult life when she would hopefully become a mother herself.

Listening to her fluid Italian speech, I finally connected with the little Francesca. Like any other young girl, she had created her idea of marriage. In that ideal representation, maintained by a rich cultural imagery, she was to wear white, and her parents would be there. The reality was different. Her parents were gone, the white wedding dress was not compulsory. Also bearing a child at her age was nothing abnormal in today's world. Now the vomit image made sense as well. She associated it with pregnancy nausea, with her anxiety about not being able to be a good mum, or even not to be able to bear a child at all. As she was sharing her fears with me, Francesca felt slightly nauseous. She recognised this sensation in her throat as something she had been experiencing lately. She had been repressing it successfully but could now understand the reason for it. Finally, I asked Francesca to go back to her dream and play it *de novo* in the "here-and-now", being free to change from the initial version. Playing with its own imagery was a breakthrough for Francesca to re-write her own story at this rich stage of her life. This time, she decided to stop searching for her white wedding gown, realising that it was more important for her at this point to get to the church, where Alain may be starting to worry. In this new refabricated dream, as she ran through the fields towards the church, dressed in her old jeans and a jumper, she reported feeling young and liberated; excitement had replaced anxiety.

Compartmentalisation is a psychological strategy that is naturally adopted by emigrants. Francesca's world was divided in two well-separated realms: her early life in Italy before her expatriation, and her "new" independent adult life in Paris and then London. Up until that session, using mainly English, we had been engaging with the latter; the young Italian girl had been left behind. Indeed, Francesca felt abandoned by her mother who had gone too suddenly and too soon. Sticking to English, I may have reinforced this narrative, leaving the little Francesca to a sad and lonely past. On the other hand, had Francesca told me about her dream in Italian only, we would have done a good job eventually; possibly an easier one. But having access to both "parts" of her through connecting with the symbolic aspects of her dream in both languages had enriched our work.

Working with dreams in therapy is a deeply relational activity. Clients do not just recount their dreams (as they do in a dream journal), but they let us enter its realm, and re-experience it with them. The language we use for dreamwork has a meaning, and the multilingual facets of the client's experiences often come through their dreams. In the case of Francesca, this "stereo" dreamwork had not only allowed me to see her more fully, but our therapeutic relationship had deepened; her younger and more vulnerable self was now invited to the therapy room rather than being left out.

Dreamwork moves therapy forward, especially with highly cognitive clients. The multilingual perspective goes one step further restoring a missing stereo effect to the music heard by the therapist. Being openly curious about the multifaceted self that these clients possess not only enriches the therapeutic work, but also models the value of such an inclusive stance. Inclusiveness is always a sensitive area for displaced individuals. They have all felt excluded from their realms at some point. In therapy, every chance to address this part of the displacement trauma is precious, and the use of a client's multilingualism, even if it is not shared by his therapist, offers plenty of such opportunities.

15 When the therapist does not speak her client's language

Any therapist expanding her practice into the broader online space will meet clients whose culture and language are unfamiliar. The inability to understand our client's mother tongue naturally triggers discomfort and shame. A natural defence is to deny this issue altogether. Clients' desire to move away from their first language, as a way of distancing from the original trauma or assimilating into the new culture, will naturally support this avoidance. But excluding their mother tongue from the therapeutic space may be a real loss. This facet of cross-cultural practice was explored by writers from the psychoanalytical tradition at a time when bilingual therapeutic dyads were rare, and the technology had not yet made the cross-cultural work more common. With an inspiring élan, Rosemarie Pérez-Foster, a Latin American psychoanalyst, proposes The Psycholinguistic History, a form of psychodynamic inquiry that can help monolingual therapists attend to their bilingual client's needs (Pérez-Foster, in Pérez-Foster et al., 1996). This simple map consists in paying attention to when, where and with whom each language has been acquired and used. She also insists on investigating the context of the use of the current language—whether with others or with oneself, in dreams, fantasies and self-talk. She has proposed a frame of inquiry that suggests, above all, a curious stance vis-à-vis the client's languages and the way he uses them. If we let clients know that their "other" tongues are welcomed, they start bringing in words, expressions, and sayings in their mother tongue. At the start, these rare additions will be used to quote a relative or a friend with whom they use that particular language, but later on, this may move into a more personal space, as clients start referring to their own self-talk or their intimate thoughts or dreams.

An inclusive attitude to the client's original language or other significant languages that we do not speak shifts the power distribution towards greater equality; as the client takes on the role of a guide, leading their therapist into their original world. Cairo, an American multilingual analyst originating from Argentina, is attentive to occurrences in which the patient feels "an intense need to express themselves in their mother tongue" (Cairo in Beltsiou, 2015: 137). His psychoanalytical perspective leads to the use of this linguistic context as an additional frustrating element: "This development (emerging of the mother tongue not spoken by the analyst) was not only inevitable but perhaps essential to an analytic process that exerts a pressure on the patient beyond the usual deprivations of the setting" (Cairo in Beltsiou, 2015: 136). The language distribution has an obvious impact on the power dynamics played out in the therapeutic dyad. The-one-who-does-not-speak-the-language (no matter which one) loses some power and control, and this loss of control can result in anxiety. The alienation that results from such linguistic exclusion always manifests in a feeling of shame. It is a powerful therapeutic act to invite into the therapy room the "other" language(s) mastered by our client but not by us. This cannot be achieved without the therapist's capacity to understand her own shame triggered in the process.

16　Language and shame

> I feel a tightness in my chest. I hear my pulse in my ears. I feel my face get hot and sweat breaks out all over me. As soon as I'm no longer calm, I stop perceiving French words and start hearing unintelligible sounds. As a result, I stop being able to identify even a few keywords so that I can finish. I start searching for my own French vocabulary, but I find myself with a mental block. Suddenly, all those French vocabulary words that I studied or those sentences I rehearsed vanish from my mind. As a result, these "encounters" often wrap themselves up silently when the French speaker realizes I don't speak French or the French speaker swaps tactics and begins asking only closed questions that require a "oui/non/c'est ca/c'est bon" response. I normally need at least an hour to calm down after this panic. I also have to stop the internal voice that starts up telling me that I'm an idiot.

These words were written by one of my expatriate clients (used here with her permission), in a reflexive assignment that I often suggest when I feel that they are struggling with what I identify as linguistic shame. This is a totally overlooked phenomenon in the literature of therapy, although it is well reported in the expatriate literature.

Somebody familiar with the field of education and language learning would probably frame this client's emotional experience as Second Language Anxiety. A therapist reading these words would identify the underlying emotion as shame. Both anxiety and shame are responsible for the struggles of many displaced individuals, for whom mastering a new language becomes an existential survival task. Second language anxiety is a well-researched topic in the field of education and multilingualism (Horwitz, 2010; 2002; 1995; Horwitz et al., 1996; MacIntyre & Gardner, 1989). In her review Horwitz (2010) concludes that anxiety is a cause of poor language learning in some individuals (Horwitz, 2010). More recently some educational researchers outlined different subtypes of second language anxiety and investigated the origins of emotions experienced by a public speaker using a foreign language (Lee et al., 2020; Kralova & Tanistrakova, 2017). Garcia and colleagues bring to our attention the fact that research has largely focused on second language learners rather than immigrants (Garcia de Blakeley et al., 2017). Their study suggests that second language anxiety is an intrinsic part of any immigrant's life, no matter the gender, education level, duration of residency, or emotional stability. It is therefore crucial for therapists working with displaced individuals to understand this anxiety.

A particular linguistic shame might also be an intrinsic part of the process when a client or his therapist use their second language. It can only slow down the therapeutic work, and as often, awareness and the willingness to take the risk and address this feeling openly with the client might be the key to a greater therapeutic alliance. A therapist's ability to tolerate her own linguistic shame has important modelling potential for her displaced clients, who generally have had to learn a new language, thus opening an opportunity for further growth.

Have you ever blushed when hearing a blatantly inaccurate simultaneous translation at a conference? Or have you ever experienced discomfort when a colleague or friend supposedly fluent in a foreign language mispronounces a word? Our own linguistic shame can be easily triggered in circumstances when we witness somebody else making a linguistic misstep.

Stéphanie, a French client of mine, once reported being deeply unsettled by an interaction she witnessed between her mother-in-law and a Polish salesgirl in a shop in London. The mother-in-law spectacularly shamed the salesgirl with a cruel remark about her English language skills. Stéphanie's English was not perfect either—she reported an impression of "sinking into the ground" as the young woman blushed with humiliation. The mother-in-law was half-French half-British and bilingual, having moved to England as a child with her parents. She had previously confided in Stéphanie about how much she had struggled then, having to learn a new language that her parents were not speaking at home in France. She had a British grandmother, a distinguished lady, who was shaming her frequently for her unperfect English. She openly disapproved her son's choice of marrying a French farmer's daughter. In the shop, Stéphanie felt shocked by how unkind her usually generous mother-in-law was being. The young Polish girl looked hurt and muted. Clearly, Stéphanie's her mother-in-law, whose early linguistic shame had dented her self-esteem at the most important developmental stage, knew too well where the "shame button" of another emigrant was placed (English in Goldberg, 1991). Probably unaware of the impact her rebuke was also having on her daughter-in-law, she was still trying to get rid of her own unbearable shame, passing it onto the vulnerable Polish girl, whose current experience was painfully similar to her own past struggle.

In my practice, I have witnessed writers, English language teachers, lawyers, therapists, and other highly educated professionals feeling disempowered by their encounter with the new language that comes with displacement. It does not allow an accurate representation of their sophisticated thoughts and emotions, making them feel under-skilled and devalued. Individuals originating from worlds in which parental validation was subject to academic achievement are particularly vulnerable to this plight.

As a striking example, Vladimir Nabokov refused to lecture or be interviewed extemporaneously, insisting on writing out every word beforehand with the help of dictionaries and grammars. He modestly explained: "I think like a genius, I write like a distinguished author, and I speak like a child" (Pinker, 2015: 289).

Learning a language as an adult cannot happen without shame. The level of vulnerability and exposure one must risk mastering a new language is similar to that which one experiences when declaring one's love to another human being for the first time. At the initial stages, our love is not returned by the language, resulting in a debilitating feeling of shame. Or, again in one of my expatriate client's words:

> I've always prided myself on being an intelligent person. I have succeeded in every intellectual endeavour I've undertaken. I haven't just succeeded, I have excelled. But for the first time, it feels like I've taken on a subject that I may never conquer, and I am embarrassed and feeling stupid for the first time in my life. [...] Occasionally, French speakers tell me that they think I've really improved and come a long way. They try to be encouraging. But I can't take their words. Instead, I have found myself in a continuous cycle of believing I'm stupid and will never learn French and believing that I'm intelligent and just need more time. Then, the thought of dedicating more time to French overwhelms me because I already feel spread too thin [...]. It's a vicious cycle.

Another client, whose first language is English and who started learning French when he expatriated to France for work, wrote in an assignment that the loss of linguistic agency results in "feeling stupid"; the stable source of his pride—his articulateness—gives way to a deep feeling of inadequacy. Ultimately his displacement experience turns into an existential threat to his identity. This stumbling block can create a great deal of additional anxiety and pressure, especially when it is a professional or personal necessity to learn the language of the new place.

Writers from the psychoanalytical tradition have noticed that the acquisition of the new language by immigrants is in many ways similar to when a child learns how to speak (Grinberg & Grinberg, 1984; Cairo in Beltsiou, 2015: 136). It is a regressive experience in its very nature, and the emotion of shame is an unavoidable part of this endeavour. Exclusion is always the worst punishment, resulting in deep shame. The chasm that separates these two different points on the life span for learning a language is rooted in human biology. In his reflections on language acquisition, Steven Pinker concludes philosophically

> This language acquisition might be like other biological functions. The linguistic clumsiness of tourists and students might be the price we pay for the linguistic genius we displayed as babies, just as the decrepitude of age is the price we pay for the vigour of youth.
>
> (Pinker, 2015: 294)

But what about emigrants? Despite the obvious obstacles, including shame, are they pushing through, learning, wrestling with a new language that they were not lucky enough to learn during the optimum biological window before the age of four? The good news is that neuroplasticity is still there, particularly if learning the language is a question of survival. The exhilaration that results from meeting this challenge and eventually recovering the lost mastery in its renewed form is perfectly conveyed by Jhumpa Lahiri:

> Confronting a foreign language as an adult is a considerable challenge. And yet, the many doors I've had to open in Italian have [been] flung wide, giving onto a sweeping, splendid view. The Italian language did not simply change my life; it gave me a second life, an extra life.
>
> (Lahiri, 2022: 15)

Researchers and writers (Nathanson, 1992; Burgo, 2018; Caplovitz Barrett, 2005) agree on the value of persistence and joy of achievement in building self-esteem: "When you work long and hard for something that matters to you, when you finally achieve your goal, perhaps after enduring frustration and repeated setbacks, the experience of pride and pleasure will lay down memories that last a lifetime" (Burgo, 2018: 264). Mastery of a new language is one of the great achievements that can pave the way for improved self-esteem.

My client Jane simultaneously wrestled with French and the shame that her displacement from England to France had brought up. She once exclaimed: "If I finally learn this damn language, it somehow means that I am not worthless, and I am able to make it in this world!" For several years, I saw her stubbornly pushing forward, despite the internal and external obstacles and setbacks. I saw her giving up a few times, leaving the language school, retreating into the comfort of her mother tongue and shame, only to rebound again, and give it another go. Reflecting on her wrestling with French and on the importance of this task was an important part in co-creating a more congruent self-narrative. Eventually, French started to make its way into our sessions, slowly but steadily giving Jane a stronger sense of self and a means to think about her future beyond of the restrictive boundaries of her original context.

In the *Cambridge Encyclopaedia of Language* (Crystal, 2011), the intrinsic link between the human emotion of shame and language is clarified by Crystal in his sub-chapter on the functions of language: "Its sole function is to provide a mean of avoiding a situation which both parties might otherwise find embarrassing" (Crystal, 2011: 10). Examples of such use of language include British weather-talk, or any kind of polite exchange that any culture has woven into the social expectations of politeness associated with any given language. This suggests that the language which has a powerful potential for making us feel shame also encapsulates the potential for alleviating this shame. As any therapist knows, expressions like "me too" or "same here" have the power to alleviate shame.

The relationship that ties emigrants to their second language is rarely a neutral one. Exploring its history and nature will therefore always bring grist to the therapeutic mill. Some will fall in love with the new language that represents a liberation, a way out and away from an original shame that is associated with the learning of their mother tongue. Others will develop a conflicted relationship with the new language, experiencing shame as they engage with it. The complex set of emotional links between the first and second language(s) acquisition creates a system of its own.

In a previous book, I presented a short story about a British expat, Claire, who struggled with learning French (Piatakhina Giré, 2022). Her initial complaint pertained to her unexplainable inability to learn French, which she badly needed to succeed in a professional assignment that had brought her to Paris. An ambitious and articulate person, Claire could not make sense of her being so "French deaf". As we embarked on exploring her resistance, some older traumatic memories emerged that she had repressed altogether. Addressing her earlier trauma led Claire to challenge her earlier beliefs about herself, and to make important changes in her present life. Claire's therapy could have been a shallow run, had we not dug into her emotional response to learning French.

Whilst engaging with a new language later in life always creates an opportunity for reparation, it also comes with the risk of re-experiencing early shame linked to childhood exclusions and rejections. When we venture into the unclear waters of an unfamiliar language, we secretly hope to be included into the new community, and eventually accepted and loved by some of its members. This powerful healing potential is felt by many emigrants who meet this challenge. The American writer David Sedaris felt that Parisians were cruel to him when he spoke French. He offers a striking example of how an earlier experience of shame can resurface in displacement, as he was mocked for sounding "like a girl".[1] With his self-deprecating humour, Sedaris knows too well how to be cruel to himself, making sure he laughs at his lack of fluency before any French could laugh at him. By telling the story of his linguistic misadventures in France in his flawless English, Sedaris takes his revenge making fun of the French.

Some emigrants live in their new country for years without learning the local language. One of my clients Dimitry, a Russian emigrant, managed to spend 20 years in Paris without speaking any French. He used to heavily rely on his bilingual wife and children for whom France was home. In his native Russian, Dimitry was well read and articulate. His resistance to learning French was astounding. At first, he insisted that he did not need to learn French; then, as we developed some trust, he started recognising the limitations that not speaking French imposed on his life. His wife had to bear the weight of all administrative tasks that came with their family's daily life, and she resented him for that. What was behind his stubborn refusal? I could sense that Dimitry felt threatened by the French, and his resistance felt like self-protection. At some point, he had decided again to reach out to a French teacher but failed again to do so. He murmured "I don't know why this is so hard ... I just feel so bad". He was clearly taken by a powerful emotion that I had never seen in him before. Digging beyond his usual self-confident persona we discovered a deep sense of insecurity going back to his childhood; he remembered feeling deeply confused back then. That confusion was the result of his father cutting off his own Jewish father and changing his name for his more Russian-sounding mother's name. With that, Dimitry's name was also changed, without much warning nor explanation. The grandfather died when Dimitry was in his early teens, and since then had rarely been mentioned by the family. Dimitry remembered his grandfather as a loving person, who sang sweet songs to him when he was little. Only now, after years of living abroad could he verbalise his feelings of loss and shame associated with the part of his identity gone with his grandfather's name. This family secret rooted in the internalised antisemitism of his father resulted in the shame that Dimitry felt about having to side with his father, never rebelling against what he now believed to have been cruel. I asked him about his grandfather's name, his own former name. As Dimitry pronounced it, tears finally broke to the surface. It took us more sessions to address his identity loss and start recovering its fragments. French language came along ... at first Dimitry was wary, but soon he started enjoying his meetings with his French teacher. "Maybe one day we have our session in French", he joked one day, bewildered by his own audacity. Indeed, we could, I thought as I smiled at him. "Would you like that?" I asked, and he stayed silent and suddenly serious for a while "No, not really, but my grandfather probably would ... you see ... he was a French teacher and loved all things French". Dimitry met my eyes, and suddenly everything was coming together. Learning French was an act of recovery after all.

Attrition of the first language is another part of the psychology of displacement and multilingualism, where shame plays an important role. Language attrition is about loss and changes in the use of the first language as a result of its declining use by individuals who have changed their linguistic environment. To this day little is known about loss or attrition of language (Schmid, 2016).

Translingual writers provide a clue to the kind of emotional experience that comes with language attrition. As Lahiri engages more fully with her second language (Italian), her first language (English) suffers a setback:

> Why don't I feel more at home in English? How is it that the language I learnt to read and write in doesn't consider me? What happened, and what does it mean? The estrangement, the disenchantment confuses, disturbs me. I feel more than ever that I am a writer without a definitive language, without origin, without definition. Whether it's an advantage or a disadvantage I wouldn't know.

(Lahiri, 2017: 129–131)

We are all loyal to our mother tongue. It is unsettling to somehow lose our natural ease in using it, and the feeling of comfort, of being at home, that we had with our first language.

For displaced clients the risk of losing their mother tongue brings up an array of emotions, from relief to terror. Many emigrant therapists like myself, whose professional identity is based on their second language, are familiar with this destabilising realisation that our first language is slipping away— ironically right in front of our fellow emigrant clients with whom we communicate in our shared mother tongue. By the time I welcomed my first Russian client into my virtual therapy room, I had been working in English and French for a while. That session was one of the most difficult of my practice, and not because of the issues it brought up, but simply because she spoke in my mother tongue, which at the time I was distancing myself from. I sat through that endless session feeling deeply inarticulate, unprofessional, and simply stupid—all clear indicators of linguistic shame in action. Only later, as I was writing my notes (in the safer English language of course), was I able to put my confusing experience into words. Understanding this phenomenon helps us to better relate to our displaced clients who may stumble on the same experience as they keep reinventing themselves and building connections in their second language.

17 Addressing linguistic shame in therapy with displaced couples

The displacement rabbit ears mentioned above in this and previous chapters are useful when counselling displaced couples, in particular to detect the presence of linguistic shame and other language-related dynamics that generally crop up in multilingual couples' dynamics. Each partner will probably display their own emotional response—rooted in his or her linguistic history—to the language of the new place. These linguistic attitudes, interwoven with their feelings about their new place itself and its people, drive a complex dynamic that has to be understood before we start modifying any of its elements.

Displaced multilingual couples are special in many ways. Similar to individual therapy with multilinguals, inquiring into their use of languages is a sure path towards a better understanding of their attachment styles, their displacement histories, and their relational dynamics.

What languages does each speak? Which of these is their first? Which language(s) do they use together? These questions can also be included in the intake questionnaire. As the partners fill the questionnaire individually, it serves as a preparation, sets the tone, and hints at which areas will be addressed in the first session. For couples with children, this inquiry should include questions about what language(s) they speak with their children (one "family" language, or each partner's language in their individual interactions with children, or any other blended variation). How these choices were initially made—consciously, collectively, organically—is also an important element of the equation. Displaced partners of such unions often feel strongly about their mother tongues, and how each of these tongues is included into their family communication fabric. If one partner displays protective or defensive attitudes to his first language, this may indicate that he or she feels threatened, and these feelings should be openly explored sooner rather than later.

For multilingual couples, the choice of a therapist is never an easy task. Any current linguistic tensions impact it, and the way the partners resolve the conflict arising in the choice process offers precious information about how such conflicts are typically dealt with. Do they go for a completely "neutral" therapist who does not carry any of their mother tongues or cultural background and prefer to put their respective first tongues aside and stick to their lingua franca for all interactions? Or do they end up with a therapist who represents one of their cultural and linguistic backgrounds? Any path they choose will affect the dynamics of the therapeutic alliance that they establish with their couples therapist. When the couple reaches out for counselling, these choices have already been made, and the therapist can only inquire into the underlying reasons, the partners' feelings about it, and invite them to reflect on how it is impacting their interactions and relational dynamics.

In the case discussed earlier of Dimitry, the first couple of sessions were actually with his wife, for a couples therapy, before moving to individual therapy for Dimitry only. From the start they made it clear that they only wanted a therapist who spoke Russian, even if an English-speaking practitioner might be easier to find in Paris. This set-up brought us closer: we were all fellow Russian emigrants, talking about our relationship with our new home and the French language. Not having to deal with an additional burden of communicating in a second language, they were both visibly relieved. They knew I could relate to their experience. Going back to our mother tongue allowed us the necessary distance, and Dimitry was finally able to verbalise his shame about not being able to speak French, which naturally led us to reflect on the broader dynamics of their relationship.

Attentive observation in the "here-and-now" of the session of both partners' use of language to communicate with one another is another key ingredient of therapy with displaced couples. When all participants are multilingual—which tends to be the norm for displaced therapists and clients who are naturally drawn to them—linguistic material for observation is endlessly rich and loaded with emotional charge. In some particularly complex linguistic situations, I have had to step in and "play translator" for a partner whose skills in the couple's common language were rudimentary.

Many displaced couples experience an unbalanced linguistic set-up. As in the case of Victoire (French) and Ben (British), they use the mother tongue of one of them, and the first language of the other partner naturally moves down the linguistic ladder of relevance, even if the other partner knows that language, for the simple reason that it is less useful. Victoire's English was good.

They had met in London before moving to France to settle down and "start a family". This decision to relocate was taken collaboratively, and Ben had found time for intensive French lessons ahead of the move. From the start, they had agreed that their children would speak both languages and grow up bilingual. Both had initially looked forward to their common French future. Things did not go exactly as planned. The prompt arrival of a son was straining their resources, and the French childcare system was not up to their expectations. Victoire spent long hours at the office. Ben was struggling to find a job. They both looked exhausted and dissatisfied with their family life. In our first session, Ben complained about Victoire's constant bad temper and her lack of patience with him as well as with their son. Victoire shot back: "You never make an effort to speak French!" She looked angry and offended. I was guessing that her words might sound rude to a British ear. "I do, but with other people, not with you!" he replied, hurt. "Why is that so?" I asked. "Because I am too afraid, she will mock me or despise me!" Now even Ben, who was usually cool, was getting visibly upset. When I asked him how exactly he felt when he spoke French with his wife or in her presence, he described feeling "like a toddler", whom she was ready to scold "Do you often feel this way in your relationship?" was my next line of inquiry. He did; her dismissive and judgemental attitude left him constantly feeling infantilised, diminished. Ben, challenged by the unexpected realities of his first expatriation, was slowly sinking into deep waters of shame. Victoire, with her perfectionism and her personality that Ben was finding "unforgiving" was not making things easier. This linguistic prelude opened a path to the core of their relational "dance". As we progressed, after several sessions, Ben was ready to take a risk and try to introduce French into our conversations. By this point we had established that behind Victoire's bitterness, she was just needing to be seen and empathised with, but with Ben retreating into shame and shielded behind the comfort of his mother tongue, this level of intimacy was out of reach. Language was actually an appropriate ground for them to practise modifying the dance in which they were currently stuck. Before taking that plunge, we agreed that Victoire would be more patient and kinder with Ben's imperfect French, and Ben committed to making an effort to meet her need for being heard and empathised with. When we switched to French, and as Ben started expressing his feelings for Victoire, she visibly relaxed. For the first time I saw her deeply touched by his words. When she replied, I noticed how kinder and more nuanced she sounded in French. When I asked Ben about this, he acknowledged that he also did not sense judgement in her tone. This linguistic experiment led to more good work that this couple was ready to make to improve their relationship.

Research shows that toddlers experience embarrassment as early as aged 18 months (Caplovitz Barrett, 2005). The feeling of not being good enough at expressing our thoughts is present from an early age. Is this the reason why language and shame appear deeply interlinked? After all, when adults, no matter how articulate, feel shame, they suddenly become speechless or lost for words. In these moments, fluency is out of reach, and it takes a lot of self-awareness, self-compassion, and patience to recognise what is going on. With multilingual couples, these moments of regression and visible difficulty with expressing thoughts and feelings are common. This kind of couple always carries a displacement-related burden of shame. Language is always a precious conductor into this area of partners' emotional lives. It is interesting to see, during a session, what happens when one partner goes through an acute episode of linguistic shame. The therapist may want to rescue them by switching to a more comfortable language, or translating for them. It is always informative to observe how the other, more fluent partner responds to their companion's struggle with shame. Do they rescue? Do they judge? Do they let the other sink alone? This emotional response shows the level of empathy and connection that the couple is currently capable of. It offers great "here-and-now" material that can be used to address the issue in the session.

Fluent multilingual people often use their languages for play in their relationships. This playful and creative use of their tongues and the different facets of their identities that come with such linguistic proficiency can also lead to manipulative games. When we share a language (especially the mother tongue) with one of the partners, he or she may want to use it to exclude, punish, or manipulate the other. This often happens in highly conflictual contexts, or when one of the partners has a personality disorder. To avoid colluding in such games, the communication rules should be clearly established from the start. For example: all relational matters have to be addressed in the session, email is only used for logistics, with both partners copied into the mail exchange. Despite this initial rule, it is not rare to be contacted by one of the partners, leaving the other partner outside of a "parallel" communication channel, in a language they have not mastered. In this case, the therapist has to be particularly attentive to not collude with the manipulative partner and gently re-state the rules. If possible, later on, and with mutual agreement, these kind of short-cut attempts can be explored in the session. Bringing these tactics to the couple's awareness can help them reflect on other games they may unconsciously play in their relationship.

18 Practising psychotherapy in the second language

There is little research on therapists using their second language for their work, even though with the spread of online counselling translingual therapy has become increasingly common. Everything that was mentioned before about clients using their second language for therapy is, in a way, relevant for therapists who make a similar choice. The rationale behind it varies, but some form of displacement is usually part of their individual context—some grew up in multilingual families (Costa, 2020), others dislocated themselves voluntarily (Akhtar, 2004) or had to live in exile (Grinberg & Grinberg, 1984).

When Jhumpa Lahiri reflects on reading in her second language, she hints at what may lie behind the professional choice of translingual therapists: "When I read in Italian, I am a more active reader, more involved, even if less skilled. I like the effort. I prefer the limitations. I know that in some way my ignorance is useful to me" (Lahiri, 2017: 43). I could easily paraphrase this statement and apply it to the field of therapy. In English, I am also a more involved therapist, even if less articulate. I also know that in some ways my ignorance is useful. But how exactly?

As discussed earlier, the second language offers a safe distance from intense emotional material for both therapist and client. Taghi Modaressi, an Iranian novelist and child psychiatrist, refers to his translating his own novels from Farsi to English as: "writing with an accent" (Modaressi in Beltsiou, 2015). The therapeutic dance performed "with an accent" offers endless opportunities for collusion and avoidance (Costa, 2020), hence the importance of facing this topic in self-reflection and bringing it up in supervision. In online therapy, this freeing effect is amplified by the disinhibiting effect of online communication (Suler, 2004). A decade of "doing therapy with an accent" has taught me humility. I have also developed a stubborn resilience to linguistic shame. In my first year of practice, I blushed and wanted to sink into my armchair every time my client asked me to repeat what I had just elaborated. With a lot of blushing and sinking, I learnt to recognise my emotional response. Acknowledging the now familiar sting of embarrassment, I moved on to rephrase in simpler words, aiming at maximum clarity. If these instances came up frequently with the same client, I would then inquire into their experience of working with me, a non-native speaker of the language they had chosen for therapy. This helped assess the therapeutic alliance and the client's satisfaction or lack thereof with the process.

The context in which we have learnt our second language and the relationship we have developed with it obviously impact our professional persona. What does speaking this language mean to me? How does it change the way I feel and relate to others? Ewa Hryniewicz-Yarbrough, a Polish American essayist and translator, offers an account that parallels the role that French language played for me:

> Just as Mrs B personified the grace and refinement I aspired to, English turned for me into a symbol of everything that was missing in Poland at the time. It promised an escape from the constraints of a provincial environment into the larger world that I knew existed.
>
> (Hryniewicz-Yarbrough, 2016)

In the same way, for those displaced clients who leave behind an oppressing reality, the language of the seemingly freer place means inner liberation.

Whilst many therapists use the liberating potential of their second language, its promise of emotional distance from disturbing historical facts turns language into a perfect shield. One can hide behind the second "professional" language as behind a professional uniform—somehow like a doctor or a soldier. Professional garments provide reassurance, but also a safe emotional distance. The obvious risk with uniforms is that they do not let our vulnerability shine through, potentially hindering the establishment of the therapeutic relationship.

We have seen how multilingual clients always benefit from reflecting on their relationship to their second language. To open that reflection, we must develop a better understanding of our own linguistic history and language-related processes. This can avoid blindly stumbling across our own material.

Research suggests that many non-native language teachers experience foreign language anxiety, with negative consequences for their teaching (Horwitz, 1996). Linguistic anxiety in therapy has received less attention than in teaching, but some therapists have acknowledged their anxiety about working in their second language (Gulina & Dobroliubova, 2018). The first remark about some discomfort related to practising in the second language comes from Freud (Gay, 2006: 388); thus making therapist's linguistic shame as old as their profession. A few psychoanalysts, mainly emigrants themselves, have openly addressed the topic (Greenson, 1950; Flegenheimer, 1989; Lijtmaer, 1999). Their accounts, echoing Freud, mostly dealt with the feeling of anger and frustration resulting from the additional effort that working in a second language involved. This was probably part of the broader psychological landscape of the early psychoanalysts, rooted in its founder's personal experience of displacement. After all, psychoanalysis itself "survived on foreign shores" and was "severed from its own past" (Makari, 2008).

The work we did with Nathalie, one of my multilingual British clients, demonstrates how recognising my own shame triggered in the process, helped us move forward. Every time I saw Nathalie I felt inarticulate. Usually this discomfort would develop gradually—a few minutes into the session I would start searching for words, and by the mid-session I would feel exhausted and would realise I was struggling to express myself in English. This strange experience repeated itself at every single session with Nathalie. She was teaching English and was fluent in her other two languages. I had experienced other clients who taught English, but this had never impressed me to the point of not being able to articulate my thoughts. I shared that haunting feeling with her, and she told me she often felt this way—ashamed of how she used words, not articulate enough, a "fraud", in each of her three languages. With this disclosure in mind, we started looking back into her story, trying to make sense of this shared "speechlessness". Soon enough we stumbled across the obvious: as a child growing up in a multilingual, ever-shifting environment with her mobile family (moving every few years following her mother's assignments), she often felt confused and inarticulate—an eternal newcomer to every school, where she would never stay long enough to make close friends. "The New Girl" was her most frequent nickname. The adult Nathalie inherited her multilingualism from that little girl. Nobody could guess that deep inside she still felt inarticulate and often speechless. She learnt how to hide her shame; to express herself with transcultural ease. She even became an English teacher. Her linguistic shame resonated with mine, amplified in the process. Once we had untangled this feeling, I regained my English. Shame dissipated naturally, allowing space for more understanding and closeness.

The path away from linguistic shame stretches out in the direction of multilingual pride. It often leads us through the fields of creativity. Bilingual therapists have recently expanded their reflections on their use of a second language towards a more embracing and creative stance (Pérez-Foster & Moskowitz, 1996; Connolly, 2002; Amati Mehler, 1995; Szekacs-Weisz, 2004): "I am a psychologist with one brain and two minds" declares Szekacs-Weisz (2004). Beverly Costa has made a timely call for integration of multilingual therapists' languages with their complex professional identity (Costa, 2020). The current spread of online counselling and the expansion of psychotherapy into an increasingly cross-cultural and cross-lingual field is propelling this topic to the forefront, creating an increasing need for a training that includes modules for fostering the understanding of displacement-related and multilingual issues. The same goes for specific supervision aimed at supporting therapists working with bilingual clients or in a translingual context.

Note

1 Glass, Ira (Host), July 28, 2000. "Americans in Paris", 165. Audio podcast episode. *This American Life*, WBEZ, Chicago https://www.thisamericanlife.org/165/america ns-in-paris

References

Aciman, A. (2000). *False papers*. New York: Picador.

Ainslie, R. C., Tummala-Narra, P., Harlem, A., Barbanel, L., & Ruth, R. (2013). Contemporary psychoanalytic views on the experience of immigration. *Psychoanalytic Psychology*, 30(4), 663.

Akhtar, S. (2004). *Immigration and identity: Turmoil, treatment, and transformation*. Lanham MD and London: Rowman & Littlefield.

Amati-Mehler, J. A, Argentieri, S., Canestri, J., & Whitelaw-Cucco, J. T. (1993). *The babel of the unconscious: Mother tongue and foreign languages in the psychoanalytic dimension*. New York: International Universities Press.

Amati-Mehler, J. A. (1995). The exiled language. *Canadian Journal of Psychoanalysis*, 3(1), 87.

Ansaldo, A. I., Marcotte, K., Scherer, L., & Raboyeau, G. (2008). Language therapy and bilingual aphasia: Clinical implications of psycholinguistic and neuroimaging research. *Journal of Neurolinguistics*, 21(6), 539–557. doi:10.1016/j.jneuroling.2008.02.001

Barthes, R. (1990). *The pleasure of the text*. London: Blackwell.

Beltsiou, J. (Ed.) (2015). *Immigration in psychoanalysis: Locating ourselves.* London and New York: Routledge.

Boym, S. (1996). Estrangement as a lifestyle: Shklovsky and Brodsky. *Poetics Today,* 17(4), 511–530. doi:10.2307/1773211

Brodsky, J. (2011). *Less than one: Selected essays.* London: Penguin Books.

Burck, C. (2011). Living in several languages: Language, gender and identities. *European Journal of Women's Studies,* 18(4), 361–378. doi:10.1177/1350506811415196

Burgo, J. (2012). *Why do I do that?: Psychological defense mechanisms and the hidden ways they shape our lives.* Chapel Hill NC: New Rise Press.

Burgo, J. (2018). *Shame: Free yourself, find joy, and build true self-esteem.* New York: St. Martin's Press.

Busch, B. (2012). The linguistic repertoire revisited. *Applied Linguistics,* 33(5), 503–523. doi:10.1093/applin/ams056.

Busch, B. (2015). Expanding the notion of the linguistic repertoire: On the concept of spracherleben —The lived experience of language. *Applied Linguistics,* amv030. doi:10.1093/applin/amv030.

Buxbaum, E. (1949). The role of a second language in the formation of ego and superego. *The Psychoanalytic Quarterly,* 18(3), 279.

Byford, A. (2015). Lost and gained in translation: The impact of bilingual clients' choice of language in psychotherapy. *British Journal of Psychotherapy,* 31(3), 333–347. doi:10.1111/bjp.12148

Caplovitz Barrett, K. (2005). The origins of social emotions and self-regulation in toddlerhood: New evidence. *Cognition and Emotion,* 19(7), 953–979. doi:10.1080/02699930500172515.

Casement, P. (1985). *On learning from the patient.* London: Routledge.

Connolly, A. (2002). To speak in tongues: Language, diversity and psychoanalysis. *Journal of Analytical Psychology,* 47(3), 359–382. doi:10.1111/1465-5922.00325

Casanave, C. P., & Vandrick, S. (2003). *Writing for scholarly publication: Behind the scenes in language education.* London: Routledge.

Costa, B. , & Dewaele, J. (2012). Psychotherapy across languages: Beliefs, attitudes and practices of monolingual and multilingual therapists with their multilingual patients. *Language and Psychoanalysis,* 1(1), 19–41. doi:10.7565/landp.2012.0003

Costa, B. , & Dewaele, J. (2014). Psychotherapy across languages: Beliefs, attitudes and practices of monolingual and multilingual therapists with their multilingual patients. *Counselling and Psychotherapy Research,* 14(3), 235–244. doi:10.1080/14733145.2013.838338

Costa, B. (2020). *Other tongues: Psychological therapies in a multilingual world.* Monmouth UK: PCCS Books.

Courtney, B. H., Cody, J. M., Bertolo, M., Lee-Rubin, H., Amir, D., Constance, M. B., … Samuel, A. M. (2021). *Acoustic regularities in infant-directed speech and song across cultures.* Cold Spring Harbor NY: Cold Spring Harbor Laboratory Press. doi:10.1101/2020.04.09.032995.

Crystal, B., & Crystal, D. (2015). *You say potato.* Pan Books.

Crystal, D. (2011). *The Cambridge encyclopedia of the English language* (3rd edn). Cambridge: Cambridge University Press.

Dewaele, J., & Pavlenko, A. (2002). Emotion vocabulary in interlanguage. *Language Learning,* 52(2), 263–322. doi:10.1111/0023-8333.00185

Epstein, M. (2012). *The transformative humanities: A manifesto.* London: Bloomsbury.

Etchegoyen, L., & Mehler, J. A. (2004). Language and affects in the analytic practice. *The International Journal of Psychoanalysis*, 85(6), 1479–1483.

Ferrante, E. (2018, February 24). Elena Ferrante: 'Yes, I'm Italian—but I'm not loud, I don't gesticulate and I'm not good with pizza'. *The Guardian*. Retrieved from http s://www.theguardian.com/lifeandstyle/2018/feb/24/elena-ferrante-on-italian-langua ge-identity.

Flegenheimer, F. A. (1989). Languages and psychoanalysis: The polyglot patient and the polyglot analyst. *International Review of Psycho-Analysis*, 16, 377–383.

Foster, R. P. (1996). The bilingual self duet in two voices. *Psychoanalytic Dialogues*, 6 (1), 99–121.

Garcia de Blakeley, M., Ford, R., & Casey, L. (2017). Second language anxiety among Latino American immigrants in Australia. *International Journal of Bilingual Education and Bilingualism*, 20(7), 759–772. doi:10.1080/13670050.2015.1083533

Gay, P. (2006). *Freud: A life for our time*. New York: Norton.

Goldberg, C. (1991). *Understanding shame*. Northvale NJ and London: Jason Aronson.

Goldschmidt, G., & de Rubercy, E. (2006). Freud et la langue allemande. *Revue Des Deux Mondes*, 16–28. Retrieved from http://www.jstor.org/stable/44194115.

Gordon, C. (2009). *Making meanings, creating family: Intertextuality and framing in family interaction*. New York: Oxford University Press.

Greenson, R. R. (1950). The mother tongue and the mother. *The International Journal of Psycho-Analysis*, 31, 18.

Grinberg, L., & Grinberg, R. (1984). *Psychoanalytic perspectives on migration and exile*. New Haven CT & London: Yale University Press.

Grosjean, F. (2010). *Bilingual: Life and reality*. Cambridge MA: Harvard University Press.

Gulina, M., & Dobrolioubova, V. (2018). One language and two mother tongues in the consulting room: Dilemmas of a bilingual psychotherapist. *British Journal of Psychotherapy*, 34(1), 3–24. doi:10.1111/bjp.12350

Gumperz, J. J. (1964). Linguistic and social interaction in two communities. *American Anthropologist*, 66(6), 137–153.

Gumperz, J. J. (1970). *Verbal strategies in multilingual communication*. Berkeley: University of California, Institute of International Studies.

Horwitz, E. (2002). Language anxiety and achievement. *Annual Review of Applied Linguistics*, 21, 112–126. doi:10.1017/s0267190501000071

Horwitz, E. K. (1995). Foreign language anxiety. *International Journal of Educational Research*, 23(7), 575.

Horwitz, E. K. (1996). Even teachers get the blues: Recognizing and alleviating language teachers' feelings of foreign language anxiety. *Foreign Language Annals*, 29 (3), 365–372. doi:10.1111/j.1944-9720.1996.tb01248.x

Horwitz, E. K. (2010). Foreign and second language anxiety. *Language Teaching*, 43 (2), 154–167. doi:10.1017/S026144480999036X

Horwitz, E. K., Horwitz, M. B., & Cope, J. (1986). Foreign language classroom anxiety. *The Modern Language Journal* [Boulder CO], 70(2), 125–132. doi:10.1111/ j.1540-4781.1986.tb05256.x

Hryniewicz-Yarbrough, E. (2016). To leave your mother tongue is to love it more. *The American Scolar*. Retrieved from https://theamericanscholar.org/issues/autum n-2016/

Ivaz, L., Griffin, K. L., & Duñabeitia, J. A. (2019). Self-bias and the emotionality of foreign languages. *Quarterly Journal of Experimental Psychology* [2006]; *Q J Exp Psychol* [Hove, UK], 72(1), 76–89. doi:10.1177/1747021818781017

Kellman, S. (2017). Jhumpa Lahiri goes Italian. *New England Review*, 38(2), 121–204.

Kellman, S. G. (Ed.) (2003). *Switching languages: Translingual writers reflect on their craft.* Lincoln NE and London: University of Nebraska Press.

Kogan, I. (2010). Migration and identity: Different perspectives. *International Journal of Psycho-Analysis*, 91(5), 1206.

Kralova, Z., & Tanistrakova, G. (2017). The subtypes of foreign language anxiety. *Slavonic Pedagogical Studies Journal*, 6(2), 347–358. doi:10.18355/PG.2017.6.2.12

Kristof, A. (2004). *L'analphabète: Récit autobiographique.* Geneva: Editions Zoe.

Krynicki, R. (2017). *Magnetic point: Selected poems.* New York: New Directions.

Lacan, J. (1968). *The language of the self: The function of language in psychoanalysis.* Baltimore MD: Johns Hopkins University Press.

Lacan, J., Sheridan, A., & Bowie, M. (2020). The function and field of speech and language in psychoanalysis. *Écrits* (pp. 33–125). Abingdon: Routledge.

Lahiri, J. (2015, November 29). Teach yourself Italian: For a writer, a foreign language is a new kind of adventure. *The New Yorker.* Retrieved from https://www.new yorker.com/magazine/2015/12/07/teach-yourself-italian.

Lahiri, J. (2017). *In other words.* London: Bloomsbury Paperbacks.

Lahiri, J. (2021). Where I find myself: On self-translation. *Words without Borders*, 27.

Lahiri, J. (2022). *Translating myself and others.* Princeton NJ: Princeton University Press.

Lee, H., Mandalapu, V., Kleinsmith, A., & Gong, J. (2020). *Distinguishing anxiety subtypes of english language learners towards augmented emotional clarity.* Cham, Switzerland: Springer International. doi:10.1007/978-3-030-52240-7_29

Lijtmaer, R. M. (1999). Language shift and bilinguals: Transference and counter-transference implications. *Journal of the American Academy of Psychoanalysis*, 27 (4), 611.

Li Wei, 2011. Moment analysis and trans-linguaging space: Discursive construction of identities by multilingual Chinese youth in Britain. *Journal of Pragmatics*, 43, 1222–1235.

MacIntyre, P. D., & Gardner, R. C. (1989). Anxiety and second-language learning: Toward a theoretical clarification. *Language Learning*, 39(2), 251–275. doi:10.1111/j.1467-1770.1989.tb00423.x

Makari, G. (2008). *Revolution in mind.* New York: HarperCollins.

Marciano, F. (2015). *The other language.* London: Vintage Contemporaries.

Miller, S. D., Duncan, B. L., & Hubble, M. A. (1997). Escape from babel: Toward a unifying language for psychotherapy practice. *Adolescence*, 32(125), 247.

Mirsky, J. (1991). Language in migration: Separation individuation conflicts in relation to the mother tongue and the new language. *Psychotherapy: Theory, Research, Practice, Training*, 28, 618–624. doi:10.1037/0033-3204.28.4.618.

Moser, B. (2022). Jhumpa Lahiri leaves her comfort zone. *The New York Times*, May 17.

Nabokov, V. (2019). *Think, write, speak.* London: Penguin Books.

Nabokov, V. (2000). *Speak, memory.* London: Penguin Books.

Nathanson, D. L. (1992). *Shame and pride: Affect, sex, and the birth of the self.* New York and London: W. W. Norton.

Nesdale, D., & Rooney, R. (1996). Evaluations and stereotyping of accented speakers by pre-adolescent children. *Journal of Language and Social Psychology*, 15(2), 133–154. doi:10.1177/0261927X960152002

Ogden, T. H. (2016). On language and truth in psychoanalysis. *The Psychoanalytic Quarterly*, 85(2), 411–426.

Pavlenko, A. (2007). Autobiographic narratives as data in applied linguistics. *Applied Linguistics*, 28(2), 163–188. doi:10.1093/applin/amm008

Pavlenko, A. (2014). *The bilingual mind: And what it tells us about language and thought*. Cambridge: Cambridge University Press.

Pérez-Foster, R., & Moskowitz, M. (1996). *Reaching across boundaries of culture and class: Widening the scope of psychotherapy*. New York: Jason Aronson.

Phillipson, R. (1997). Realities and myths of linguistic imperialism. *Journal of Multilingual and Multicultural Development*, 18(3), 238–248.

Phillipson, R. (2012). Linguistic imperialism. *The encyclopedia of applied linguistics* (pp. 1–7). Chichester: Wiley.

Phillipson, R., & Skutnabb-Kangas, T. (2012). Linguistic imperialism and endangered languages. *The handbook of bilingualism and multilingualism* (pp. 495–516). Chichester: Wiley.

Phipps, A. (2019). *Decolonising multilingualism struggles to decreate*. Bristol: Multilingual Matters.

Piatakhina Giré, A. (2022). *Unlocked: Online therapy stories*. London: Confer Books.

Piatakhina Giré, A. (2015, March 31). In treatment, but in which language? *New York Times*. Retrieved from https://archive.nytimes.com/opinionator.blogs.nytimes.com/2015/03/31/in-treatment-but-in-which-language/.

Pinker, S. (2015). *The language instinct: How the mind creates language*. London: Penguin Random House.

Rampton, B. (1995). Language crossing and the problematisation of ethnicity and socialisation. *Pragmatics*, 5(4), 485–513.

Rolland, L., Dewaele, J., & Costa, B. (2017). Multilingualism and psychotherapy: Exploring multilingual clients' experiences of language practices in psychotherapy. *International Journal of Multilingualism, 14*(1), 69–85. doi:10.1080/14790718.2017.1259009

Schmid, M. S. (2016). First language attrition . *Language Teaching*, 49(2), 186–212. doi:10.1017/S0261444815000476

Schrauf, R. W. (2000). Bilingual autobiographical memory: Experimental studies and clinical cases. *Culture & Psychology*, 6(4), 387–417. doi:10.1177/1354067X0064001

Stavans, I. (2001). *Art and anger: Essays on politics and the imagination*. Basingstoke: Palgrave Macmillan.

Sugarman, A., & Wilson, A. (1995). Introduction to the section: Contemporary structural analysts critique relational theories. *Psychoanalytic Psychology*, 12, 1–8. doi:10.1037/h0079606.

Suler, J. (2004). The online disinhibition effect. *CyberPsychology & Behavior*, 7(3), 321–326. doi:10.1089/1094931041291295

Szekacs-Weisz, J. (2004). How to be a bi-lingual psychotherapist. *Lost childhood and the language of exile* (pp. 21–28). London: Imago East West and the Freud Museum.

Szekacs-Weisz, J., & Ward, I. (Eds.) (2022). *Lost childhood and the language of exile* (2nd edn). Manila, Philippines: Phoenix Publishing House.

Walcott, D. (2019). *The poetry of Derek Walcott 1948–2013*. London: Faber & Faber.

Wei, L. (2011). Moment analysis and translanguaging space: Discursive construction of identities by multilingual Chinese youth in Britain. *Journal of Pragmatics*, 43(5), 1222–1235.

Yalom, I. D. (2002). *The gift of therapy: Reflections on being a therapist*. London: Piatkus.

Chapter 7

Displacement and shame

Why shame?

Guilt is a well-acknowledged topic in the literature dedicated to the psychology of displacement (Grinberg & Grinberg, 1984), but little or nothing is written about shame and the ways it manifests for those who deal with displacement. However, the on-going inquiry that I undertake in my therapy room with emigrant clients continuously confirms the link between their experience of dislocation and the family of shame-related emotions: "I am constantly feeling like a fraud and a misfit", my emigrant clients often complain. No matter how much success they achieve in their personal or professional life, no matter how well they integrate into their new place, the feeling haunts them as a malevolent ghost lurking among their most mundane daily experiences.

Any personal experience of shame will be influenced by an individual's life, including one's family, neighbourhood, nation, culture, or the era in which one grew up (Nathanson, 1987). But for emigrants it will also be impacted by their unique displacement history. As the early shame scholar Helen Lynd (1999) stated, the power of shame comes from the fear of being excluded, banished from one's attachment figures or the group to which one belongs. Here the attachment perspective becomes useful again, as such exclusion from one's place and one's people is at the core of the displacement experience. From this perspective, displacement is a condition that results from the rejection one has experienced from one's original place or/and one's original family. Pervasive shame is the natural psychological response to such a rejection by early attachment figures, be they caregivers or a place. This confers on shame an unquestionable central place in the displacement psychology. Therapists working with such clients, online or in person, should be prepared to actively explore this emotion in their work.

Being a refugee or an exile feels too close to being an outcast—so we tend to deny and avoid this self-definition. To be displaced often feels like being misplaced or out-of-place altogether. In the literature, a rare recognition of displacement-related shame comes from Dowd:

DOI: 10.4324/9781003144588-7

It is common in my experience for the dis-located to feel shame at their seeming inability to manage their re-location. The manic defensive system erected to protect against their own lost-ness and sense of foreignness in the new often alienating environment are profound; the aim being to seem as if it never happened, as if they already "belong" as one of "us".

(Dowd, 2019)

The striking manifesto written in 1943 on behalf of Jewish refugees of the Second World War by Hannah Arendt, the Jewish American political philosopher, starts with an opening line that puts the underlying shame of the displacement condition to the centre of her discourse: "In the first place, we don't like to be called 'refugees'. We ourselves call each other 'newcomers' or 'immigrants'" (Arendt, 2007: 264). The pages of this powerful essay are infused with the confusion and the identity struggle typical of those who fled their original places to escape persecution and death during the Holocaust. To this day, the painful sentiment behind Arendt's account keeps resonating for many individuals displaced by wars and other life-threatening circumstances. Anger, hurt, resentment, and shame emanate from these pages—"If we are saved, we feel humiliated and if we are helped, we feel degraded"—Arendt continues describing the collective experience of exile, consistently avoiding the word "shame" throughout her text. Further, Arendt clarifies her opening line: "we don't want to be refugees because we don't want to be Jews" (Arendt, 2007: 272). This alienation from the self and the desire to escape one's own skin is at the core of a debilitating shame. Individuals belonging to any marginalised and persecuted group will almost unavoidably suffer from it. Many clients turning today to online therapy may be experiencing less dramatic forms of displacement, but they carry a similar emotional load.

A well-hidden emotion

The Indo-European root at the base of the word "shame" is *skem*, or *sham*, meaning "to hide" (OED). This "secret", hidden quality of the emotions from the shame family (from mild embarrassment to humiliation) makes them difficult to identify; and shame is thus often over-looked in therapy (Goldberg, 1991). This phenomenon may explain why the emotion is nearly absent from the literature dedicated to psychology of displacement.

With writings of authors from different mental health horizons such as Nathanson, Goldberg, Wheeler, Bradshaw, Brown, and more recently Burgo, Epstein, and Cundy, shame has been central to the psychological inquiry for decades. My scope here is to place shame in the context of displacement, looking at the specific aspects of this emotional experience that make it relevant for a displacement-oriented practice. Shame, experienced by emigrants at different stages of their journey, leads to acute psychological discomfort and a heightened self-introspection. Even unrecognised and unnamed, it brings many otherwise functional displaced individuals to therapy, creating a precious window for personal work and change.

Shame is a primary and pervasive source of human discomfort (Nathanson, 1992). "The pain of shame uniquely draws attention to who one is and how one appears, to oneself and to others" (Burgo, 2018). It is all about feeling painfully "self-conscious" (Tangney & Fischer, 1995). This particular quality of chronic shame was recently summed up in a powerful metaphor by Chefetz, who compares the person suffering from this feeling to "a bird plucked clean of its feathers while still alive: naked and unrecognizable, completely vulnerable, devalued, unable to flee, unable to hide" (Chefetz in Epstein, 2021).

The psychological discomfort that comes with change is the intrinsic part of the displaced individual's reality. At the initial stages of any expatriation, we find ourselves unqualified, uncertain of local rules and practices, inarticulate in the new language. Nevertheless, as Boym points out, "to confront the unknown, particular and unpredictable, one had to risk embarrassment, the loss of mastery and composure" (Boym, 2001: 354). By embracing the foreign, we instantly become a foreigner; and naturally stumble on the emotion of shame. This is the price people pay for expanding the limits of their original world. For those already imprinted with toxic shame from their pre-displacement past, that price can be extremely high, even unaffordable in some rare cases.

Authors who have written extensively about shame (Goldberg, 1991; Burgo, 2018) point out the peculiar irony of this human emotion—it is embarrassing to feel shame, and we tend to avoid naming it, often replacing the straightforward "shame" by a milder, less threatening word. When I first name as "shame" what my clients describe as "feeling bad", their initial reaction is to back-up, minimise or deny it: "Shame is maybe a little strong. It was just embarrassing". This confirms Burgo's observation: "When shame walks into my consulting room, it nearly always shows up in disguise: to shield themselves from their pain, these clients have masked the shame they feel, hiding it from themselves and from other people" (Burgo, 2018: 16). But when a therapist recognises the shame lurking behind the mask, it often leads to a deeper and better therapy. As Elisabeth Howell insists, "one of the psychotherapist's important tasks: that of de-shaming shame" (Howell in Epstein, 2021).

With displaced clients, shame cannot and should not be kept out of the room, be it a physical or virtual therapy room. Older emigrants or freshly arrived expats may step into a therapist's office bringing with them a whole array of shame-provoking experiences. There is a risk for any therapist, especially if she has remained in one place for long enough, of slipping into the expert's role. It is a comfortable one, mostly aligned with our clients' expectations. But wearing an expert mask can undermine the impact of our work as it creates a chasm, which may only reinforce client's alienation: if we are experts, they are inept, goes the thought. Luckily, there is no way for a cross-cultural therapist, no matter how experienced or good willed, to avoid clumsy culture-related mistakes. Using them as opportunities to learn more about a client's culture and better understand their experience can lead to a better therapy. After all, any such therapist is skating on thin ice—constantly unsteady on the slippery surface, losing her footing, and then catching herself, committed to repair any cultural missteps.

Therapy with multilingual displaced couples offers some particularly fascinating opportunities for such high-risk/high-benefit therapeutic interventions. When I met with Claudia and Hassan for the first time in person, it was during Ramadan. They lived in Dubai (Claudia was Italian, Hassan was from Afghanistan), and we had been meeting online until their Paris trip. It was particularly hot, that summer's day. Like most old Parisian buildings my office does not have air conditioning. As they settled into their chairs, I poured them some fresh water. "No, thank you, we are fasting", Hassan responded with a slightly indulgent half-smile, as he pushed his glass away. I felt stupid for a second: how could I forget about Ramadan, such an important time in their religious tradition? Instead of masking my embarrassment and moving on, I recognised my misstep and used it as an opportunity to inquire further. Was Claudia fasting too? I knew from our previous sessions that their cultural and religious differences (she came from a stern Catholic background) were causing them both numerous concerns. Indeed, Claudia had been fasting, and this was the first time she felt that she was fasting for her own good, not just to please her partner. This brought us to discuss their progress towards a decision to build a life together. My initial clumsiness highlighted the fact that, just like Claudia, I was not raised in the religion that was now dominant for this couple—they were both practising Islam. My initial clumsiness helped Claudia to connect with her feeling of not being a good enough Muslim. By recognising my misstep and not letting it turn into a separation wall, we were able to model a possibility for closeness despite the deep differences in their cultural and religious backgrounds.

For those dealing with displacement, shame pops up in the most unexpected places. There may be a natural temptation for therapists to use their empathy to help their clients avoid shame. Such collusion with a client's avoidance or denial is unhelpful or even, at worse, harmful. Acknowledging the shame triggered in the "here-and-now" of the session is the best way of helping clients out of their lonely shame-filled place. When a client stumbles onto shame, his therapist ought to be there, with her displacement rabbit ears out, ready to catch the opportunity to address some of these painful and often unexpressed feelings.

My client Citra is a young Indonesian woman and now an American academic. During an early session she reported being terribly upset after a karaoke night with friends that had just taken place. She had been living in the USA for a decade and was married to an American. She had attended international schools for all of her childhood. She was truly bilingual. Unpacking the experience for me in the session, she was still visibly upset. Tears in her eyes, she said: "I felt completely alien and out of place". She was a skilful singer and a music theory scholar, but what she had expected to be an enjoyable evening soon turned into "torture". She knew the tunes and most of the lyrics, but these pop songs were not the ones she had grown up with. Hearing others sing joyfully, she felt lonely, and painfully missed her old friends and her four sisters. This activity, for her American friends something of a communion, was for her about exclusion. Karaoke is all about self-exposure to shame in a regulated safe environment, and for Citra, because of her history of displacement, that space felt anything but safe. Talking about that evening opened another issue in her displacement's Pandora's box: "And some people even sung out of tune!" she added bitterly. Their lack of shame made her angry as she, a trained musician, was sitting there mute and humiliated. "Something seemed wrong with them … Are they even human?" she wondered jokingly but with tears of anger. Her words seemed harsh but reflected the emotional experience that had crystallised in her during that karaoke evening—she felt alien and un-human. Behind her well-adjusted, well-educated, and perfectly articulate façade, she kept feeling inadequate.

Later, reflecting on that karaoke night, she said that sharing her humiliation with me and sitting with her anger and her sense of shame during that session had somehow made a difference. "Nobody ever gets this", she often commented when we spoke openly about the chasm between her well-adjusted appearance of "a successful emigrant", and her constant deep sense of being out of place. Citra's feeling of being "an outsider and a fraud" is familiar to many apparently successful and otherwise thriving emigrants.

Shame and the decision to leave

The experience of not fitting in, not belonging to their original environment, and a more general feeling of being out-of-place, are reported by several emigrant writers. The opening paragraph to Edward Said's memoir is a striking example:

> All families invent their parents and children, give each of them a story, a character, fate, and even a language. There was always something wrong with how I was invented and meant to fit in with the world of my parents and four sisters. Whether this was because I constantly misread my part or because of some deep flaw in my being I could not tell for most of my early life. Sometimes I was intransigent and proud of it. At other times I seemed to myself to be neatly devoid of any character at all, timid, uncertain, without will. Yet the over-riding sensation I had was of always being out of place.
>
> (Said, 1999: 3)

His reported feeling of being deeply flawed, constantly uncertain, and confused about his own worth are all indicators of various degrees of shame, an emotional palette that is familiar to many displaced clients.

Burgo insists that:

> Unreciprocated affection or interest will always stir emotions from the shame family. As part of our genetic inheritance, we want to connect with a loved one who will love us in return; when our longing is disappointed, when we fail to connect, we inevitably experience shame, however we name the feeling.
>
> (Burgo, 2018: 35)

This interpersonal perspective on shame is deeply rooted in Bowlby's recognition of the fact that secure relationships are the bedrock of affect regulation. As Epstein sums up: "Shame seems to emerge as a consequence of neglect, alongside criticising and humiliating caregiving and other attachment related traumas" (Epstein in Epstein, 2021).

Many emigrant clients present an insecure attachment to their original place. A motherland that does not return our affection is like a parent that fails to meet our expectations of unconditional love. Both of these unfortunate early circumstances may result in a feeling that something is deeply wrong with us. It is not possible to change the family where one was born, but one can always change countries, expatriate oneself to somewhere else. Wishing "to have the ground open and swallow you up" is the most natural response to shame (Alonso & Rutan, 1988), and leaving is often the most efficient way of enacting this disappearance. A decision to leave can often be unconsciously driven by the need to avoid the shame from a discordance between who we are and who we are expected to be in our original environment. In many cases, the choice to leave home is the best survival strategy.

An extreme example is for queer individuals in countries that reject and punish homosexuality: they can only flee if they want to freely live their lives in the way that feels right to them.

Many emigrants mention "the call" when reflecting on their decision to leave their home country (Madison, 2011). "I simply had to go", some of my clients explain when we discuss their original move. The feeling of unfitness was not verbalised at the time of departure; its processing can only be done later, when they are safe enough in a new place and can afford to look back. Displacement-sensitive therapy should offer an opportunity for such a processing to take place.

Re-experiencing shame in displacement

One of the most powerful sources of shame is the painful awareness of being different from others who reject us based on this divergence. "Different" is dangerously close to "inferior" or "faulty". This feeling is an intrinsic part of the emotional experience associated with displacement. Children who grow up in emigrant families, with parents who do not look or sound like most other parents, are exposed early to the experience of self-as-different. They may end up with internalised shame. In her recent book, *Weird* (Khazan, 2020), Olga Khazan tells stories of people who felt like outsiders, "too weird to fit in", alongside her own experience of growing up in a Russian emigrant family in Texas. The title of her book sums up such childhood experience. Weirdness means alienation, loneliness, shame.

Recently emigrated adults experience a similar estrangement that often leaves them speechless and confused, and their adult self-confidence threatened. In the early stages of displacement emigrants constantly face situations in which they commit missteps, misunderstanding the local language or local rules. Feeling like a fool becomes an emotional background, feeding self-loathing thoughts and self-deprecating language. This internal experience can turn the most outgoing individual into an insecure, awkward loner, threatening his social integration in the new place. In 1921, the young Nabokov shared with his fellow emigrants in Berlin his impressions about Cambridge.

> There is no shortage of these rules, and a newcomer will inevitably put his foot in it from time to time. If a wild foreigner nonetheless behaves his own way, at first people will marvel at him—what an odd-ball, a barbarian—but then they will start to avoid him, not to recognize him on the streets. Sometimes, it is true, a kind soul with a weakness for exotic creatures will come your way, but he will only approach you in a secluded spot, fearfully looking around him, and, having satisfied his curiosity, will disappear forever. This is why, at times, your heart swells with sorrow, feeling that it won't find a true friend here.
>
> (Nabokov, 2019: 5)

This essay is filled with nostalgic feelings about the warmth of a home that does not exist anymore, and with the sense of discomfiture that one is exposed to in a foreign place.

Displacement is also about not fitting in, sticking out in a rather unpleasant or embarrassing way. No matter how long ago we moved to the new place, displacement-related shame is not far away. To misunderstand a joke, to mispronounce a word, to make a childish misstep, are all part of any emigrant's daily life. The American writer David Sedaris describes his experience of life in France as an endless series of more or less mild humiliations (Sedaris, 2001). Even experienced emigrants, who tend to think that the shameful struggles of the first days are behind them, can stumble on this sinking feeling again, overwhelmed by the desire to disappear. Triggers can vary: a new job, a new fitness club, or a new flat to share with somebody not yet well known and trusted. Situations where one joins an established group of people are the perfect setting for our older shame story to be re-enacted.

In my practice, I witness heart-breaking examples of how a displaced person can be caught up in the familiar struggle of alienation. For Hao, a young Asian gay man, settling in Paris had been a dream come true, achieved through hard work. In his country of origin he had experienced a considerable amount of stigma and rejection because of his homosexuality. At last, he would be desirable to a small community of gay friends. He was self-confident, popular, and felt "cute". On his arrival in France, he was elated by the new experience of being more accepted as a gay man, but then as he started dating online, a new reality descended on him like a cold shower: in the local community of gay men, to which he craved to belong, he was undesirable. Asian men were not in demand. Back home Hao had felt rejected by the wider community, but desired by a smaller LGBT sub-group. At least he belonged there. Here in Paris, he was more generally welcomed as a gay man, but rejected on racial grounds by the particular community he longed to join. The cruel irony of this situation was the topic of many sessions with Hao. His shame was an intrinsic part of this period of his new life in France. As we stumbled through his self-consciousness, his tendency to withdraw and self-isolate, or his fear of being ugly, Hao reckoned how much he had internalised the very racism he was experiencing. Was his own desire shaped by this internalised prejudice? The tricky question about the nature and origins of our desire was recently explored by Shrinivasan, a British philosopher, who notes that racism and heteronormativity extend into the intimate sphere of romance and sex, protected by the logic of the personal preference (Shrinivasan, 2021).

"Are you attracted to Asian men?" I asked at one point as I noticed his tendency to obsess over some unreachable French men. "I am … some of them are very cute", he responded. As he explored these slightly less obvious routes, he started to recover from the shame he was initially made to feel: "If I find them cute, it means others may find me cute as well", he reasoned. It took him a while to connect with other gay men of Asian origin, and finally develop meaningful bonds in Paris. It was central to the therapeutic work with Hao that he recognise how his pre-existing shame about being gay was being amplified by his experience of displacement and discrimination in the community he wanted to belong to.

Home may be left behind in the hope of escaping shame, but displacement then creates a context in which our worst fears about being faulty are confirmed. This can be partly explained by Freud's concept of repetition compulsion (Freud, 1961). That being said, a strong desire to change is a great drive—towards a better life in a new place, or to become a better person. As a Japanese proverb sums it up: "When travelling, shame should be thrown away". Displacement has a freeing potential. In moving online one may feel liberated from some social norms and personal rules; in moving to a different culture, such a disinhibition effect exists as well. Some inexperienced travellers will start getting drunk as soon as they board the plane to their holiday destination, some usually shy people will sing karaoke in a foreign bar, and others will engage in rule-breaking activities that would be judged shameful and out of order in their home country.

An interesting example of such a benefit of emigration comes from Julia Beltsiou, an American psychoanalyst who grew up in a Greek family who emigrated to Germany. Due to that background, some people had limited expectations for her and did not seem to value who she was. After emigrating to the US as a young adult, she was finally able to develop her professional identity in this new world, in which her European background typically carried cachet, not stigma (Beltsiou, 2015).

With the 2022 invasion of Ukraine ordered by Putin, I was brutally reminded of how a country left behind almost three decades before can catch up with you and create an abyss of shame. Russians from inside and outside Russia will have to carry the shame for this war for years to come. The days that followed the beginning of the war sent shockwaves through my life and my therapy practice. Most of my Russian clients were in disbelief. Some of them attended street protests, some just sat in their kitchen all night until the grey Moscow morning, drinking and talking with their friends, sharing their confusion, their fear, but mostly trying to cope with their shame. With their lives wrecked by the war initiated by their motherland, Russians were wrestling with the immediate questions of survival, not only pragmatic but also psychological. They found different ways to cope with their humiliation. Some left Russia in a desperate attempt to escape this feeling, as well as a regime once more becoming totalitarian. Other nationalities were affected as well. Of course, Ukrainians, attacked in their flesh and forced by the situation to run for their life or fight. But other Europeans who had become used to peace on their continent were also affected.

Therapists dealing with Russians all over the world will have to listen to this shame, trying to learn from it to help their client. The only way we, human therapists and human clients, can make this war a little less senseless is to let it impact us, push us to change something deeper in the way we live our lives, in the way we make our choices, or handle the responsibility, or hand over power to others.

Other wars have resulted in collective shame. In the aftermath of the Second World War, Germans had to process their shame about the Shoah. In 1940s mainland Europe the—mostly Jewish—psychoanalysts had been forced to flee, and the talking therapy was not widely available. Today technology has broadened the outreach of talking therapies, making them available to displaced populations. Therapy can play an important role in processing such a shame, one individual at a time.

Loneliness and shame

Loneliness is a common condition associated with a variety of negative health effects (Hawkley & Cacioppo, 2010; Masi et al., 2011). It is associated with poor sleep, high blood pressure, cognitive and immunity decline, depression, and early death (Cacioppo et al., 2014). Whilst it is a chronic state for approximately 15–30% of the general population (Reis, 2001; Hawkley & Cacioppo, 2010), with the loss of social connections and the language barrier, displaced individuals take loneliness experience to a different level. It can easily turn into alienation for many expatriates who struggle to make connections in their new place, for various reasons such as natural shyness or a pre-existent social anxiety. Many of these generally recently expatriated clients come to therapy feeling that something is deeply wrong with them. When Cooper (Mearns & Cooper, 2018) describes this facet of extreme isolation, he does not go as far as naming it shame, but the character he chooses to illustrate this desperate loneliness is a blood-sucking monster, a vampire:

> And, as with Nosferatu, some clients may feel that it is something intrinsic to them—something hidden and unspoken—that destroys any chance of connection. They, they sense, are the infection that kills the thing they most desperately yearn for: no wonder it is the most abject pain.
>
> (Mearns & Cooper, 2018: 23)

This monstrous quality that one attributes oneself when feeling rejected is what causes shame, the most painful self-conscious human emotion. Many expatriate clients, beyond the loneliness that goes with their displaced condition, end up fearing that there is something wrong about them that makes them unlikable to others. After all, from unlike to unlikable there is only a short emotional step. This chronic loneliness is too embarrassing a burden to be shared, especially when there are no close friends or family members around anyway. This emotional reality remains unspoken, perpetuating the vicious cycle of "loneliness-shame-loneliness".

Even the most well-adapted emigrants, who seem to be beyond these earlier struggles, occasionally slip back into this painful emotional place. When they bring these disorientating experiences to therapy, it opens another opportunity to work through a shame that is reinforced by displacement.

Mei for instance, a young client of mine, came upset and angry to one of our sessions. A Vietnamese emigrant to the United States, despite her successful career, solid friendships, and happy marriage to an American woman, she often felt lonely and misunderstood. For Mei, this feeling of sinking loneliness, often associated with sudden nostalgia for her native place, was a familiar emotional place. But this time it hit her hard and seemed to come out of nowhere. The fact that she felt this way again, after all these years of emigration, was discouraging. It stirred up more shame. As we started unpacking what had provoked this emotional crisis, Mei talked about the post-pandemic remote job she had started recently. With her new colleagues all located in different states, she felt "cut-off", disconnected. "And even in my therapy group, I felt like an alien again", she told me with tears in her voice. This online group had been an important source of support and stability in her life for the past few years. When she shared how lonely she was feeling in front of her screen, her group therapist acknowledged her loneliness and summarised her relational geography: "Your brother is in Canada, your sister in England, your parents in Vietnam, your therapist in Paris, and I am in Berlin". And even though he was stating the obvious, his words produced another wave of shame in Mei. "Why am I constantly putting myself through this? It is stupid". Answering this question was an important task in Mei's therapy. This time again, we had to revisit all the reasons why she had decided to leave her country behind. She had always felt out of place in her traditional family, which rejected her homosexuality and expected her to marry a well-to-do man and take care of her aging parents. These waves of loneliness mixed with shame were familiar blocks she would stumble on every so often. With time, Mei developed ways of coping with the feelings that would earlier overwhelm her. Instead of retreating into comforting consumer goods from her native place—from television to food—she turned to her wife for support, and they went on long hikes, to reconnect with the nature and with the beauty of their new place. She also talked more openly in her therapy group about her alienation. It opened a path to other members who recognised her emotional experience and resonated with it in their own ways. These were like "mild colds" that she had to live with, she once commented, and the more we talked about them in therapy, the more she was able to accept this fact of her displaced life. She eventually developed a resilience that helped her to get over these periods of loneliness and reach out to her significant others, strengthening their intimate bonds.

In her book *The Lonely Cities* Olivia Laing (2016), a British writer freshly arrived in New York, explores the particular feeling of being lonely in a big crowded foreign city:

> Though I made myself venture each day for a walk by the river, I was spending increasing hours sprawled on the orange couch in my apartment, my laptop propped against my legs, sometimes writing emails or talking on Skype, but more often just prowling the endless chambers of the internet, watching music videos from my teenage years or spending eye-damaging hours scrolling through racks of clothes on the websites of labels I couldn't afford. I would have been lost without my MacBook, which promised to bring connection and, in the meantime, filled and filled the vacuum left by love.
>
> (Laing, 2016: 65)

Ironically, Laing's book, dedicated to loneliness, is really about shame. The experience of isolation and lack of belonging naturally results in the feeling of shame. She mentions Andy Warhol's experience of loneliness and his peculiar relationship to then developing technology, which "liberated him from the burden of needing other people" (Laing, 2016: 62). When somebody so accustomed to seeking in technology a relief from acute loneliness and shame turns to online therapy, it may offer them what it usually does not—an unexpected gift of connectedness and intimacy.

The existential solitude—the inescapable fact that we will all face our death alone—usually successfully suppressed for an optimal functioning in daily life— pops up to the surface when an emigrant's home country is going through a major crisis, such as a war, a revolution, or a natural disaster. For example, Russian emigrants have been experiencing an alienation from their own country after it invaded Ukraine. One of my clients, Irina, who had been living in Europe for two decades, and had a successful career in academia, was slowly falling into depression. Usually an extremely sociable person, she was slowly sinking into a kind of solitude, exacerbated by the feeling of shame about what her original country was becoming. Her loving partner and her close friends, all unfamiliar with her Russian world, were unable to understand the level at which this war was impacting her psychologically. She would spend long hours watching the opposition journalists and thinkers. Connecting with these people, who were also deeply impacted by the events, seemed to alleviate her loneliness. As a result, she was going through the motions of her day, detached, sleep-deprived, anxious, and increasingly lonely. She was trying to understand the history of her complex country, processing the horror of the war, feeling the unavoidable guilt and shame, all in isolation. "I just feel so alone and guilty", she would say with tears in her eyes. Her obsessive consumption of the grim news and her detachment from her local friends and her partner were perpetuating the loneliness-shame-loneliness cycle. On the other side of the screen, I was resonating with her struggle. The "Russian shame" that we both carried was necessary to remain decent human beings. The space that we had co-created during several years of therapy work was allowing us both to feel less alienated. In this case, the shared cultural background was particularly beneficial, as the kinship and the parallel process naturally facilitated working at relational depth.

The healing of shame requires the opportunity for intimacy. Since we live in community with others and generally achieve our moments of greatest satisfaction in other people's company, the highest aim of humanity, as Aristotle indicated long ago, may lie within genuine friendship. People who lack trusted friendships are vulnerable to the devastating effects of shame (Goldberg, 1991). Displaced individuals do not have immediate access to their family members and friends; they learn about their friends' important milestones—from a new job to the birth of a child—from their social media accounts. The nature of these online realms is such that the information they receive comes with a biased filter. The lives of their distant friends appear surreal, removed from the warm and imperfect reality made clear with physical proximity. This creates an alienating effect: in comparison their unsettled upside-down lives are the exact opposite of the digital constructs that look perfectly arranged from a distance, on a phone screen.

"My friends are so photogenic!" Kirsty exclaimed in total disarray. Following her recent move from Edinburgh to Paris, her life felt like "a total mess". As she was trying hard to put in place the pieces of her existence, long ago disrupted by drinking, she managed to quit alcohol but developed an addiction to social media. She would scroll endlessly, desperately looking for some connection, but end up even more convinced of her incompetence as a human being.

Any deeply rooted shame goes back to a relationship—with a caregiver, a parent, a teacher, or a community. This is why the therapeutic alliance is so central in the treatment. As Lee and Wheeler insist,

> Even when shame is experienced in solitude, it is experienced relationally with reference to the feelings, desires, standards, rules, principles, limitations, and so on of a larger relational context—friend, lover, colleague, spouse, family, community, ethnic or social or professional group, social class, country and so on.
>
> (Lee & Wheeler, 2003: 7)

In his recent volume, Epstein stresses the unique value of meaningful human contact for any form of repair to take place (Epstein, 2021). "Until or as long as there is no parent to make reparation self-generated shame is irresolvable" and healing can only take place through "acceptance and physical contact from primary attachment or powerful social figures" (Solomon in Epstein, 2021). Shame experienced in displacement is precisely associated with a difficulty to maintain stable social bonds and therefore isolation, thus making it even harder to repair. A meaningful therapeutic relationship is a powerful tool here, for modelling an honest relationship in which both therapist and their client can display vulnerability that does not result in additional shame.

Potential of group therapy for displaced clients

As the earlier example of Mei suggests, displaced clients can greatly benefit from group therapy. Whilst research confirms that the group therapy modality is at least as effective as individual therapy (Burlingame et al., 2003; McRoberts et al., 1998), its application to displaced groups is under-researched, understated, and the displacement-focused approach in group therapy seems to be mainly missing from the field of group therapy. Specific benefits of interpersonal group therapy may be superior to individual therapy in aspects that pertain to its social quality: a group offers members a social microcosm with its potential for social support and relational learning—both elements that are central for better coping with the displaced condition.

Even if not broadly discussed until relatively recently (Weber & Gans, 2003), shame is central to the group therapy process. Shame is often experienced in secrecy and in isolation, and clients are reluctant to bring it up in therapy for fear of generating even greater shame (Alonso & Rutan, 1988). In contrast to clients in individual therapy, therapy group members get an opportunity to experiment with opening up about their feelings of inadequacy in front of other displaced individuals who may resonate with their shame with the most healing "same here" response. If any group setting offers specific advantages for the treatment of shame (Alonso & Rutan, 1988), groups for displaced clients become a perfect stage for resolving shame-related issues. In such groups, shame-related material will take an even more prominent place.

Similarly, whilst the therapist's shame is an unavoidable element of any group process, when the therapist is displaced herself and facilitates the group in her second language, her shame naturally takes centre-stage. Such a set-up offers endless opportunities for modelling facing shame and, whilst avoiding its debilitating grip, using its power for one's progress. Whilst shame often sets people apart, once acknowledged, the poison turns into a cure, bringing group members closer, showing them the path for opening up for more intimacy and closeness in their outside relationships.

Leszcz and Yalom (2005) propose a three-step path for designing a specialised therapy group based on their process-oriented existential model, which includes assessment of the clinical situation; formulation of appropriate clinical goals; and modification of the traditional techniques to the new clinical situation and the relevant clinical goals (Leszcz and Yalom, 2005). With good "displacement rabbit ears" on, an efficient interpersonal displacement-oriented group can be formed in any clinical setting, from an institution or a smaller clinic to a private practice.

One of the widely recognised therapeutic factors of psychodynamic group treatment is cohesiveness (Bernard et al., 2008), or that feeling of trust and togetherness that develops between the members of a mature well-functioning group (Leszcz and Yalom (2005). The emotional experience of togetherness that is naturally sought by humans is of further vital importance for those wrestling with displacement. In the initial stages of expatriation, when social links are fragile or non-existent, and shame is constantly around the corner, joining a local in-person group can accelerate the development of links with the place and its people. Emigrants are often suspended between places; a group will bring them an opportunity to belong. Therapy groups with a particular focus on displacement or cross-cultural groups can be of particular value to displaced clients. There, the universality of the emotional experience is enhanced by the fact that members feel united in their all too human struggle, no matter the differences in cultural, social, or linguistic backgrounds. For emigrants, often alienated from their new reality (and in many cases from their original realities as well), this existential aspect of the group can become a powerful ally on the path to change. A group mixing locals and expats offers valuable therapeutic opportunities for the emigrant members: in that safe space, displacement issues will not be the only focus and they can work on inter-personal dynamics, and also opportunities will appear to address cross-cultural tensions.

The Covid-19 pandemic accelerated groups' transition to the online world. Research confirms that the online group can be as effective as the traditional formats, and even more effective for some individuals (Weinberg & Rolnick, 2020). Displaced clients probably represent one of the groups that may use this space to their benefit. Like Mei, many of them crave validation of their struggle; this validation can come from both sides of the dividing barrier that is omnipresent in their existence—from others who experience some form of dislocation or from the "locals".

Shame of the privileged

Shame about their privileged position compared to other displaced groups, such as refugees of war or other life-threatening disasters, is a common theme amongst expatriates who relocated for professional reasons. The word "expat" itself is tainted with disdain. Many therapists who simultaneously work with other, less privileged groups, can unconsciously collude in this self-loathing. This is where working at the relational depth and at the existential level is necessary to avoid slipping into the trap of reducing the person to their displacement status.

"This is another first-world problem". Marc often started our sessions with this statement. We had been working together for a few months, and his shame was never far away from our virtual therapy room. When he first reached out to me, Marc described himself as a "trailing spouse". He was that indeed, but he was also a committed artist, a painter who was making money from his art, although with no regularity. His wife had a steady job in a big American corporation that Marc mockingly called an "expat bonanza". He was excellent at using a self-deprecating kind of humour, while minimising his own struggle. Before marrying, he had spent years surviving with low-paying jobs, so as to continue painting. Now that his wife's career in finance was booming, Marc could relax into his newly found financial security. But he was not particularly good at relaxing. He grew increasingly angry with his wife for making so much money. As the cracks in their relationship developed, Marc retreated into his studio more and more often, drinking more and more. As I listened to Marc's self-loathing, I was also aware that his wife's income probably paid for his therapy. Listening to his shame led us to appreciate how important it was for Marc to use their wealth in a meaningful manner. As they did not have children, they started exploring adoption. This was a long and emotionally challenging journey, but when they finally decided to adopt two brothers, one of whom had a disability, their relationship was in a much better place, and Marc felt that he was doing something to make this world a better place, at least for two human beings.

Shame and the choice of online therapy

Apart from practicality, relatability, and mobility, which we have discussed as key reasons driving clients to online therapy, some deeper psychological factors can have an impact. Clients may wrestle with their own internalised shame. In some cultural contexts, it can be amplified by the stigma attached to mental health struggle, which can make reaching out for support nearly impossible. When the potential support is just one click away, and there is no physical exposure involved, the step is easier to take. The disinhibiting effect of the online setting, acknowledged in literature (Suler, 2004), opens a gateway to treatment that would otherwise be avoided because of shame. In addition, as mentioned in previous chapters, the online setting broadens clients' choice, connecting them with potential therapists from different racial, cultural, and social backgrounds. They may also use their second language, to transgress the shame that inhibits them when using their mother tongue.

In his memoir, Irvin Yalom mentions his first experience of therapy via Skype. His client lived in an extremely isolated place, to which she had deliberately chosen to emigrate after a painful rupture: "She felt so raw that, if she lived nearby, I am certain she would not have been willing to meet me, or any other therapist, face-to-face in an office" (Yalom 2017: 306). Rejection by a loved one naturally triggers what Burgo calls "shame as unrequited love" (Burgo, 2018). Instead of withdrawing further from human connection and intimacy—perceived as an "antidote" to shame, reaching out to a less threatening remote therapist can break the vicious cycle in which many get stuck for years.

Clients who chose online therapy can often use its idiosyncratic properties creatively. Those who struggle with shame may keep their camera switched off, or, when encouraged to show their face, play with the lighting and positioning in order to avoid being fully seen. Such "hiding" tactics are a great indicator of the presence of shame. One of my online clients, Tim, a policeman from Ireland, had always suffered from shyness. When I first met with him online, I could barely see him. His pale face was floating in the dark window of my screen, and his glasses reflected the bluish light from his screen—my own face, I guessed, as in Velazquez's mirror. Tim had grown up in a narcissistic family, and naturally ended up with a deep sense of not being good enough. His father openly referred to him as a "failure" and the "biggest disappointment of his life". Tim had previously sought traditional face-to-face therapy whilst struggling with drinking and depression, but had not trusted the therapist enough to open up and expose himself, as he feared being judged. He felt that his parents never really saw him. Any close emotional or physical contact seemed unbearable for him. Bound by shame, he had retreated into loneliness, his only safe space. In the early sessions, Tim would talk "at me" and seek little input. His camera would focus on a far corner of the room, avoiding his face, re-enacting his desire to flee. As we discussed the reasons for his choice of online therapy with a Russian therapist based in Paris, Tim recognised that he felt safer that way. The physical distance between us and the difference in our cultural backgrounds made him feel more relaxed. He could control and regulate his level of exposure.

Therapists who opt for practising online instead of in-person may be driven by practical reasons: the flexibility it allows, saving the rent of an office space, the expansion of their practice to broader and more diverse populations. Others will just find working online easier or more comfortable, simply preferring the technology-mediated or slightly "indirect" way of communicating with their clients. A blended practice is nevertheless attractive to many (including myself), who seek a balance of online and in-person interactions. In any case, it is fruitful to explore the deep motivations for the choice of the online setting by a therapist. The very shame that can sometimes drive our clients' inclination to the online setting can also apply to us, leading us to unconsciously seek a potential for concealment in the online setting. Such collusion with shame-ridden clients' avoidance of intimacy can undermine the therapeutic relationship that should offer them a safe ground for experimenting with closeness and connection.

With Covid-19's social interaction restrictions and lockdowns, most therapists were forced to transition abruptly to digital technology in order to keep supporting their clients. Many embraced the unfamiliar space and adapted their practice accordingly. This transition exposed even the most settled practitioners to the unsettling reality of displacement. Indeed, this is exactly what it is all about—unsettling oneself, meeting the different and the unfamiliar, despite the discomfort and shame that come with such dislocation and expansion.

Recognising defence strategies

On the path to a better understanding of the role shame plays in our client's displacement journey, it is crucial to examine the array of strategies humans use to defend against this painful emotion. Based on the earlier psychodynamic understanding of shame defences, Burgo identifies three primary strategies that people use to defend against shame: avoidance, denial, and control (Burgo, 2018). All three are common masks that displaced clients wear when entering a physical or virtual therapy room. Learning how to recognise these defences and look beyond them enables us to reach deeper layers of any individual's displacement experience.

Avoidance is probably the most common protective shield that displaced clients will use when reaching out to a therapist. As mentioned earlier, individuals who opt for online therapy are often good at hiding. They may also be skilled at avoiding shame, or rather avoiding situations that would expose them to that unbearable emotion to which dislocation has made them more sensitive.

Becca, one of my emigrant clients, had been living in Paris for nearly a decade. Her home was a few metro stations from my office, but she preferred meeting online, "at least initially". It took her months of weekly online meetings before she felt able to make the short journey to my therapy room. Her initial complaint was her writing block. Inspired by a tradition for American writers to spend time in Paris, she had quit her publishing job in

New York and moved to Paris with a project to write a book. Almost ten years later, her book was still unwritten. Becca was making a living as an English teacher. Despite her frequent accounts of social outings and drinks, I was struck by how secluded and lonely her life was. Her small flat was "a mess", and she felt "too embarrassed" to invite anybody in. Consequently, she was not invited anywhere either, and her relationships never crossed the invisible threshold into a real friendship. She was intimate with no one. After years in Paris all her acquaintances were expats like herself. They all spoke English. As Becca admitted that she had not been able to learn French during those 10 years, her tone was full of self-mockery, barely concealing her embarrassment. In her stubborn refusal to engage with the French or use her timid language skills for anything beyond ordering drinks, Becca avoided what she saw as worse—being publicly shamed about her accent, her mistakes, or her social clumsiness. As Becca finally came to my office, I could see that her refusal to take risks extended to her clothing. She would later confirm that she shopped for clothes exclusively online. In local shops—that attract visitors from all over the world—"nothing would fit me"; she was "too fat for the Parisians", and the shop assistants scared her with their slim frames, condescending looks, and speedy French language.

Our main challenge in Becca's therapy was to help her recognise that she felt inadequate. This feeling, which she initially was able to relate to her dislocation, was of an older, developmental nature. The feeling of not being good enough or not fitting in, made worse by her displacement, was a familiar feature of her American childhood. She grew up with two successful journalists as parents. They travelled, got involved in important and exciting matters, were opinionated. She was often left with her grandmother, who was cold and uninterested in her. Becca felt like a nuisance, lonely, and unfit for her parents' beautiful and exciting world. On rare occasions, when as an awkward teenager she was invited to join her parents at a party, everybody around her seemed elegant, comfortable, and articulate. Everybody except for her. Her experience in Paris seemed like an endless repetition of these nightmarish gatherings in her parents' elegant Manhattan flat.

Recognising her shame and tracing it back to her childhood helped Becca to make some changes to her life. She managed to remove the stumbling blocks—her drinking and her lack of discipline—to finally advance towards a more meaningful existence.

Just like Becca, many expatriates display a similar refusal to engage with their new environment. They end up in a bubble of isolation or shallow relationships, "socialising" in groups of fellow expatriates, promoted as communities for bonding and connection, but offering little more than fleeting interactions for their unsettled members. With their hopes for an accepting community shattered, they stumble on the familiar shame "Everybody in this group has more friends and speaks the language better. What is wrong with me?"

Arrogance, haughtiness, disdain for the accomplishments of others, jea-
lousy, envy, and greed are only a few of the defensive attitudes and emotions that characterize those for whom self-awareness is more painful
than pleasant. For those whose lives are ruled by shame, anything that
can reduce the self-esteem of others can assist them to feel better about
themselves in relation to those others.

(Nathanson, 1992: 87)

In displacement, "others" are often represented by "the locals", who naturally
have everything the newly displaced person does not—language skills, family,
friends, and a secure roof over their heads. They become a perfect object for
these defensive strategies. It is not unusual for some of my expatriate clients
to express a deep and disturbing envy of the locals.

Sarah, a young British woman who came as an au-pair to Paris with hopes
of creating a brighter future for herself, experienced a devastating outburst of
envy towards her hosts. She had grown up in a reduced family consisting of
her mother and herself. Her mother always held several jobs, as an office
cleaner or a cashier in a supermarket. She would always come home exhausted. Sarah felt deeply unhappy in their small town where they had no other
family. Her mother had never returned to Ireland, which she had left when
pregnant with Sarah. In Paris, Sarah found herself in a well-off family. The
children she was taking care of had everything she had not had—their parents' attention, expensive clothes and toys, a big family that would often
gather for elaborate meals on the terrace with a view of the Eiffel Tower.
Sarah's envy made her despise herself. "I am a terrible person", she concluded
disconsolately. She was terrified by her own destructive thoughts, and by her
nightmares in which she would find one of the children dead, or by magic
become one of them. Sarah actually loved spending time with them. She was
enjoying the trust their parents granted her, but the more trust and affection
for her they showed, the more she retreated into shame, knowing that as "a
terrible person" she did not deserve any of it. Inquiring into these feelings, we
stumbled onto her early history. Her mother had to flee her native place
because of her unexpected pregnancy at the age of eighteen, a source of
shame for her family. Somehow Sarah had always known that she was the
cause of her mother's loneliness and despair—she was the shameful child. She
felt jealous of other kids who had fathers, grandparents, and proper family
gatherings. Her decision to become an au-pair was an obvious attempt to get
what she had not had. Her mother did not try to conceal her scorn about
"being left behind", shaming her for that.

Now, in Paris, she felt all these feelings all over again—she was the odd
one, unfit for this sophisticated life, and painfully aware of her inadequacy.
Only when Sarah recognised that the envy that she was feeling was a defensive reaction to shame, could she work it through and talk more honestly with
her hosts. With time, she grew more and more attached to the children, learnt

French, and managed to save some money that her "French parents" helped her invest in further education. They agreed that once their youngest was ready for school, she would leave them to enrol in a prestigious institution for training professional nannies. Once recognised and faced, shame had given Sarah the emotional strength to make better choices and advance in life with pride.

Denial is another common way of shielding from shame, and many displaced clients will make sure that nobody can guess their inner struggle, by displaying certainty and a flawless or grandiose version of themselves to the world.

When Pavel, the only child of a wealthy Russian industrial tycoon, turned twelve, his parents enrolled him in a high-end British boarding school. Now in his mid-20s, he possessed a flawless British accent and a master's degree from a prestigious American law school. He was seeking treatment because of his "problematic" relationships. In our first session, it became apparent that behind his shiny and arrogant façade, Pavel felt lonely. When I asked what other people might dislike about him, he refused to give it any thought. It was an easy guess, though. Already, during that first session with Pavel, I was feeling belittled by his dismissive tone and contemptuous gaze. My eclectic English could not compete with his perfect enunciation, and he clearly enjoyed the contrast. "Where did you say you studied?" he asked with little curiosity for an answer. Pretentiousness, arrogance, blame, and self-righteousness are all strategies for offloading unconscious shame and forcing other people to feel it. It was a major risk for Pavel to admit he did not always feel great about himself and his life; his parents—who had acquired their wealth rather unexpectedly during the chaotic economic and societal changes of the 1990s in post-Soviet Russia—had made it clear from when he was very young that he had no other option than to be perfect. Pavel was a good son. Despite his obvious lack of emotional connection to his father, he promoted him as a powerful and generous "self-made man", rejecting any of my attempts to dig deeper into their relationship. Not giving any weight to our therapeutic relationship was another way for Pavel to protect his original world and the nature of his family bonds. The early imprint of growing up in a narcissistic family had left Pavel with a sense of inner isolation and little self-worth. This deeply rooted shame had been amplified by his consecutive displacement. When boarding, he had always felt an unbridgeable chasm between himself, the child of a newly enriched, unsophisticated man, and his polished British peers from "old money" families with inherited wealth and education through several generations.

Pavel had been relocated by his American company to Paris where he had an influential position. To his bewilderment, being in Paris did not feel as "great" as he expected. His French was basic, and his polished English and his impressive resumé did not impress people who were more interested in asking him about his hobbies, his family, and his friends. His constant chasing after a perfect career did not leave much space for friendship, and he was rather uncomfortable talking about his family; he felt that nobody here could relate to their story. In Paris, Pavel felt exactly as he had felt as a teenager at the boarding school—alienated, lonely, and strangely homesick. Getting in touch with the original shame was a daunting task for him, but focusing on his current emigrant experience led us to inquire into the feelings that lay below the surface of his artificial pride. When Pavel trusted our alliance enough to be radically honest, he said that he had not done anything special to gain his place in the world—this was rather the result of his father's money, something he would be reminded about occasionally when talking with his father. Pavel felt paralysed in front of others who might discover that he was a fraud. Once he realised that his shame was preventing him from developing intimacy with anybody, he could finally reflect on the defensive strategies he put in place to keep "others" at a safe distance. At this later stage of our work, Pavel became a perfect candidate for group therapy, and joined an online group with displaced individuals like him. There, he learnt more about how he functioned with other people, and eventually started experimenting with closeness and a more honest presentation of himself. When Pavel saw that the humbler version of himself was bringing other members of the group closer, he experimented with displaying his vulnerability outside of the group.

Individuals who choose control over avoidance or denial

> try to cope with unbearable and unpredictable shame by controlling when and how they experience it. Self-pity, self-hatred, masochism, and various types of self-deprecating humor all represent strategies for submitting to shame while making it a known and predictable experience rather than a surprising one.
>
> (Burgo, 2018: 19)

Some defend against displacement-related shame by rejecting the local language, expressing contempt for everything local. Others take the opposite route—they embrace, learn, and eventually master the art of self-metamorphosis. Like chameleons, they adapt to any surroundings quickly and efficiently.

The way in which emigrants engage with the local language is often an indicator of the deeper processes that animate them. Rachel avoided a potential linguistic shame by not learning French for ten years, although she knew it would have helped her life in Paris. Pavel's impressive British accent had been a perfect shield against the possibility of feeling "inferior".

From cross-cultural to transcultural (online) practice

Since the early days of psychotherapy therapists have worked with clients from backgrounds ethnically or culturally different from their own. When these clients come to their therapist's physical office, the therapist is on her "home ground", often in her original country, whilst the client may be a foreigner, dealing with the subtleties of social interaction in an unfamiliar place. Part of the therapist's job is then to understand how cultural differences, codes, and nuances of emotional expression can impact her clients' relationships.

For therapists expanding their practice beyond the physical borders of their country, meeting with clients from elsewhere is a norm. Connecting online, from two different physical realities, they meet upon a third ground that is neutral. The cultural perspective of one does not prevail over the other. In developing a shared vocabulary through which to communicate, each one must adapt to the other to some degree. This relational stretch, the effort that each of them must make to make the connection possible and their collaboration viable, accelerates the development of a therapeutic alliance and propels therapy forward.

According to Mikhail Bakhtin, "the most intense and productive life of cultures takes place on the boundaries of its individual areas and not in places where these areas have become enclosed in their own specificity" (Bakhtin, 1986: 2). This view on intercultural relations echoes gestalt therapy's concept of the interpersonal boundary, which is where contact takes place, allowing a distinction between self and non-self. Any relationship, including the therapeutic one, happens on the margins of selves, at this invisible boundary between individuals and the cultures that they carry. The Russian-American thinker and humanist Mikhail Epstein wonders whether we can move from the model of "difference" that dominated the humanities from the 1970s to the 1990s, to a model of interference (Epstein, 2012: 59). This question is central to a cross-cultural and cross-lingual practice of psychotherapy. The interferential model no longer isolates cultures from each other but rather it opens perspectives for their self-differentiation and mutual involvement. When therapists, no matter their professional orientation, open their practice to displaced clients and those from a different culture, they respond to Bakhtin's call to foster humility and openness towards the other, rather than revel in the pride of self-identity.

"By emphasizing the life of cultures on the boundaries, we can conclude that they are inherently insufficient when isolated from one another", Epstein develops further (Epstein, 2012: 60). This dialogical approach leads us from the multicultural model of practising psychotherapy to a transcultural one, which is not based on the value of "outsidedness", but rather focuses on locating oneself in the interaction with the different "other" at the very crossroads of cultures.

Here our displacement "rabbit ears" become extremely useful again, and the online transcultural practice abounds in opportunities for using them for clients' benefit. An example of such use comes from a recent session I had with Amanda, a British expat in Italy. We were a few sessions into our work, and Amanda had only recently moved to the south of Italy, where she was now settling with her husband and their two young children. After a typical "honeymoon" period, Amanda, who had grown up in London and was a successful children's author, was now struggling to adapt to life in a small Sicilian town. She was also wrestling with learning Italian. As her camera switched on, Amanda was on her phone, making a quick apologetic gesture to me. She was trying to give her address to somebody in Italian. Probably the removal people or a craftsman, I guessed, as the chaos of boxes behind her seemed to suggest. Amanda knew I spoke Italian, and she grimaced, indicating her embarrassment. "J-o-n-e-s", she spelled her name in Italian (neither that name nor "Amanda" is my client's real name of course). Pronouncing this name would be no problem for a Briton, but quite a challenge indeed for her Sicilian interlocutor apparently! She finally hung up, sweating and red-faced: "Sorry". The slightly surreal conversation that she had me witness became a perfect opportunity to talk about her emigrant experience. Her name sounded suddenly exotic, illustrating her uncanny experience in the new place. Here in Sicily, she was an illiterate foreigner who "always got it wrong". The tension on the boundary between her and Italian culture was generating anxiety and conflict, but it was also leading to the birth of a new expanded identity—multilingual and multicultural. Now, that metamorphosis was painful, and in that precise moment, Amanda could not access the deeper meaning of her displacement. She eventually would, and she would fall in love with Sicily.

Any therapeutic relationship starts with a name. For therapists working cross-culturally, their new client's name may sound unfamiliar and difficult to pronounce. That simple situation creates a potential for embarrassment. The same goes for the client reaching out to a therapist with whom they do not share a common cultural background. Addressing this situation in the first session gives the therapeutic alliance a good start. I fondly remember one of my first clients who initially contacted me through a voicemail. I listened to her first name over and over but could not decode it. I was worried, how not to feel inadequate in such a situation? When we finally met, and her beautiful face filled my screen, I acknowledged that I had not understood her name on the voicemail. Smiling, she responded in her Scottish accent: "Nathalie"!

For emigrants, dislocation often complicates the relationship with their own name. Some will change their name to make it sound more "local", some will defiantly maintain their original names, leaving to others the task of figuring out its pronunciation. Several of my Asian clients initially introduced themselves with a Western, Christian first name, and then, after our relationship had developed, shared their original name, generally an entirely different one. This is often a marker that a new stage in the therapeutic alliance has been reached.

As a fascinating literary example, Vladimir Nabokov's exiled characters often experience various complications with their names: from not being named at all to being named wrongly. This consistent name conundrum is an illustration of their displacement-induced identity issues (Connolly in Bevan, 1990). Nabokov's particular way of distributing names to his displaced characters is far from being neutral: some of them lack a surname, others are only given a first name so that "the acquisition of a name becomes an epic accomplishment for the author-protagonist" (Kellman, 1976). This situation is shared by many emigrant writers. Edward Said carries two names associated with his two cultures and languages: "Thus it took me about fifty years to become accustomed to, or, more exactly, to feel less uncomfortable with 'Edward', a foolishly English name yoked forcibly to the unmistakably Arabic family name Said ... For years, and depending on the exact circumstances, I would rush past 'Edward' and emphasize 'Said'; at other times I would do the reverse, or to connect these two to each other so quickly that neither would be clear" (Said, 1999: 3). For displaced clients as well, to settle for the version of their name that fits with their current self-narrative is often an important task, which can be facilitated in therapy. When the therapist enquires into their choice of name or notices the change in the way their clients sign their written messages, she should invite them to reflect on their metamorphosis, opening a dialogue about their identity struggle.

The transcultural online set-up brings up an exciting set of challenges that can be turned into opportunities. Any cross-cultural therapeutic relationship comes with an important modelling potential—creating a precedent of a healthy and satisfying relationship that is possible despite cultural differences. This is particularly helpful to those clients who in their past experienced disruptive, abusive, or unsatisfying relationships with a person from a different race or culture. As a result, they learn how to better negotiate such a relationship, and eventually experience a higher degree of openness and inclusion.

Another valuable effect of cross-cultural counselling, enhanced by the online setting, is the de-trivialisation. Sometimes psychologically challenging conditions, typical for a certain culture, become socially trivialised. For example, in Russia, growing up in a family where at least one person suffers from alcohol addiction is not uncommon. A client with such a backstory coming to therapy will often minimise the impact on his development of what seems a normal background. The same can be said about clients who as children were left behind by a parent who had to emigrate to make a living elsewhere. The absent parent has become a social norm in many poorer countries. In therapy, what seemed trivial and not dramatic suddenly becomes de-trivialised, re-discovered not only through the eyes of a different person but also through the lens of a different culture.

The call for a dialogical encounter between cultures made by Mikhail Bakhtin in the early 20th century resonates with a renewed urgency: "Only in the eyes of an alien culture, does another culture open itself in a fuller and deeper way" (Bakhtin in Epstein, 2012: 60). Mikhail Epstein insists on the re-evaluation of Bakhtin's dialogical model for the humanities in general, and this call is of crucial importance to psychotherapy, which is nothing else than applied humanities. His interferential model shifts the focus to the boundary, the between, or the "here-and-now", fostering transcultural dialogue in therapy (Epstein, 2012). In one of his late interviews, Bakhtin summarises:

In order to understand, it is immensely important for the person who understands to be located outside the object of his or her creative under-standing—in time, in space, in culture. For one cannot even really see one's own exterior and comprehend it as a whole, and no mirrors or photographs can help; our real exterior can be seen and understood only by other people, because they are located outside us in space, and because they are others.

(Bakhtin in Gratchev & Marinova, 2019)

In cross-cultural therapy we practise daily the use of the "dialogical" quality of the human mind, for our client's benefit.

Displaced individuals constantly feel disempowered by every kind of loss of competency: linguistic, parental, professional. This facet of their condition opens another developmental opportunity for displacement-sensitive therapy: in handing over to them a guiding role, we empower these clients to take the lead, to get back in touch with the competent self that belongs to their pre-expatriation period. Even for those therapists who have never left their origi-nal place, a curious and respectful stance will help to connect with their cli-ents despite this displacement gap, and build a relational bridge where at first there was no bridge. By moving online and adopting a displacement-sensitive stance, a therapist who is not displaced in technical terms, is opening herself to the experience of displacement. In a way, this is an act of courage, as dis-placement is uncomfortable and makes us vulnerable to loss of expertise and authority. And, as therapists, we owe that to our clients: taking the risk, showing the path, initiating the dialogue against all odds—the distance, the difference, the language barrier.

The transcultural therapeutic relationship and shame

One of the crucial tasks of any therapeutic relationship is to help clients to heal, to recover from their original shame; with clients in displacement, this goes to a new level. No matter when their feelings of inadequacy developed, addressing them within the therapeutic relationship will benefit the client.

Any person, client or therapist, who steps into a therapy room to face a person from a different cultural background will be instantly sensitive to shame-related emotional responses. The same may happen in therapeutic situations in which one person clearly differs from the other in some obvious ways—for example race, social "level", or a physical disability. These emo-tional responses can hardly be avoided, therefore there is a benefit in explor-ing them head-on.

In addressing these feelings in the "here-and-now" of the session, the therapist seizes the opportunity for modelling how to own embarrassment without retreating into self-isolation. This usually results in a strengthened therapeutic alliance.

With clients whose culture is different from our own, we ought to recognise situations in which shame is likely to arise for both parties, such as mis-pronouncing a word when using our second language or not understanding an "obvious" cultural reference made by the other party, and other subtle trig-gers. When we stumble on our shame, there is always a great temptation to simply deny or avoid it. Nevertheless, our displaced clients will not be fooled by these seemingly invisible defensive strategies, attuned as they are to this situation.

Now there is a common problem of interpreting this or that word. Some-thing profound can be lost in translation, particularly because different cul-tures associate different words with the exact same feeling. Researchers have worked on how culture affects the experience and the expression of emotional distress. The term "idioms of distress," as used in medical anthropology, puts forward socially and culturally mediated ways of experiencing and expressing distress (Nichter, 2010; 2022). Despite some slightly utopian attempts to compare cultures by identifying key words in languages to translate them into a universal semantic metalanguage (Wierzbicka, 1997), there is no straight-forward measuring stick for such benchmarking. Transcultural therapists have to rely on their curiosity, their ability to listen, and their empathy, to tune into their displaced clients' individual experience of universally strong emotions. This constant dance between uniqueness and universality is always performed to the specific music of the client's culture and language.

The impact of culture on ways we experience shame is probably an area of displacement-sensitive practice that demands closer attention. Nathanson warns that "we must be careful to avoid the trap of saying that our under-standing of any emotion is better or more valid than that of one who grew up differently" (Nathanson, 1992: 20). Inquiring into the ways in which shame is understood and experienced in our client's original culture is an important part of our inquiry into their emotional life. This can be achieved by direct questioning about their perception of shame. It always starts with paying close attention to the language they use to describe their feelings of inade-quacy and self-deprecation. As discussed earlier (Chapter 6), when practising with multilingual clients or using a second language for conducting therapy, we ought to be particularly attentive to our clients' choice of words, especially the "key words", or the words that describe their emotional state or carry an important emotional charge. Terms that clients use to describe their feelings of not being good enough, being unworthy, faulty, weird, or simply "bad" are indicators of shame-related distress that needs attention. The common apprehension about using the exact word "shame" (or any closest equivalents in the language we use to communicate with our clients) is illustrative of how painful the emotional experience of shame is, as if the very utterance of the word could deepen the discomfort that stems from the feeling.

Inquiring into the experience of shame can take an even more dramatic turn when a lingua franca is used for therapy. For example, with Da, a

Chinese art student in Italy, with whom we spoke English, we quickly stumbled on an inner discomfort that he seemed embarrassed about. Da was a gifted and passionate artist. As he tried to describe what he had felt at a drawing class, when a Chinese model turned up for a nude drawing session, his face went blank. Usually articulate in both English and Italian, Da seemed short of words. From his expression and what I already knew about his background, I sensed that he was struggling with complex emotions, probably shame. "Could you maybe say it in Chinese?" I asked. He let out a few Chinese words, his face relaxed. Now that he had verbalised his experience, I asked for some translation in Italian or English, and from there we were able to scrutinise and elaborate on what had happened. Looking at the Chinese naked man, Da had felt exposed. He was the only Asian man in a class of white European students. He therefore fantasised that, as his classmates were drawing the nude model, they were thinking about his own body hidden behind the light fabric of his clothing. With this sudden exposure, he wanted to sink into the floor, disappear from the well-lit room in which he felt there was nowhere for him to hide. That incident led us to explore and recognise Da's earlier childhood experience of being inadequate. A gay, sensitive boy, he felt pressured and judged by his family environment, in which what was expected from him was to perform academically, make it into a good business school, and eventually make a good living to support his parents in their old age. Even though Da had been allowed to pursue studies in art, the bitter taste of failing his original world's expectations had stayed with him, resulting in constant self-doubt and the debilitating belief that for his parents he was a failure.

Achieving pride in displacement

If shame is a central process for any psyche dealing with displacement, achieving pride naturally becomes the ultimate task.

Dislocation comes with challenges of various nature. When an emigrant manages to successfully navigate these challenges, and moves towards a more meaningful life, displacement can turn into a great source of joy. This is how Nathanson describes a particular kind of joy that we may encourage our clients to pursue:

> Success, especially in an exciting venture, triggers joy; the pattern or sequence of these events is known to us as healthy pride. Along with this joy will come our memory of previous experiences of competence pleasure, making for some of the complex emotionality of pride.
>
> (Nathanson, 1992: 85)

There are at least as many opportunities for finding joy in displacement as there are obstacles. Acquiring competence in the new language and culture are among the most evident challenges for any migrant, but there can be many other more personal challenges depending on each individual. Joseph Burgo insists that

> the road to authentic self-esteem inevitably passes through the land of shame and never entirely leaves it. Along the way, joy and pride in achievement, especially when shared with the other people who matter most to us, will often transform our encounters with shame from painful defeats into opportunities for growth and self-fulfillment.
>
> (Burgo, 2018: 7)

For displaced clients, the potential of sharing shame is proportionate to the amount of shame they experience. As they acquire more competence in therapy and develop trust in their therapist, they also develop relational skills that are crucial. In the case of cross-cultural therapeutic dyads, the potential for a parallel process naturally arises—as clients negotiate the challenges of their expatriate reality, they simultaneously learn how to thrive in a transcultural relationship. In a successful emigration, similarly to a successful therapeutic journey, one has a chance to turn a struggle into a victory. Displaced clients often enter therapy feeling disempowered in face of the challenges of dislocation, and their therapists' task is to travel alongside them to a point in their journey where they can feel pride in their achievements.

Among the great examples of emigrant writings about journeys from shame to pride, there is the autobiographical account of the Ukrainian-American professor of applied linguistics Aneta Pavlenko. As an immigrant from the former USSR myself, reading her autobiography I felt greatly inspired, for instance by her take on academic writing in a second language despite the shame this process naturally triggers. "Whereas for some aspiring scholars it can be a source of disempowerment, for others, myself included, being a refugee, an immigrant, and a female is a privilege and an ultimate source of strength, critical consciousness, and multiple perspective" (Pavlenko, 2001: 178). Another powerful example comes from Olga Khazan, an American journalist and author, who grew up in a family of Russian immigrants. Khazan's book *Weird* is a study and a celebration of diversity and the ways in which its characters find power in their difference (Khazan, 2020). She reflects on her own story, one greatly impacted by her early emigration, and exemplifies how pride can come out of recognising and owning the original experience of the displacement-related shame.

In displacement, how can one transition from a restraining shame to an empowering pride? There are many routes, but creativity can be one. Many emigrant artists show us a path for transcending displacement-related shame through creative endeavour. A remarkable example of collective conquering of a new place came from l'Ecole de Paris, an artistic movement of the mid-1920s. It emerged from La Ruche (the Hive)—a complex of cheap studio apartments in the Montparnasse neighbourhood of Paris. It housed freshly arrived emigrant artists, many from Eastern Europe. La Ruche was a friendly, welcoming place, which not only offered them a roof and a workshop, but also a community of fellow emigrants; the latter being probably even more crucial for their stumbling self-esteem. One of the inhabitants of La Ruche was Haim Soutine, a Jewish refugee from Russia, who later painted his famous series of bellboys and other hotel staff. In most of these portraits, painted over a decade, especially the earliest of the series, the models have awkward positions, clutch their hands, and seem to struggle with crippling shyness, just like Soutine himself. The models were badly paid emigrant workers, and the load of shame they were all carrying can be felt. The empathy that emanates from Soutine's portraits suggests how familiar and recognisable the displacement-related shame was to the painter. In later portraits of this series, Soutine asks his subjects to pose in a different, more assertive posture—their hands firmly planted on their hips (*The Little Pastry Cook*, 1927). What does Soutine seek to represent by this intentionally set posture? Does he suggest that they are drawing their pride from their craft? Or does he depict their pride in their ability to survive, to master their surroundings for a better life? This evolution coincides with Soutine's well-deserved rise to recognition and financial security through his own art.

As we progress on the therapeutic journey with our displaced clients, we celebrate their victories on the way, no matter how small or insignificant they may look from outside. Managing a phone conversation with a French clerk, progressing one level up in the English class, surviving a job interview in their second language, asking a girl out in the foreign city … all these seemingly easy acts turn into challenges for the displaced. They can either crush their self-esteem or pave the way to a more confident version of self.

I can hardly find a better way to conclude this chapter than Masha Gessen's motivational message:

> I wish I could finish on a hopeful note, by saying something like: If only we insist on making choices, we will succeed in keeping darkness at bay. I'm not convinced that that's the case. But I do think that making choices and, more important, imagining other, better choices, will give us the best chance possible of coming out of the darkness better than we were when we went in. It's a bit like emigrating that way: the choice to leave rarely feels free, but choices we make about inhabiting new landscapes (or changed bodies) demand an imagination.
>
> (Gessen, 2018)

For therapists, travelling alongside their clients on their displacement journey through the trauma of dislocation demands an effort of imagination. Re-inventing better ways of being in their new reality is the noble task of any displacement-sensitive therapy.

References

Alonso, A., & Rutan, J. S. (1988). The experience of shame and the restoration of self-respect in group therapy. *International Journal of Group Psychotherapy*, 38(1), 3–14. doi:10.1080/00207284.1988.11491080.

Arendt, H. (2007). *The Jewish writings*. New York: Schocken Books.

Badkhen, A. (2018). An anatomy of lostness. *World Literature Today*, November.

Bakhtin, M. (1986). *Speech genres and other late essays*. Eds. Emerson, C. & Holquist, M. Trans. McGee, V. W. Austin: University of Texas Press.

Beltsiou, J. (Ed.) (2015). *Immigration in psychoanalysis. locating ourselves*. London and New York: Routledge.

Bernard, H., Burlingame, G., Flores, P., Greene, L., Joyce, A., Kobos, J. C., ... Feirman, D. (2008). Clinical practice guidelines for group psychotherapy. *International Journal of Group Psychotherapy*, 58(4), 455–542. doi:10.1521/ijgp.2008.58.4.455.

Bevan, D. (1990). *Literature and exile*. Amsterdam and Atlanta GA: Rodopi.

Boym, S. (2001). *The future of nostalgia*. New York: Basic Books.

Burgo, J. (2018). *Shame: Free yourself, find joy, and build true self-esteem*. New York: St. Martin's Press.

Burlingame, G. M., Fuhriman, A., & Mosier, J. (2003). The differential effectiveness of group psychotherapy: A meta-analytic perspective. *Group Dynamics*, 7(1), 3–12. doi:10.1037/1089-2699.7.1.3.

Cacioppo, S., Capitanio, J. P., & Cacioppo, J. T. (2014). Toward a neurology of loneliness. *Psychological Bulletin*, 140(6), 1464–1504. doi:10.1037/a0037618.

Dowd, A. (2019). Uprooted minds: Displacement, trauma and dissociation. *Journal of Analytical Psychology*, 64(2), 244–269. doi:10.1111/1468-5922.12481.

Epstein, M. (2012). *The transformative humanities: A manifesto*. London: Bloomsbury.

Epstein, O. B. (2021). *Shame matters: Attachment and relational perspectives for psychotherapists*. Abingdon: Routledge.

Freud, S. (1961). *Beyond the pleasure principle*. New York: Liveright.

Gessen, M. (2018). To be, or not to be. *The New York Review*, February 8.

Goldberg, C. (1991). *Understanding shame*. Northvale NJ and London: Jason Aronson.

Gratchev, S., & Marinova, M. (Eds.) (2019). *Mikhail Bakhtin: The Duvakin interviews, 1973*. Lewisburg PA: Bucknell University Press.

Grinberg, L., & Grinberg, R. (1984). *Psychoanalytic perspectives on migration and exile*. New Haven and London: Yale University Press.

Hawkley, L. C., & Cacioppo, J. T. (2010). Loneliness matters: A theoretical and empirical review of consequences and mechanisms. *Annals of Behavioral Medicine*, 40(2), 218–227.

Kellman, S. G. (1976). The fiction of self-begetting. *MLN*, 91(6), 1243–1256.

Khazan, O. (2020). *Weird: The power of being an outsider in an insider world*. Paris: Hachette.

Laing, O. (2016). *The lonely city: Adventures in the art of being alone*. New York: Picador.

Lee, R. G., & Wheeler, G. (Eds.) (2003). *The voice of shame: Silence and connection in psychotherapy*. Cambridge MA: Gestalt Press.

Leszcz, M., & Yalom, I. (2005). *Theory and practice of group psychotherapy* (5th edn). New York: Basic Books.

Lynd, H. M. (1999). *On shame and the search for identity*. London: Routledge.

Madison, G. A. (2011). *The end of belonging: Untold stories of leaving home and the psychology of global relocation.* London: CreateSpace.

Masi, C. M., Chen, H., Hawkley, L. C., & Cacioppo, J. T. (2011). A meta-analysis of interventions to reduce loneliness. *Personality and Social Psychology Review*, 15(3), 219–266.

McRoberts, C., Burlingame, G. M., & Hoag, M. J. (1998). Comparative efficacy of individual and group psychotherapy: A meta-analytic perspective. *Group Dynamics*, 2(2), 101–117. doi:10.1037/1089-2699.2.2.101.

Mearns, D., & Cooper, M. (2018). *Working at relational depth* (2nd edn). London: Sage.

Nabokov, V. (2019). *Think, write, speak.* London: Penguin Books.

Nathanson, D. (Ed.) (1987). *The many faces of shame.* New York: Guilford Press.

Nathanson, D. L. (1992). *Shame and pride: Affect, sex, and the birth of the self.* New York and London: W. W. Norton.

Nichter, M. (2010). Idioms of distress revisited. *Culture, Medicine and Psychiatry*, 34(2), 401–416. doi:10.1007/s11013-010-9179-6.

Nichter, M. (2022). From idioms of distress, concern, and care to moral distress leading to moral injury in the time of covid. *Transcultural Psychiatry*, 59(4), 551–567. doi:10.1177/13634615221115540.

Pavlenko, A. (2001). "In the world of the tradition, I was unimagined": Negotiation of identities in cross-cultural autobiographies. *International Journal of Bilingualism: Cross-Disciplinary, Cross-Linguistic Studies of Language Behavior*, 5(3), 317–344. doi:10.1177/13670069010050030401

Reis, H. T. (2001). Relationship experiences and emotional well-being. In Ryff, C. D., & Singer, B. H. (Eds.), *Emotion, Social Relationships, and Health* (pp. 57–86). Oxford and New York: Oxford University Press.

Said, E. W. (1999). *Out of place: A memoir* (1st edn). New York: Knopf.

Schrauf, R. W., Pavlenko, A., & Dewaele, J. (2003). Bilingual episodic memory: An introduction. *International Journal of Bilingualism*, 7(3), 221–233. doi:10.1177/13670069030070030101.

Sedaris, D. (2001). *Me talk pretty one day.* New York: Back Bay Books.

Shrinivasan, A. (2021). *The right to sex.* London: Bloomsbury.

Stavans, I. (2001). *Art and anger: Essays on politics and the imagination.* Basingstoke: Palgrave Macmillan.

Suler, J. (2004). The online disinhibition effect. *CyberPsychology & Behavior*, 7(3), 321–326. doi:10.1089/1094931041291295.

Tangney, J. P. E., & Fischer, K. W. (1995). *Self-conscious emotions: The psychology of shame, guilt, embarrassment, and pride.* New York: Guilford Press. [The idea for this volume grew out of two pivotal conferences. The first, on Emotion and Cognition in Development, was held in Winter Park, CO Park, CO, Summer 1985. The second, on Shame and Other Self-Conscious Emotions, was held in Asilomar, CA, December 1988].

Weber, R. L., & Gans, J. S. (2003). The group therapist's shame: A much undiscussed topic. *International Journal of Group Psychotherapy*, 53(4), 395–416. doi:10.1521/ijgp.53.4.395.42833.

Weinberg, H., & Rolnick, A. (2020). *Theory and practice of online therapy.* New York: Routledge.

Wierzbicka, A. (1997). *Understanding cultures through their key words: English, Russian, Polish, German, and Japanese.* New York: Oxford University Press.

Yalom, I. (2017). *Becoming myself.* New York: Basic Books.

Chapter 8

The distance therapeutic relationship

The therapeutic relationship goes remote

One of the most significant developments in contemporary psychotherapy, across different approaches, has been the move towards the centrality of the therapeutic relationship (Evans & Gilbert in Charura & Paul, 2014). Outcome research suggests that the quality of the therapeutic alliance is more essential for the progress of the therapeutic relationship than the choice of modality (Del Re et al., 2021; Finsrud et al., 2022). Even if research has not entirely caught up with the rapid technological developments and the post-Covid mentality shift, it is not too far-fetched to extrapolate these conclusions to the delivery method as well.

The rapid expansion of online therapy triggered preoccupations about the therapeutic relationship being altered by the online setting (Dunn in Weitz, 2014; Russell, 2015; Reeves in Cundy, 2015). The remote therapeutic relationship was generally envisaged through the lens of the traditional in-person therapeutic alliance (Wright in Charura & Paul, 2014). With the take-off of online psychotherapy, the specificities of the online therapeutic alliance have begun to be studied (Dunn in Weitz, 2014), and the post-pandemic research has confirmed that the transition to teletherapy has not affected the quality of a therapeutic alliance previously established during in-person sessions (Eichenberg et al., 2022). Research dedicated to an older kind of remote therapy—that delivered by the traditional telephone—can also inform our understanding of other technology-mediated types of delivery. A systematic review identified 15 studies exploring the interactional process-related differences between telephone and face-to-face therapy (Irvine et al., 2020). The review found no evidence of significant differences between the modes for any of the six variables save for the duration of sessions, which tended to be shorter over the phone. The other five variables, all relating in different degrees to the therapeutic relationship—therapeutic alliance, client disclosure, empathy, attentiveness, and client participation—were similar for both delivery methods. The therapeutic alliance, measured by the Working Alliance Inventory (WAI), showed a slightly better rating for telephone interventions.

DOI: 10.4324/9781003144588-8

These are rather reassuring findings for those therapists who are uncomfortable with losing the clues that the client's embodied presence in the room offers. On the other hand, in video therapy, we access visual clues, not only from our client's face and upper body but also from his surroundings. This suggests greater chances to build a strong alliance than relying solely on the information captured through the client's voice.

Another study (Treanor, 2017), conducted as part of the Doctorate in Counselling Psychology at the University of Roehampton, researched the general doubts of some relationally focused practitioners about online therapy; Treanor studied the extent to which relational depth can be reached in online therapy and its facilitating and inhibiting factors. Despite the small size of this mixed-methods study (13 participants for the survey part and 7 for the subsequent interviews), the findings offer a glimpse into clients' experience of relational depth in the online sessions. All participants were on long-term therapy via videoconferencing. Treanor used the Relational Depth Inventory (RDI) developed by Sue Price, asking clients to focus on one significant event; and the Relational Depth Frequency Scale (RDFS) that measures the therapeutic relationship's overall setting (Di Malta et al., 2020). The same metrics had been previously used in studying the relational depth of the traditional in-person setting (Wiggins et al., 2012). Treanor's research suggests that clients can experience relational depth in online therapies at levels similar to those reported in the in-person setting by Knox (Knox, 2008).

Humans are deeply social animals and are wired to build the reliable relationships necessary for their survival. This biological reality is probably what makes people seek meaningful relationships, no matter how much void they are facing; silence or absence is interpreted as a promise of intimacy by those experiencing an unsatisfied relational longing. This existential reality, which makes us human, is responsible for the relative success of such "dehumanised" therapy delivery methods as the computerised therapist ELIZA created in 1966 by Weizenbaum, or the more recent applications of virtual reality for cybertherapy. It is also behind many clients' stubborn use of online dating platforms despite their frustration with the non-meaningful relationships they find there.

But what makes the online therapeutic relationship work?

Presence is one of the elements of relational dynamics that persist in the therapeutic interaction, even when the therapist is not physically there with the client—a phenomenon routinely associated with the strength and effectiveness of the therapeutic alliance (Geller & Porges, 2014; Hayes & Vinca, 2017). Therapeutic presence is more about ways of being with a client than it is about technical aspects of therapy. It involves therapists bringing their whole self to the encounter and being fully in the moment on a multitude of levels (Geller, 2017; Geller, 2021). Porges' (2022) recent polyvagal theory clarifies neurophysiological reasons behind the magic of presence: when a therapist is attuned to her client in the "here-and-now", her receptive way of being sends a neurophysiological message to the client that he is being heard, met, and understood (Geller & Porges, 2014). In Geller's words, the therapist's presence is "like an antenna, reading the experience of the moment by resonating with clients' experience and attuning to their own felt experience of the moment" (Geller, 2021). The online setting somehow removes the bodies and the shared place from the interaction; it makes presence an illusive phenomenon. Therapists' ability to express their presence with their full body is therefore greatly reduced, as is their capacity to attune their rhythms and bodily movements to those of their clients. This may limit their ability to attune, to convey a sense of safety and to build trust through presence (Geller, 2017; 2021). All therapists working through videoconferencing systems are familiar with the frustration of not being able to fully meet their patients' gaze, which is part of the sophisticated system of attunement to the other in the in-person communication. There have been multiple attempts to describe or define presence in relation to human digital activities (Lombard & Ditton, 1997), and the term of "telepresence" has been brought forward more recently and seems to imply that it "reflects that the therapist forgets about being in an online context, feels absorbed in the session, and the therapist interacts with the client as if they were in the same room" (Rathenau et al., 2022). Telepresence and therapeutic presence are separate concepts that overlap in the online therapy context: if a therapist is not fully present with her client, no matter whether they share a physical room or a virtual space—being technology savvy will not make a difference. This brings us back to the question of what makes the therapeutic presence persist in therapy performed through videoconferencing? Amongst multiple descriptions of what constitutes presence, one stands out: it is supported by research in neurology and is summarised by Riva as "subject is 'present' in the space—real or virtual—where he/she can act in" (Riva, 2011: 3). This leads to the paramount question of impact and back to the relational dimension of the therapeutic process: how much impact we have on the other will probably define the level of presence we will experience in the online interaction. This is relevant for both parties—therapist and client—as they both need to witness the impact that they are making on each other during the session. When the client is sharing his pain or his anger, he needs to see on his therapist's face the reflection of his emotional experience. In therapy through videoconferencing this can be easily achieved, as we mainly have access to each other's faces, with a close-up. I have noticed how I tend to compensate for the loss of physical presence by unconsciously exaggerating my facial expressions. At the end of any particularly busy day of working online, my facial muscles are sore. Similar mechanisms may explain why therapists report feeling more tired and experiencing professional self-doubt and loss of confidence when transitioning their work to their screens (Békés & Aafjes-Van Doorn, 2022).

Having an impact on the other person is cited amongst the relational human needs which are the component parts of a universal human desire for intimate relationships and secure attachments (Erskine, 2011; 1998). The centrality of impact to the experience of presence is what makes online work with some withdrawn or depressed clients particularly challenging, compared to in-person therapy where we have access to their body posture and can rely on other sensory information. With clients who have difficulty accessing their emotions, we must walk the extra mile in inquiring actively into their emotional experience there and then, in the "here-and-now" of the session. With Mel, one of my online patients, his tuned-down facial expressions made our early work particularly hard and frustrating for both parties. A young American man, he lived out of his suitcase, drifting from one place to another with not much obvious direction. As he appeared again and again, with robotic punctuality, on my screen, I always felt a sting of apprehension. With his perfectly groomed hair, his neat shirt, and his grey transparent eyes, he looked machinelike himself. He worked remotely as a programmer and spent his life in front of his screen, locked away from the outside world. When, after a few months of skimming the surface of his life struggles, Mel shared for the first time the cruel facts of his early life, I could barely contain my tears. As he promptly noticed my eyes tearing up, I could see his reflexive response—he backed away from the screen, and for a split-second a wave of confusion and disgust animated his usually impassive face. "What has just happened?" I asked, and he immediately froze back into his emotionless shell. As his usually intense gaze moved away from the camera, I could see that he was embarrassed by my emotional disclosure. We had to perform this "emotional impact" dance many times before he was finally able to accept that his emotional states were resonating with me, touching me deeply. As he started owning the fact that he was making a visible impact, we both started to feel more present, more engaged during our interactions. Regardless of our mutual frustration, we stumbled forward. At the same time Mel was experimenting with online dating. He described to me how he wrote to a few girls, but after a few exchanges and often one single in-person drink, he would feel absolutely no interest in them and would quickly disengage, quickly moving to the next candidate. And yet, he craved a relationship, something deeper, something different from anything he had ever experienced before. When I asked Mel to describe what he was hoping for, he struggled to describe anything more than a vague desire to "have a good time" and "have great sex". Learning how to be in a meaningful relationship soon crystallised into the main focus of his therapy. This was the most difficult task for Mel, who had grown up in a total emotional solitude; his two parents were addicted to drugs and alcohol. During his developmental years, he simply had not learnt how to emotionally impact others or to be impacted by them. In his adult life, this had led to an inability to develop satisfying relationships. In our work, seeing on his large screen the emotions from my face triggered by his stories and emotions, was a major part of this learning process. At this later stage, Mel was ready to take more relational risks and joined an interpersonal online therapy group, where he could experiment, in the "here-and-now" of each session, with how to engage with others in more open and empathic ways.

Just like Mel, many of those who seek therapy online are simultaneously dealing with a variety of distance relationships. Their emotional attachments often extend beyond borders. With the increased mobility, these displaced clients face more losses and separations. In this relational context, engaging in therapy with an online therapist, they find themselves committed to yet another distance relationship. This distance is unavoidably re-enacted in remote therapy. It should be properly addressed, since the way we negotiate this relationship can add much reparative value to the work, as does the level of trust and intimacy we can build despite the distance and cultural differences. Based on my own clinical observations, I can echo Reeves' experience:

> In the engagement with these clients, we have experienced rupture and repair, we have discussed the effects of distance and the clients' sense of instant access to me the therapist, and we have felt each other and experienced the real depth that in no way seems less to me than the experience of connectedness I feel with my face-to-face clients.
>
> (Reeves in Cundy, 2015)

In the same way as clients are experts in the therapeutic relationship (Haugh & Paul, 2008), displaced clients are certainly experts in the long-distance therapeutic relationship. Or at least, their experience in building and maintaining meaningful and intimate remote relationships is crucial to building the online therapeutic alliance. Of course, many clients who come to therapy have a far-from-ideal relational history. Many complain about their lack of strong and stable relationships, which tend to shrink with every consecutive move. Their expertise is often about what does not work, and these clients can be deeply ambivalent: hoping for the best, they also feel mistrustful and resistant to investing in building yet another remote relationship. "Can a distance relationship be a reliable source of care and support?" they secretly wonder. With such clients, the therapist is challenged to prove that the relational magic works despite the distance and other potential obstacles that lie in the way of an online cross-cultural therapeutic dyad. Depending on their current relational agenda and their attachment history, this challenge will prove harder for some clients than for others.

Connection is broadly considered as another marker of the therapeutic alliance. Some studies went to a considerable length to measure the level of connection that therapists and their clients experience during their sessions (Cooper, 2012; Sexton et al., 2005). But no matter how well-designed and thorough these studies are, connection and presence remain hard-to-capture phenomena. In their clinical work, therapists will have to rely on their best judgement, intuition, and all kinds of gut feelings, to assess where they are in relation to their clients. Ironically, as digital communications technology developed, the term "connection" moved into our everyday language. We are all accustomed to measure the quality of connection that our devices have. In online therapy this opens a channel for an active exploration of the quality of the intrapersonal connection during the sessions. "When you shared that your mother neglected you, leaving you to cry for hunger for hours in your dirty bed, I felt connected and sad", I responded to Mel's sharing of his childhood's grim realities. Based on his perplexed look, this was probably the first time he heard "connected" in reference to him and not his computer.

As discussed earlier, one of the changes that occur in the therapeutic relational dynamics is the power shift, which transfers more control to the client. Not only by moving online do clients acquire more freedom in choosing their therapist, but they also have more control over their space and their use of therapy. Paradoxically, clients seem to be quicker in using online delivery methods creatively, intuitively turning what the professional community had initially seen as pitfalls into opportunities for getting better. They turn to the seemingly "safer" remote therapists for support despite their shame; they use the disinhibition effect of the online communication (Suler, 2004) for their benefit, disclosing uncomfortable emotional material earlier in the process; they choose online therapists who do not share their cultural backgrounds in order to explore tensions with their home countries; or reach out to therapists in their second language, exploiting its neutrality to feel freer in their risky personal quest.

Irvin Yalom describes the therapist and her client as being "fellow travellers" (Yalom, 2002: 6). This existential metaphor is particularly appropriate when working with displaced or highly mobile individuals. They bring their talking-head-therapists with them (on their devices' screens) through the time zones and the fleeting backgrounds of their temporary places. There is something moving in the way these clients welcome us into their uprooted realities, as we experiment together with the distance—putting the right distance between us—just enough to feel fleeting intimacy but also to allow them to feel safe in their reassuring independence. Here again, Olga Tokarczuk's poetic description of her wandering characters' experience in her book *Flights* offers the most accurate account of this particular kind of relational dance that the distance therapeutic dyad performs from session to session:

> the only way to survive [...] is to keep your distance, a kind of dance that consists in approaching and retreating, one step forward, one step back, one step to the left, one to the right—easy enough steps to remember. And the bigger the world gets, the more distance you can dance out of this way, immigrating out across seven seas, two languages, an entire faith.
>
> (Tokarczuk, 2018: 59)

The dance of the remote therapeutic relationship can cause frustration and anxiety for both parties. Depending on their personality and their personal displacement background, some therapists will find it more manageable than others. For example highly mobile clients will frequently need to postpone sessions, sometimes at the last minute, because of a cancelled flight, a trip that has come up, or a child care issue. They will challenge the traditional notion of consistency, pushing our boundaries, and testing our capacity to endlessly adapt to their movable needs. But in my experience, if we keep being there, no matter how much moving parts are in play, and maintain some sort of consistency, then the sparkles of relational depth will move therapy forward.

Working at relational depth

Relational depth is a crucial component of any meaningful relationship in our lives and our clients' lives. It has the potential to change us, be it a friendship, a romantic partnership, or a therapeutic alliance. It builds on moments of intense contact and enduring experiences of connectedness (Mearns & Cooper, 2018). This dynamic phenomenon resists a simple definition:

> Such experiences of engagement can be very difficult to put into words. How does one describe, for instance, those moments of connection and intimacy with a client when each person's words seem to flow from the other's and all self-consciousness is lost?
>
> (Mearns & Cooper, 2018: xi)

However, any person who has ever engaged fully in therapy, as a therapist or as a client, easily recognises those blissful moments,

> when we really meet people at a very deep level. Where we feel totally tuned in to the other and we experience a common humanity and sense that, existentially, we are not alone: that we are part of a community, connected with another, thrown into this world together and both striving alongside each other, not alone, to try to find our way. And it is a magical feeling of safety and certainty and excitement and engagement and togetherness.
>
> (Cooper in Mearns & Cooper, 2018: x)

These precious moments usually coincide with major shifts in the process, in clients' attitudes to therapy, starting sometimes subtly but eventually translating in major changes. Clients finally commit to what previously felt emotionally unaffordable, take decisions that have the potential of changing the course of their lives. In brief, these fleeting moments are at the core of any meaningful and lasting change occurring in therapy. Like tiny but powerful relational sparks, they shed light on our shared journey through the "dark tunnel"—the over-used metaphor that many clients draw upon to describe their experience of life situations where they feel lost and disempowered. These sparks we create in a shared relational effort make the therapy journey more manageable; they eventually turn into a broader light that announces the exit from the "dark tunnel".

Working at relational depth strengthens the therapeutic alliance and may keep both parties' motivation high. But the phenomenon is hard to measure, and rarely mentioned in research on dropouts as reason why clients leave therapy prematurely. Studies on predictors and reasons for adherence to online therapeutic interventions suggest that guided interventions—those which include a human on the other side of the screen—are associated with increased adherence, confirming the intuitive conclusion that lack of human contact is associated with low adherence (Beatty & Binnion, 2016). There is no clear indication in the literature about higher dropout rates in online therapy compared to in-person treatment. It is easier to "terminate" with a click, by sending an email or a text to a therapist whom one has never met in person. Online therapy may be an easier way into treatment for many clients, especially for men for whom stigma and embarrassment are major obstacles to seeking treatment (Richards & Bedi, 2015; Springer & Bedi, 2021), but it can also be an easier way out. There are certainly various ways to mitigate this situation, but one of the most powerful tools in a therapist's reach is to aim at relational depth.

The current understanding of relational depth stems from Rogerian and person-centred modalities and is the result of a fruitful collaboration between two therapists—Dave Mearns and Mick Cooper. Mearns, a Rogerian therapist, has been writing about relational depth since the mid-1990s (Mearns, 1997), turning the core Rogerian conditions (empathy, congruence, and unconditional positive regard) into a universal stance for a deeper therapeutic work. In 2002 Cooper, rooted in a person-centered school, joined Mearns and the two collaborated on their acclaimed volume, *Working at Relational Depth*, which has gone through several editions since 2005. Through this collaboration, the concept of working at relational depth has evolved into one congruent relational stance for working across modalities. Mearns and Cooper (2018) suggest that process features that are necessary to achieving relational depth are realness, empathy, affirmation, presence, and mutuality.

Let us look at some of these elements through the lens of displacement-sensitive practice. Being genuine or real with the other is about not putting on a mask and letting the other person know what is genuinely going on for us (Mearns & Cooper, 2018). When their perception of the client is limited by the screen and its bidimensional quality, therapists may naturally start hiding, colluding with their client's tendency to conceal parts of themselves that they are uncomfortable with. Even if this behaviour is at odds with their deeper human desire to be seen fully, the shame they may feel about their incompetency could take over. As discussed earlier (Chapters 5 & 7), those clients who when presented with a choice opt for online therapy, may be in the grip of shame that results in this kind of internal conflict. Their online therapist's task is then to make sure to invite all parts, even the most hidden, into the encounter. This can only be achieved by one's own full presence and the presentation of an integrated self. In addition, in cross-cultural encounters, therapists burdened by shame resulting from their difference or lack of knowledge of their client's culture or language, may feel tempted to step back, to efface themselves from the interaction. In this way they collude with those client's parts that go into hiding, and they risk failing to meet their deeper relational need to be fully seen. This self-effacing stance impoverishes presence and undermines the strength of the contact.

This raises the question of self-disclosure in a cross-cultural online encounter.

I recently met with Maria; an Italian based in Paris. When she initially contacted me, she was still seeing another therapist. When I asked her what pushed her to "shop around", she mumbled something about her feeling that their work, that lasted for a few years, was over. Only when we later started working together, and she came for her first in-person session to my office, were we able to dig deeper into her reasons for changing therapists. She sat in one of the two armchairs and looked around at the bookshelves: "I read your book, *Unlocked* ... so I knew you had a dog", she volunteered, glancing at my dachshund sleeping under my desk. "So, how do you feel about seeing the person who wrote the book?" I inquired. Maria felt simultaneously excited about meeting the therapist that she had imagined when she was reading the book, as well as threatened and uneasy. With her previous therapist they only spoke Italian—their shared mother tongue—and the neutral background behind her back was not giving away anything. "I did not know anything about her", Maria added, clearly uncomfortable at knowing so much about me already. I was taken aback by her reaction, as the book she was talking about had limited personal details and no other clients ever seemed burdened by what they had learnt. So, what was it all about? Moving on, Maria verbalised how uncomfortable she usually was when offered any form of intimacy. Her previous therapist, with her neutral stance and presence limited by the screen, was a safe option, even though not an entirely satisfying one. Maria's relational history was extremely scarce; at the age of 33 she was painfully single. But the work they had done together allowed Maria to feel the need to experiment with in-person therapy and ultimately ask for more. With clients like Maria, who transition from one method of delivery to another, it is always interesting to explore the reasons behind their choice and pay attention to the impact of that change. Looking back at the work Maria had done previously with her online therapist, it became clearer to me that self-disclosure is all the more important when working online. Irvin Yalom (2009) delineates three categories of disclosure—about the process of therapy; about "here-and-now" feelings; and about therapist's personal life. The necessity to be clear about what clients should expect from therapy and a contiguous effort at transparency are crucial, and probably even more so when the therapeutic process is framed by a screen and impacted by the use of technology. For example, in acknowledging that the online interaction may speed up the self-disclosure and make us move faster by bypassing embarrassment can help clients to use this quality of the online interaction more mindfully. A client's lack of curiosity about their therapist's personal life or opinions is rarely questioned and often dismissed as normal, expected: a "good" client's behaviour. Now, as Maria's example illustrates, this easy acceptance of therapist's "blankness" can reveal an avoidant strategy of those who are uncomfortable with intimacy. For a few years Maria had been perfectly happy with not knowing anything about her therapist, until she realised that the human behind a therapist's blankness does matter to her. She took a risk, reaching out for a more natural and enriching human contact, and a closeness that she was so painfully lacking in her displaced life.

There are certainly numerous ways for achieving relational depth in therapy. The paths may vary from one medium to another, but at the core they are probably common to any delivery method. In my experience, there are two main avenues that help to achieve relational depth in therapy: existential stance on one side, focus on the "here-and-now" on the other. The former stresses the universality of client's experience and, by paying attention to the core existential preoccupations (death, freedom, isolation, and meaninglessness), we can recognise our shared predicaments of the human condition. When therapist is capable of recognising her own existential struggles in those shared by the client, it can only lead to more honesty and trust, and therefore to a strengthened therapeutic alliance. In Cooper's words,

> relational depth takes us back into the heart of things and to the heart of what is often most meaningful for us: deep, common, relating; the joy of being with others. It is a reminder of who and what we most fundamentally are.
>
> (Cooper in Mearns & Cooper, 2018: xi)

Meeting with the client in our shared humanness is probably at the core of any existential work, as well as a required part of working at relational depth. Each is inseparable from the other.

The second concrete path for achieving relational depth is active use of the "here-and-now", which in Yalom's definition refers to "the immediate events of the therapeutic hour, to what is happening here (in the office, in the relationship, in the in-betweenness—the space between me and you) and now, in this immediate hour" (Yalom, 2002: 47). Such a focus on the interpersonal process during the session brings both therapist and client back to their shared space. In an online encounter, this space is not shaped by any concrete place, which puts a stronger accent on interpersonal dynamics. That shift from place to relationships also happens naturally in any successful displacement.

The potential of the here-and-now derives from the fact that ultimately in their relationship with their therapist, clients behave as in the outside world. The session is a reduction of the real world, and success in experimenting or rehearsing changes in some behaviours and attitudes during the session can be reused in real life by the client. All therapists do this more or less consciously, but they less often invite clients to openly reflect on these dynamics.

My work with Caroline is an illustration of an active use of the "here and how" equivalents of our clients' interpersonal attitudes. This was early in her therapy; I had only seen her twice before. Caroline was French, with flawless English after a decade living in the US and then the UK before moving back to France. Since our first session, I felt Caroline was distant. Despite her superficial willingness to talk about herself, I could sense that she was holding back, carefully, and skilfully managing her narrative, delivering a story that looked good enough. Her choice of online therapy and her use of English for our communication were shields she used to protect her intimate emotional truth, which I intuited differed from the smoother version she was presenting to the world. As I was waiting in front of my screen for Caroline to join our session, I realised that I hardly remembered her face. The facts of her life that she had shared with me the week before were clear in my mind, but her personality was slipping away for me. After two hours with Caroline, I could hardly figure out what kind of person she was. The elements popping up related to superficial facts—her brilliant studies at Harvard, her job at a big American law firm, her perfectly groomed blonde hair ... So, when Caroline finally connected, perfectly on time, I felt a little lost about whom I was trying to help. She mentioned her isolated life, and that "friends somehow did not seem to stick around". When I asked her what the reasons might be for this solitude and lack of friendships, she shrugged: "I moved around a lot ... worked all the time". But was there anything else in the way she presented herself to others that was not inviting closeness and intimacy? During that session, Caroline talked about her frustration with the co-workers from the Paris office who did not make much effort to include her in their cohesive team. The day before she noticed that when she approached the coffee machine, the conversation, that sounded lovely from a distance, faded and people quickly left to return to their desks. Caroline seemed bewildered by their attitude and could not grasp how she might be participating in creating that drift. "Caroline", I said tentatively, "I noticed that in our conversations you seem to hold back, I have this fantasy that you are not entirely relaxed with me, which I understand as you do not know me well yet, and why should you trust a stranger?" "Yes, why would I?" she said, suddenly animated. As we established later in that session, there were not many people in this world whom Caroline trusted. The list came down to just two—her brother who lived in Canada and her old English teacher from high school days. She did not see either of them often but knew she could turn to them anytime in case of a major crisis. As we looked into the reasons for her mistrustful attitude, multiple previously hidden facts of her life came to light. Caroline was shocked as she lined them up for me—her mother lying to her about her sexuality, and coming out as gay only towards the end of her life; Caroline's boyfriend cheating on her with her best friend, her other best friend copying her college assignments … The list of these unfortunate stories was so long that it became obvious why she had slowly built defensive walls around herself, losing in the process the credulous and naïve girl she had been before. As we resuscitated that younger version of her, Caroline reverted to French, and looked vulnerable for the first time. "What would it take for you to start trusting me?" I asked. She stayed silent for a long moment. Then smiled "a very long time of not surprising me with something horrible". This was the point at which we agreed that we would be there for a longer run, and Caroline would do her best to be as truthful and open as she could. Now we had a shared interpersonal goal, and Caroline, despite her initial discomfort, learnt to recognise the potential of using the "here-and-now".

The online setting as an opportunity to re-focus on the relationship

Online therapy may offer novel ways to reach and form strong psychotherapeutic relationships (Kocsis & Yellowlees, 2018; Agar in Weinberg & Rolnick, 2020). So, no matter the modality that we practice, moving online can be turned into an opportunity to re-focus on the therapeutic relationship. As we negotiate this transition together with our clients, it is only natural to re-focus on the relationship. Moving from the physical room to the screen is like changing the lens on your camera—after a wide-angle you adopt a close-up lens. The acute face-to-face quality of this closer shot may surprise us at first by its renewed intimacy.

Buber (1958), the existential philosopher whose ideas about centrality of contact paved the way for further developments of relational approaches (Mearns & Cooper, 2018), insists that we will always move in and out of deep relating (what he calls the "I–Thou" stance), and that we need distance as well as closeness in our lives. Displaced individuals are used to experimenting with distance, and often are much less comfortable with closeness, especially those who have been living in displacement for long enough. They are familiar with how distance makes them feel—the vast array of emotional experiences can be associated with "distance", which can make them feel lonely, free, alienated, relieved, etc. The familiarity of remoteness from attachment objects is reassuring. Clients whose early relationships have gone astray may find the intimacy of therapeutic relationship suffocating and impossible to handle. The filter of the screen allows them to keep a safe distance, creating an opportunity to explore closeness at their own pace. Co-constructing the therapeutic relationship with these clients can turn into a proving process, where they will experiment. For therapists, these experiments can feel exhausting, but if we can stay present through this process, trust will eventually develop. At that stage, they may bring us a wider view into the rooms of their flats that were previously blurred from our sight, or even suggest a meeting in person if they are travelling to the city we happen to work in.

Various impingements of the online setting can become opportunities to strengthen the "togetherness" of the therapeutic endeavour. At the initial stages of cybertherapy development, therapists and clients were very dependent on technology and bandwidth and concerned with it "letting us down". This can still happen, although much less frequently, videoconferencing literacy and better internet networks having now become widespread. Nevertheless, there remains a risk of dropped calls and pauses, inaudible segments, inability to read some body language and nonverbal cues. Managing these impingements creatively can be a brilliant opportunity for strengthening the therapeutic alliance, and it is true that the therapist and her client are in the same boat facing rough seas, whereas in the face-to-face setting mishaps such as traffic jams, public transport delays or bad weather remain possible but are not faced together by the late client and the frustrated therapist. Technology can be seen as a shared adversity that the therapist and her client must overcome together—together being the key notion here.

One example of a situation in which a bad internet connection put a session at risk comes from my work with Leila, a young Saudi woman. Only a few minutes into a session, we were interrupted by her unstable internet signal. After a few failed attempts at reinitiating the call, we had to switch to Telegram—an alternative communication channel that we had previously agreed on. There was only the audio option but we agreed to continue the session. In the previous few months of her therapy, she had not mentioned her feelings about her body, but this time she brought up the topic as soon as I asked how she felt about talking over the phone. "I feel invisible and much less self-conscious", she recognised. Her feelings of unease and self-doubt had started in her teenage years, around the time when, following the Saudi tradition, she had been obliged to start covering her face in public and in the presence of unrelated men. Wearing an abaya and a hijab felt safe—she quickly got used to being invisible, and with the invisibility came shame. More recently, when she refused to meet the mother of another suitor whom her parents hoped to marry her with, her mother wondered with frustration: "Is there anything wrong with your body?" Nothing really was, but nevertheless Leila never felt beautiful or attractive. Even inside her house, where she was able to walk with her face uncovered, she had been avoiding mirrors. During that phone session Leila remembered that during one big family gathering she had realised that she did not really know how she looked. That voice-only session led us to the first honest conversation about her body shame and her identity confusion. During the following session, with the image back, I looked at her uncovered face with particular attention. Leila recognised that it had been easier to talk about her body shame over the phone and that she would not have brought it up otherwise. We also agreed that being at peace with her body was one of her goals now. A few weeks later she started sharing her photos on her private social media group of friends. This was the first time she had received compliments about her new shorter hairstyle. Around the same time, she started uncovering her face in restaurants when she lunched with her female colleagues or friends. Experimenting with showing her face was part of her broader risk-taking regarding being more honest and vulnerable in relationships. As Leila progressed with these experiments her social connections grew. Even though many of them were through the internet, just like our therapeutic relationship, Leila felt more seen and less lonely. Her earlier depression subsided and she employed her new-found energy to engage in more studying and started negotiating with her slightly open-minded parents for more freedom, such as being in a shopping mall without the constant presence of one of her brothers. In our online therapeutic endeavour, trying to find an optimal way for connecting at a deeper level within the limiting frame of the online sessions had been a precursor, despite the differences in our cultural backgrounds, and in a language that was not a mother tongue for either of us.

Another impingement of the online setting has little to do with the short-comings of technology, but rather with clients' use of the online space. More than once I was left alone in a room by my client who left the room to respond to a doorbell, to let his dog out or cat in. When clients use their mobile devices to connect for the session, they might leave me on the floor or in the car temporarily. I have had to spend long minutes contemplating old wooden floors, white ceilings, and strange corners of their rooms from impossible angles. This always gives me time to reflect, as I listen to the noises of their interiors, on the meaning of the interruption. Considering our own emotional response to such events, whether frustration or anxiety, can be useful. To mend this, not just ignore it, is an important relational task.

One of my online clients, Lisa, a single mother, always connected from her flat in Moscow. A few weeks into her therapy, in the middle of our session, her 4-year-old daughter grew impatient with waiting and started to cry outside the bedroom door. Lisa had an anxious look on her face. Then, she apologised, stood up and went to calm her child down. I found myself alone, staring at Lisa's empty living room with a dark television screen in a corner and modern artwork on the grey wall. Our sessions had been planned to take place during nursery hours until this one. Lisa was an intelligent young woman and a gifted musician. Fighting to make a living in tough environment, with no support from her family or her child's father, she longed to follow her passion for music, but made a living from playing violin at extravagant parties and writing music for TV commercials. She often felt extremely isolated, stuck in her life and in an oppressive reality. On the other side of the closed door she was trying to calm her daughter down. I could hear the child's high-pitched voice as she grew more and more upset and frustrated. My despair kept growing. I felt a strong temptation to "leave" the room by clicking on the red switch-off button. The little girl's crying reached my ears with such despair that I felt powerless and paralysed. The fact that I was physically far away, sitting in my own office, in another country, made the whole experience somehow even more powerful. In face-to-face therapy we rely mostly on our clients' words, their narrated version of their "out there" life. When practising online we witness first-hand their personal reality: we get invited, albeit virtually, into their office, their kitchen, sometimes even their bedroom. We may have a glimpse of their pets or their flatmates peeping into the room during the session. Classical psychotherapy would view such intrusions as harmful nuisance, as "breaking the frame," but in online psychotherapy, they help us gain a better insight into clients' actual experience of their world. Like other highly educated and articulate clients of mine, Lisa used elaborate talking as a way to hide, thus deflecting the attention from unbearable feelings of shame and abandonment that she could not express. When she "abandoned" me in the room, she unconsciously made me feel exactly as she had felt for most of her babyhood: alone in a pram, left in the cold outside on the kitchen balcony. In Russia at that time, this was a common practice. It was widely believed that babies slept better in the cold, breathing fresh air. This old pre-verbal experience of lying alone in the confined space of her pram, tightly swaddled and unable to move, soon came to define her general feeling in life, as she had alluded to in a previous session. Crying was pointless—nobody would come. To escape was impossible. That winter, Lisa was feeling stuck and left alone in the cold again. Her country was falling into despair with no hope of escape. When Lisa finally managed to soothe her daughter, and the notes of despair faded from the child's voice, the door I had been staring at for the long minutes finally opened, and she stepped back into the room. When her face appeared again on my screen, she looked exhausted and vulnerable. We looked into each other's eyes, or rather into the webcam on top of our screens, and I understood her much better. I had just had a chance, even for a few minutes, to connect with the feelings of despair, loneliness, and frustration with which she had been living. Lisa started to speak but suddenly stopped. In my pained expression, she recognised her own suffering. This face-to-face close-up on our screens brought a deep mirroring opportunity. At this point, the silence we shared had a different quality: we felt closer than we had ever been. This could not have unfolded with such immediacy if Lisa had been coming to my office for in-person sessions. I would never have heard her daughter's crying, which so clearly resonated with my own inner child.

Meeting online clients in person

With therapists' expanding engagement with a variety of online therapy options, acceptance of hybrid or blended approaches has been growing (Dunn & Wilson, 2021). With every transition from one medium to another, the established dynamics of the therapeutic relationship are shaken by this change. On the one hand, displaced and highly mobile clients adjust promptly; on the other, recognising what is lost and found in the process can help them reflect on other relationships challenged by their mobility. These transitions offer another opportunity for identifying the here-and-now equivalents of our clients' experiences outside of therapy.

Meeting in person with a client whom we have only seen online before breaks the well-established routine. This embodied encounter can be exploited in order to further strengthen the therapeutic alliance and bring about a further breakthrough; but in other cases, it can also threaten the therapeutic process. For the extremely avoidant clients, for example those who have been victims of sexual abuse, this sudden transformation of their therapist from a talking head into a body in the same room can be overwhelming—too much intimacy resulting from sharing the same physical space. No matter what the client's initial response may be, such transitions always generate new therapeutic opportunities.

With Keira, we had an opportunity to start meeting in person before she had to return to New York. The first session shed some light on her previous online work with another therapist. Keira was a 32-year-old American model, who was staying in Paris for a few weeks following her engagement by a French haute-couture brand. She explained her decision to meet with me by the fact that I was referred by a friend whom she trusted. This seemed like an interesting choice as Keira had no intention to settle in Paris, and all our subsequent meetings would have to take place online. When Keira stepped into my room, both my office and I shrunk. Keira was extremely tall and slim, unusually so, even for a model. Once we were settled in front of each other, Keira told me about her previous therapist, whom she had met online only, for a few years. She seemed happy with their work, which allowed her to "better understand her current issues", but somehow, she felt that it was time to change and "try something different". Despite her obvious beauty, Keira had felt like "a piece of shit" for most of her life. The sad story that she shared echoed many others that I had heard from women in the modelling business. Always the tallest girl in her school, she had constantly been singled out and bullied by other kids. She started modelling full-time at the age of 14, and her employers pretended to ignore her being under-age. Still a child, she realised that her only asset was her body, and even though she stopped feeling ashamed of her height, which was now an asset, her shame grew and soon she started to feel worthless, fat, and ugly. This early and constant objectification led Keira to body dysmorphia and addiction. It did not help that she was stuck in mainly dysfunctional relationships, despite her awareness.

This unique in-person session that Keira made sure to secure seemed extremely important to her, giving her therapist the experience that people generally have when meeting with her in person, physically looking up at her. Outside work, Keira preferred solitude, and meeting online suited her well. But this time she chose to step out of her comfort zone and expose herself more fully. Later, as we kept meeting online for a few years, Keira would often refer to this unique in-person session as an anchor which we were able to hold onto. Keira showed another example of the creativity with which clients use the possibilities of blended approaches.

Openly addressing the transition from the screen to an in-person encounter will always nurture the alliance and the work itself. What does the client feel about being in the same room? Is it any different from what they had imagined? As an example, my office happens to be a tiny room, longer than it is wide. Through the camera, the perception of the physical reality of the space is different. Some figurines or paintings near my computer are not visible online. Each client who comes in person after a long time of seeing me on their screen is surprised in one way or another. Openly inquiring into their experience of that in-person session leads us to explore their fantasies about our therapeutic relationship. When stepping into my therapy room, all will generally comment on either its view of the Paris rooftops or how smaller-than-they-thought my office actually is. These initial reactions often lead to some fascinating reflections about their experience of seeing me in person and ultimately about the work we have been doing online.

Even for those clients who will not make it to Paris (for political, economic, or other reasons), the in-person session may never be possible but fantasising about it is an important and powerful element of therapy. For those stuck in their unfriendly realities, the dream about visiting their therapist onsite brings wonderful grist to the therapeutic mill. We recognise the limitations to their freedom imposed by their circumstances, and this leads them to explore their deeper feelings of anger, sadness, and frustration about it. A powerful example of such dynamics comes from my work with women from certain Middle Eastern countries where their freedom is restricted in different ways. They are perfectly aware of the situation abroad and the differences in our situations become apparent and difficult to ignore. Mourning the impossibility of meeting in person is one important step in this grieving proces; it helps them deal with their particular situation.

When the therapeutic relationship moves from one medium to another, the feeling of shame is often part of such a transition. In both situations (from in-person to online or vice-versa), something previously hidden suddenly becomes apparent and visible to the other. In the case of moving from a physical room to the online space, this invisible part is the environment—the living arrangements of the client are disclosed to the therapist. The elements of his universe, his toddler, pets, or the messiness of a room, come to life on the therapist's screen. In the case of the opposite shift, from online to in-person, it is the body that is revealed. The shame that comes with exposure is an intrinsic part of such a transition, and therapy can be re-energised and pushed forward if that feeling is properly addressed.

In the case of Andrew, our unique in-person session was the occasion to address his body shame, which he had not managed to reveal in our earlier online encounters. I was visiting San Francisco and he made sure to fly in from Los Angeles where he lived. He was using dating sites and struggling with deceptions and failed attempts to get beyond the first date. When he showed up in my hotel lobby, where I was expecting him before leading him to a quiet corner that I had secured for this session, I was surprised by the level of discomfort and anxiety that descended onto me. It was one of the most difficult sessions for both of us. "You are much taller than I thought", he offered as a greeting. "You are also much taller than I imagined", I echoed him, taken aback by the levels of anxiety that were flooding us both. The silence that followed was awkward. We scrutinised each other for a moment. I smiled and felt vulnerable.

"It is uncomfortable, isn't it?" I asked when we finally made it through the lobby to a corner with snug armchairs. "Yes, it is weird", he concurred with visible relief. As soon as we found ourselves in the same space and at a close physical distance from each other, Andrew's shame became palpable. In an uncanny parallel process, I could sense the kind of struggle he was dealing with in his dating attempts. The hour we spent together in that dim hotel lobby opened a new avenue for the rest of his therapy. After that session, we could dialogue more openly about his shame of never having experienced proper intimacy with a woman. Behind the façade of a tall and athletic young man, Andrew was skilfully hiding a belief that somehow he was faulty and not loveable. That façade did not resist the in-person setting, especially as we had had a few sessions before it to start building a therapeutic relationship.

Some clients, despite their apparent desire, will prefer to pass up the opportunity to meet in person, even when it arises. Martin lived in New York, and we usually met online, when he took his first early coffee. When he planned to come to Paris for a few days, we agreed on meeting at my office. But he never showed up, messaging me at short notice only a few hours before the scheduled time. When, on his return to the US, Martin and I finally met again in our usual and comfortable online setting, I invited him to reflect on this missed opportunity. Stumbling, he admitted he had not wanted to meet me in the flesh, as he feared that I would realise how "fat" he was. This missed in-person session became a perfect opportunity to address his body shame, which was closely associated with his social uneasiness—the initial reason he put forward when seeking therapy in the first place.

When online clients initiate an in-person encounter, our own reaction can offer some interesting opportunities for self-reflection. The persona that we had established for our online clients may be at odds with the clutter in our office, the not-fancy-enough location, or other parts of our life that we would rather leave out. I always make sure I can meet with my online clients in person if the opportunity arises. Such in-person meetings are disruptive to an already established routine in online therapy, but they are an opportunity for growth. When the therapeutic relationship survives such a rupture, it can further develop. Clients are then presented with a unique opportunity to face their shame, as in the case of Andrew, or to experiment with more closeness and intimacy. Missing such an opportunity would be a clear loss for their therapy.

References

Beatty, L., & Binnion, C. (2016). A systematic review of predictors of, and reasons for, adherence to online psychological interventions. *International Journal of Behavioral Medicine*, 23(6), 776–794. doi:10.1007/s12529-016-9556-9.

Békés, V., & Aafjes-Van Doorn, K. (2022). Relational factors predict tele-psychotherapy acceptance in patients: The role of therapeutic relationship and attachment. *European Psychiatry*, 65, S169. doi:10.1192/j.eurpsy.2022.448.

Buber, M. (1958). What is common to all. *The Review of Metaphysics*, 359–379.

Charura, D., & Paul, S. (Eds.) (2014). *The therapeutic relationship handbook. Theory and practice*. Buckingham: Open University Press.

Cooper, M. (2012). Clients' and therapists' perceptions of intrasessional connection: An analogue study of change over time, predictor variables, and level of consensus. *Psychotherapy Research*, 22(3), 274–288. doi:10.1080/10503307.2011.647931.

Cundy, L. (2015). *Love in the age of the internet: Attachment in the digital era*. London: Karnac Books.

Del Re, A. C., Flückiger, C., Horvath, A. O., & Wampold, B. E. (2021). Examining therapist effects in the alliance–outcome relationship: A multilevel meta-analysis. *Journal of Consulting and Clinical Psychology*, 89(5), 371–378. doi:10.1037/ccp0000637.

Di Malta, G., Evans, C., & Cooper, M. (2020). Development and validation of the relational depth frequency scale. *Psychotherapy Research*, 30(2), 213–227. doi:10.1080/10503307.2019.1585590.

Dunn, K., & Wilson, J. (2021). When online and face to face counseling work together: Assessing the impact of blended or hybrid approaches, where clients move between face-to-face and online meetings. *Null*, 20(4), 312–326. doi:10.1080/14779757.2021.1993970.

Eichenberg, C., Aranyi, G., Rach, P., & Winter, L. (2022). Therapeutic alliance in psychotherapy across online and face-to-face settings: A quantitative analysis. *Internet Interventions: The Application of Information Technology in Mental and Behavioural Health*, 29, 100556. doi:10.1016/j.invent.2022.100556.

Erskine, R. G. (1998). Attunement and involvement: Therapeutic responses to relational needs. *International Journal of Psychotherapy*, 3(3), 235.

Erskine, R. G. (2011). Attachment, relational-needs, and psychotherapeutic presence. *International Journal of Integrative Psychotherapy*, 2(1)

Finsrud, I., Nissen-Lie, H., Vrabel, K., Høstmælingen, A., Wampold, B. E., & Ulvenes, P. G. (2022). It's the therapist and the treatment: The structure of common therapeutic relationship factors. *Psychotherapy Research*, 32(2), 139–150. doi:10.1080/10503307.2021.1916640.

Geller, S. (2021). Cultivating online therapeutic presence: Strengthening therapeutic relationships in teletherapy sessions. *Counselling Psychology Quarterly*, 34(3–4), 687–703. doi:10.1080/09515070.2020.1787348.

Geller, S. M. (2017). *A practical guide for cultivating therapeutic presence*. Beaverton OR: Ringgold.

Geller, S. M., & Porges, S. W. (2014). Therapeutic presence: Neurophysiological mechanisms mediating feeling safe in therapeutic relationships. *Journal of Psychotherapy Integration*, 24(3), 178–192. doi:10.1037/a0037511.

Haugh, S., & Paul, S. (2008). *The therapeutic relationship: Perspectives and themes.* Ross-on-Wye UK: PCCS.

Hayes, J. A., & Vinca, M. (2017). Therapist presence, absence, and extraordinary presence. In Castonguay, L. G. & Hill, C. E. (Eds.), *How and why are some therapists better than others?* (pp. 85–100) Washington DC: American Psychological Association. Retrieved from http://www.jstor.org/stable/j.ctv1chs4fx.10.

Irvine, A., Drew, P., Bower, P., Brooks, H., Gellatly, J., Armitage, C. J., … Bee, P. (2020). Are there interactional differences between telephone and face-to-face psychological therapy? A systematic review of comparative studies. *Journal of Affective Disorders*, 265, 120–131. doi:10.1016/j.jad.2020.01.057.

Knox, R. (2008). Clients' experiences of relational depth in person-centred counselling. *Counselling and Psychotherapy Research*, 8(3), 182–188. doi:10.1080/14733140802035005.

Kocsis, B. J., & Yellowlees, P. (2018). Telepsychotherapy and the therapeutic relationship: Principles, advantages, and case examples. *Telemedicine and E-Health*, 24(5), 329–334. doi:10.1089/tmj.2017.0088.

Lombard, M., & Ditton, T. (1997). At the heart of it all: The concept of presence. *Journal of Computer-Mediated Communication*, 3(2), JCMC321.

Mearns, D. (1997). *Person-centred counselling training.* London: Sage.

Mearns, D., & Cooper, M. (2018). *Working at relational depth* (2nd edn). London: Sage.

Porges, S. W. (2022). Polyvagal theory: A science of safety. *Frontiers in Integrative Neuroscience*, 16, 871227. doi:10.3389/fnint.2022.871227.

Rathenau, S., Sousa, D., Vaz, A., & Geller, S. (2022). The effect of attitudes toward online therapy and the difficulties perceived in online therapeutic presence. *Journal of Psychotherapy Integration*, 32(1), 19–33. doi:10.1037/int0000266.

Richards, M., & Bedi, R. P. (2015). Gaining perspective: How men describe incidents damaging the therapeutic alliance. *Psychology of Men & Masculinity*, 16 (2), 170–182. doi:10.1037/a0036924.

Riva, G. (2011). Presence, actions and emotions: A theoretical framework. *Journal of CyberTherapy and Rehabilitation*, 4(2), 204–206.

Russell, G. I. (2015). *Screen relations: The limits of computer-mediated psychoanalysys and psychotherapy.* London: Routledge.

Sexton, H., Littauer, H., Sexton, A., & Tømmerås, E. (2005). Building an alliance: Early therapy process and the client–therapist connection. *Psychotherapy Research*, 15(1–2),103–116. doi:10.1080/10503300512331327083.

Springer, K. L., & Bedi, R. P. (2021). Why do men drop out of counseling/psychotherapy? An enhanced critical incident technique analysis of male clients' experiences. *Psychology of Men & Masculinity*, 22(4), 776–786. doi:10.1037/men0000350.

Suler, J. (2004). The online disinhibition effect. *CyberPsychology & Behavior*, 7(3), 321–326. doi:10.1089/1094931041291295.

Tokarczuk, O. (2018). *Flights.* London: Fitzcarraldo Editions.

Treanor, A. (2017). The extent to which relational depth can be reached in online therapy and the factors that facilitate and inhibit that experience: A mixed methods study. Psych.D. dissertation, University of Roehampton.

Weinberg, H., & Rolnick, A. (2020). *Theory and practice of online therapy.* Abingdon: Routledge.

Weitz, P. (Ed.) (2014). *Psychotherapy.02.* London: Karnac Books.

Wiggins, S., Elliott, R., & Cooper, M. (2012). The prevalence and characteristics of relational depth events in psychotherapy. *Psychotherapy Research*, 22(2), 139–158. doi:10.1080/10503307.2011.629635.

Yalom, I. D. (2002). *The gift of therapy: Reflections on being a therapist*. London: Piatkus.

Yalom, I. D. (2009). *The gift of therapy*. London: Harper Perennial.

Yalom, I. D. (2012). *Love's executioner and other tales of psychotherapy*. New York: Perseus/BasicBooks.

Chapter 9

The gift of therapy in displacement

Many clients who seek therapy in the midst of displacement are often unaware of the psychological toll of their condition, which leaves this facet of their experience overlooked and often unaddressed in therapy. These apparently successful emigrants carry the invisible burden of a displacement trauma. Those who left their original places willingly, in search of a better life, often feel ashamed about not being "happy" in their new place. Therapists, displaced or not, run a risk of colluding with such clients in avoiding the displacement-related themes, and it takes a heightened awareness, understanding of multilingualism, and a good pair of displacement-rabbit ears to welcome them into their work. If the displacement-related elements of their experience remain locked away and are not properly addressed in therapy, these clients will stagnate and will hardly make the desired progress.

Therapy, online or in-person, helps displaced individuals to better cope with the hardship of their condition, and to make it a more meaningful experience, leading to personal growth. Svetlana Boym considers estrangement as both an artistic device and a way of life (Boym, 1996: 511–530). This poetic view on life in displacement extends to therapy with emigrant clients, turning their experience of estrangement into a powerful creative and therapeutic force.

The term "migratory practice" has been sporadically used in migration studies that promote the view on migration as a creative endeavour (Akimenko, 2018; Hack-Polay et al., 2021). The practice of therapy with displaced clients is also a migratory practice and a creative venture; the scope of which is to make sense of a client's experience of displacement, and to re-define the narrative of their dislocated life. My own therapy work is also an example of such migratory practice.

For those choosing displacement, mobility is a form of rebellion, often a silent one, or a way of giving up on something one has not managed to change. Whilst extremely efficient at the initial stage, this coping strategy often leads to further loneliness and isolation. As these serial expatriates keep running away from places where they feel alienated, they lose more social connections and become increasingly self-reliant. That vicious cycle, in which

DOI: 10.4324/9781003144588-9

many get caught up, can be broken in a displacement-attuned therapy, which uses the therapeutic alliance to heal earlier relational traumas and re-create, in a shared endeavour, different and healthier relational possibilities.

The main aim of this book has been to raise therapists' awareness of displacement and multilingualism-related issues and examine how the online setting can be particularly adapted for that particular population. Only by engaging in a dialogue about the psychological realities of displacement—these inner landscapes of abandonment and loss—can we become better therapists for those who are on the move. Svetlana Boym, reflecting on the phenomenon of nostalgia, makes a powerful remark: "Freedom in this case is not a freedom from memory but a freedom to remember, to choose the narratives of the past and remake them" (Boym, 2001: 354). These words summarise the potential of therapy in displacement; for the uprooted and the dislocated, the gift of therapy is about hope for redemption.

Creativity is a driving force behind any good therapy, both for therapists—how they approach their work, and for their clients—how they approach their lives in displacement. It can hardly exist outside of vulnerability. To open our hearts to the other, we always take a major risk—that of being rejected and shamed. Therapists should model this creative stance. To borrow the Russian composer Igor Stravinsky's words: "in order to create there must be a dynamic force, and what force is greater than love?" (Stravinsky in Barron, et al., 1997). So, love it will be. Love for the misplaced, misunderstood, and dislocated parts of us.

References

Akimenko, D. (2018). Narrative spaces: On identity work and placeness through arts-based narrative practices. Ph.D. dissertation, Faculty of Art and Design, University of Lapland.

Barron, F., Montuori, A., & Barron, A. (1997). *Creators on creating: Awakening and cultivating the imaginative mind*. New York: Jeremy P. Tarcher/Penguin.

Boym, S. (1996). Estrangement as a lifestyle: Shklovsky and Brodsky. *Poetics Today*, 17(4), 511–530. doi:10.2307/1773211.

Boym, S. (2001). *The future of nostalgia*. New York: Basic Books.

Hack-Polay, D., Mahmoud, A., Rydzik, A., Rahman, M., Igwe, P., & Bosworth, G. (2021). *Migration practice as creative practice: An interdisciplinary exploration of migration*. Leeds UK: Emerald Publishing.

Index